Teach Yourself®
WebTV®

Teach Yourself® WebTV®

Erica Sadun and Dennis R. Cohen

IDG Books Worldwide, Inc.
An International Data Group Company

Foster City, CA • Chicago, IL • Indianapolis, IN • New York, NY

Teach Yourself® WebTV®

Published by
IDG Books Worldwide, Inc.
An International Data Group Company
919 E. Hillsdale Blvd., Suite 400
Foster City, CA 94404
www.idgbooks.com (IDG Books Worldwide Web site)

ISBN: 0-7645-3397-5

Printed in the United States of America

10 9 8 7 6 5 4 3 2 1

1VH/SV/QS/QQ/IN

Distributed in the United States by IDG Books Worldwide, Inc.

Distributed by CDG Books Canada Inc. for Canada; by Transworld Publishers Limited in the United Kingdom; by IDG Norge Books for Norway; by IDG Sweden Books for Sweden; by IDG Books Australia Publishing Corporation Pty. Ltd. for Australia and New Zealand; by TransQuest Publishers Pte Ltd. for Singapore, Malaysia, Thailand, Indonesia, and Hong Kong; by Gotop Information Inc. for Taiwan; by ICG Muse, Inc. for Japan; by Intersoft for South Africa; by Eyrolles for France; by International Thomson Publishing for Germany, Austria and Switzerland; by Distribuidora Cuspide for Argentina; by LR International for Brazil; by Galileo Libros for Chile; by Ediciones ZETA S.C.R. Ltda. for Peru; by WS Computer Publishing Corporation, Inc., for the Philippines; by Contemporanea de Ediciones for Venezuela; by Express Computer Distributors for the Caribbean and West Indies; by Micronesia Media Distributor, Inc. for Micronesia; by Chips Computadoras S.A. de C.V. for Mexico; by Editorial Norma de Panama S.A. for Panama; by American Bookshops for Finland.

For general information on IDG Books Worldwide's books in the U.S., please call our Consumer Customer Service department at 800-762-2974. For reseller information, including discounts and premium sales, please call our Reseller Customer Service department at 800-434-3422.

For information on where to purchase IDG Books Worldwide's books outside the U.S., please contact our International Sales department at 317-596-5530 or fax 317-572-4002.

For consumer information on foreign language translations, please contact our Customer Service department at 800-434-3422, fax 317-572-4002, or e-mail rights@idgbooks.com.

For information on licensing foreign or domestic rights, please phone +1-650-653-7098.

For sales inquiries and special prices for bulk quantities, please contact our Order Services department at 800-434-3422 or write to the address above.

For information on using IDG Books Worldwide's books in the classroom or for ordering examination copies, please contact our Educational Sales department at 800-434-2086 or fax 317-572-4005.

For press review copies, author interviews, or other publicity information, please contact our Public Relations department at 650-653-7000 or fax 650-653-7500.

For authorization to photocopy items for corporate, personal, or educational use, please contact Copyright Clearance Center, 222 Rosewood Drive, Danvers, MA 01923, or fax 978-750-4470.

Library of Congress Cataloging-in-Publication Data

Sadun, Erica
  Teach Yourself WebTV / Erica Sadun and Dennis R. Cohen.
    p. cm.
  ISBN 0-7645-3397-5 (alk.paper)
  1. WebTV (Trademark) 2. World Wide Web.   I. Cohen, Dennis R.
  II. Title.
TK5105.8887. S23 2000
004.67'8--dc21   99-085698

 is a registered trademark or trademark under exclusive license to IDG Books Worldwide, Inc. from International Data Group, Inc. in the United States and/or other countries.

ABOUT IDG BOOKS WORLDWIDE

Welcome to the world of IDG Books Worldwide.

IDG Books Worldwide, Inc., is a subsidiary of International Data Group, the world's largest publisher of computer-related information and the leading global provider of information services on information technology. IDG was founded more than 30 years ago by Patrick J. McGovern and now employs more than 9,000 people worldwide. IDG publishes more than 290 computer publications in over 75 countries. More than 90 million people read one or more IDG publications each month.

Launched in 1990, IDG Books Worldwide is today the #1 publisher of best-selling computer books in the United States. We are proud to have received eight awards from the Computer Press Association in recognition of editorial excellence and three from Computer Currents' First Annual Readers' Choice Awards. Our best-selling ...*For Dummies*® series has more than 50 million copies in print with translations in 31 languages. IDG Books Worldwide, through a joint venture with IDG's Hi-Tech Beijing, became the first U.S. publisher to publish a computer book in the People's Republic of China. In record time, IDG Books Worldwide has become the first choice for millions of readers around the world who want to learn how to better manage their businesses.

Our mission is simple: Every one of our books is designed to bring extra value and skill-building instructions to the reader. Our books are written by experts who understand and care about our readers. The knowledge base of our editorial staff comes from years of experience in publishing, education, and journalism — experience we use to produce books to carry us into the new millennium. In short, we care about books, so we attract the best people. We devote special attention to details such as audience, interior design, use of icons, and illustrations. And because we use an efficient process of authoring, editing, and desktop publishing our books electronically, we can spend more time ensuring superior content and less time on the technicalities of making books.

You can count on our commitment to deliver high-quality books at competitive prices on topics you want to read about. At IDG Books Worldwide, we continue in the IDG tradition of delivering quality for more than 30 years. You'll find no better book on a subject than one from IDG Books Worldwide.

John Kilcullen
Chairman and CEO
IDG Books Worldwide, Inc.

*Eighth Annual
Computer Press
Awards ≥1992*

*Ninth Annual
Computer Press
Awards ≥1993*

*Tenth Annual
Computer Press
Awards ≥1994*

*Eleventh Annual
Computer Press
Awards ≥1995*

Credits

Acquisitions Editor
Michael Roney

Project Editor
Paul Winters

Technical Editors
Allen Wyatt
Discovery Computing Inc.

Copy Editors
Richard Adin
Timothy J. Borek
Laura Hester
Marti Paul

Project Coordinators
Amanda Foxworth

Graphics and Production Specialists
Amy Adrian
Jacque Schneider
Mary Jo Weis

Quality Control Specialists
Chris Weisbart
Laura Albert

Book Designers
Daniel Ziegler Design
Cátálin Dulfu
Kurt Krames

Proofreading and Indexing
York Production Services

About the Authors

Erica Sadun, Ph.D. is a user interface expert, technology consultant and computer book author. She wrote the critically acclaimed and best-selling *JavaScript Cookbook* (Charles River Media).

Dennis R. Cohen is now a freelance programmer, editor, and writer who has been developing software for over 20 years, starting with the Deep Space Network at the Jet Propulsion Laboratory, and continuing through Ashton-Tate, Claris, and Aladdin Systems. He started writing magazine articles and reviews in 1981, doing technical edits of books in 1986, and writing computer books in 1994. When he is not working, he can usually be found with his Boston terrier, Spenser.

For Lina Sadun

Welcome to
Teach Yourself

Welcome to *Teach Yourself*, a series read and trusted by millions for a decade. Although you may have seen the *Teach Yourself* name on other books, ours is the original. In addition, no *Teach Yourself* series has ever delivered more on the promise of its name than this series. That's because IDG Books Worldwide has transformed *Teach Yourself* into a new cutting-edge format that gives you all the information you need to learn quickly and easily.

Readers have told us that they want to learn by doing and that they want to learn as much as they can in as short a time as possible. We listened to you and believe that our new task-by-task format and suite of learning tools deliver the book you need to successfully teach yourself any technology topic. Features such as our Personal Workbook, which lets you practice and reinforce the skills you've just learned, help ensure that you get full value out of the time you invest in your learning. Handy cross-references to related topics and online sites broaden your knowledge and give you control over the kind of information you want, when you want it.

More Answers . . .

In designing the latest incarnation of this series, we started with the premise that people like you, who are beginning to intermediate computer users, want to take control of your own learning. To do this, you need the proper tools to find answers to questions so you can solve problems now.

In designing a series of books that provide such tools, we created a unique and concise visual format. The added bonus: *Teach Yourself* books actually pack more information into their pages than other books written on the same subjects. Skill for skill, you typically get much more information in a *Teach Yourself* book. In fact, *Teach Yourself* books, on average, cover twice the skills covered by other computer books — as many as 125 skills per book — so they're more likely to address your specific needs.

Welcome to Teach Yourself

...In Less Time

We know you don't want to spend twice the time to get all this great information, so we provide lots of timesaving features:

▶ A modular task-by-task organization of information: any task you want to perform is easy to find and includes simple-to-follow steps.

▶ A larger size than standard makes the book easy to read and convenient to use at a computer workstation. The large format also enables us to include many more illustrations — 500 screen illustrations show you how to get everything done!

▶ A Personal Workbook at the end of each chapter reinforces learning with extra practice, real-world applications for your learning, and questions and answers to test your knowledge.

▶ Cross-references appearing at the bottom of each task page refer you to related information, providing a path through the book for learning particular aspects of the software thoroughly.

▶ A Find It Online feature offers valuable ideas on where to go on the Internet to get more information or to download useful files.

▶ Take Note sidebars provide added-value information from our expert authors for more in-depth learning.

▶ An attractive, consistent organization of information helps you quickly find and learn the skills you need.

These *Teach Yourself* features are designed to help you learn the essential skills about a technology in the least amount of time, with the most benefit. We've placed these features consistently throughout the book, so you quickly learn where to go to find just the information you need — whether you work through the book from cover to cover or use it later to solve a new problem.

You will find a *Teach Yourself* book on almost any technology subject — from the Internet to Windows to Microsoft Office. Take control of your learning today, with IDG Books Worldwide's *Teach Yourself* series.

Teach Yourself

More Answers in Less Time

Search through the task headings to find the topic you want right away. To learn a new skill, search the contents, chapter opener, or the extensive index to find what you need. Then find — at a glance — the clear task heading that matches it.

Learn the concepts behind the task at hand and, more important, learn how the task is relevant in the real world. Timesaving suggestions and advice show you how to make the most of each skill.

After you learn the task at hand, you may have more questions, or you may want to read about other tasks related to the topic. Use the cross-references to find different tasks to make your learning more efficient.

► Reading a News Story

Not only does WebTV News show you the headlines, it allows you to read more about them. When a story catches your eye, you can pull up the article behind it. Move the yellow box to a headline and activate it by pressing Go or Return.

WebTV News headlines and news stories are supplied by MSNBC. When you activate a headline, you automatically move to the MSNBC news site on the World Wide Web. At this site, you can read the full article, discover related pieces, search for further information, rate stories, and so forth.

At the MSNBC site, news features typically begin with a large-font summary and a picture. At the bottom of the summary, is the option to view the COMPLETE STORY. Activate this to view the rest of the article. Use the Scroll up and Scroll down buttons to fully view the summary and article.

When WebTV moves you to a different part of a page, you may encounter a "ragged edge" effect. This looks like part of the screen has been "torn." If you see this, it means that you have moved to another part of the article. WebTV uses this effect to differentiate moving between parts of a page and moving between separate pages.

At the bottom of an article is found a collection of related items. These may include older versions of a breaking story, or support materials, or extra discussions. If interested, you can activate these with the yellow box and Go or Return.

To read the article behind another headline, use the Back button to return to WebTV News.

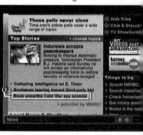

❶ On your home page, select **News** with the yellow box and activate it by pressing Go on your remote control. This will take you to the WebTV News page.

❷ Select a headline of int to you with the yellow and press Go or Return

CROSS-REFERENCE

Read more about the World Wide Web in Section II.

Ultimately, people learn by doing. Follow the clear, illustrated steps presented with every task to complete a procedure. The detailed callouts for each step show you exactly where to go and what to do to complete the task.

Welcome to Teach Yourself

Go to this area if you want special tips, cautions, and notes that provide added insight into the current task.

The current chapter name and number always appear in the top right-hand corner of every task spread, so you always know exactly where you are in the book.

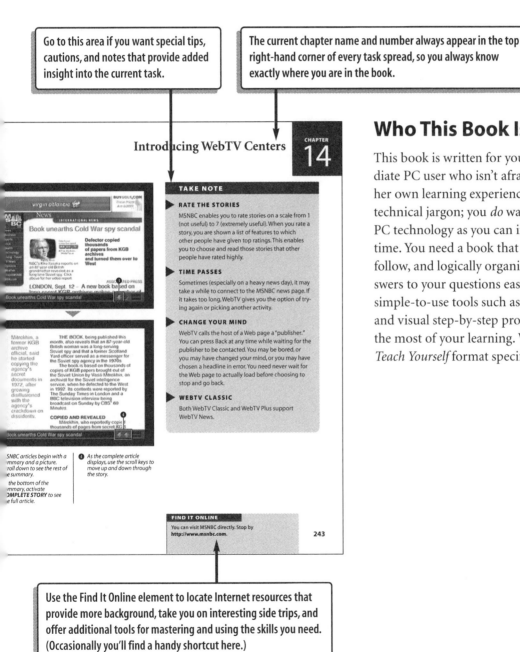

Introducing WebTV Centers

CHAPTER 14

TAKE NOTE

RATE THE STORIES

MSNBC enables you to rate stories on a scale from 1 (not useful) to 7 (extremely useful). When you rate a story, you are shown a list of features to which other people have given top ratings. This enables you to choose and read those stories that other people have rated highly.

TIME PASSES

Sometimes (especially on a heavy news day), it may take a while to connect to the MSNBC news page. If it takes too long, WebTV gives you the option of trying again or picking another activity.

CHANGE YOUR MIND

WebTV calls the host of a Web page a "publisher." You can press Back at any time while waiting for the publisher to be contacted. You may be bored, or you may have changed your mind, or you may have chosen a headline in error. You need never wait for the Web page to actually load before choosing to stop and go back.

WEBTV CLASSIC

Both WebTV Classic and WebTV Plus support WebTV News.

FIND IT ONLINE

You can visit MSNBC directly. Stop by http://www.msnbc.com.

243

Who This Book Is For

This book is written for you, a beginning to intermediate PC user who isn't afraid to take charge of his or her own learning experience. You don't want a lot of technical jargon; you *do* want to learn as much about PC technology as you can in a limited amount of time. You need a book that is straightforward, easy to follow, and logically organized, so you can find answers to your questions easily. And, you appreciate simple-to-use tools such as handy cross-references and visual step-by-step procedures that help you make the most of your learning. We have created the unique *Teach Yourself* format specifically to meet your needs.

Use the Find It Online element to locate Internet resources that provide more background, take you on interesting side trips, and offer additional tools for mastering and using the skills you need. (Occasionally you'll find a handy shortcut here.)

Personal Workbook

It's a well-known fact that much of what we learn is lost soon after we learn it if we don't reinforce our newly acquired skills with practice and repetition. That's why each *Teach Yourself* chapter ends with your own Personal Workbook. Here's where you can get extra practice, test your knowledge, and discover ideas for using what you've learned in the real world. There's even a Visual Quiz to help you remember your way around the topic's software environment.

Feedback

Please let us know what you think about this book, and whether you have any suggestions for improvements. You can send questions and comments to the *Teach Yourself* editors on the IDG Books Worldwide Web site at **www.idgbooks.com**.

Personal Workbook

Q&A

1 How do you tell WebTV that you wish to begin searching the World Wide Web?

_____

_____

_____

2 Why do you find Web pages that include only subsets of the search phrases you used?

_____

_____

_____

3 Which will produce more Web pages: a search for *burgundy* or a search for *Burgundy*?

_____

_____

4 What is the difference between searching for *top cat* and *"top cat"*?

_____

_____

5 How might you search for the Gettysburg Address, if you are unsure how to spell Gettysburg?

_____

_____

_____

6 What's a good way to search for song lyrics by Gilbert and Sullivan?

_____

_____

_____

7 If you wish to find information about the Golden Gate Bridge, which query should you use: *San Francisco attraction +golden +gate +bridge* or *+San +Francisco +attraction golden gate bridge*?

_____

_____

_____

8 How might you search for information about camels but exclude pages that talk about the cigarettes?

_____

_____

ANSWERS: PAGE 33

108

> After working through the tasks in each chapter, you can test your progress and reinforce your learning by answering the questions in the Q&A section. Then check your answers in the Personal Workbook Answers appendix at the back of the book.

Welcome to Teach Yourself

Another practical way to reinforce your skills is to do additional exercises on the same skills you just learned without the benefit of the chapter's visual steps. If you struggle with any of these exercises, it's a good idea to refer to the chapter's tasks to be sure you've mastered them.

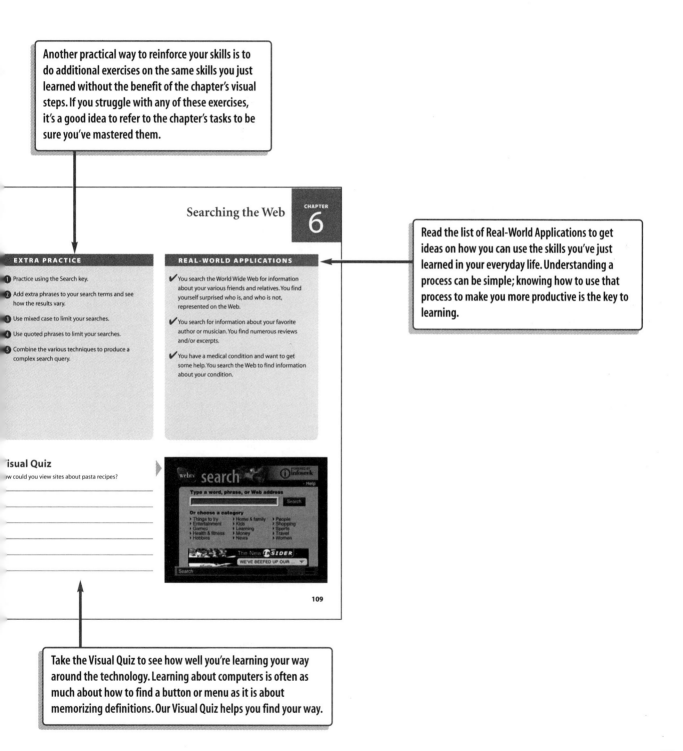

Searching the Web

CHAPTER 6

Read the list of Real-World Applications to get ideas on how you can use the skills you've just learned in your everyday life. Understanding a process can be simple; knowing how to use that process to make you more productive is the key to learning.

EXTRA PRACTICE

1. Practice using the Search key.

2. Add extra phrases to your search terms and see how the results vary.

3. Use mixed case to limit your searches.

4. Use quoted phrases to limit your searches.

5. Combine the various techniques to produce a complex search query.

REAL-WORLD APPLICATIONS

✔ You search the World Wide Web for information about your various friends and relatives. You find yourself surprised who is, and who is not, represented on the Web.

✔ You search for information about your favorite author or musician. You find numerous reviews and/or excerpts.

✔ You have a medical condition and want to get some help. You search the Web to find information about your condition.

Visual Quiz

How could you view sites about pasta recipes?

109

Take the Visual Quiz to see how well you're learning your way around the technology. Learning about computers is often as much about how to find a button or menu as it is about memorizing definitions. Our Visual Quiz helps you find your way.

Acknowledgments

Noah Siegel of Waggner Edstrom.
Neil J. Salkind and the Studio B Agency.

— Erica Sadun

I would like to recognize the assistance rendered by the folks at WebTV, in particular Richard Hay, Robert Laws, and Aaron Mata. In addition, Steve Perlman and his wife, Sandi, were of great help in aiding my understanding of the design considerations that went into the development and interface of an Internet appliance. Thanks, also, to Mike Roney and Paul Winters of IDG Books for bringing me onto this project and helping me over the hurdles of getting the material ready for your use.

— Dennis Cohen

Contents

Welcome to Teach Yourself viii

Acknowledgments xv

Part I: Introducing WebTV 2

Chapter 1: Acquiring Basic WebTV Skills 4

Powering On WebTV for the First Time 6

Signing Up for WebTV Using Your Remote Control 8

Signing Up for WebTV Using Your Keyboard 10

Introducing the Yellow Box 12

Using the Yellow Cursor 14

Using the Onscreen Keyboard 16

Touring the Keyboard 18

▶ Personal Workbook 20

Chapter 2: Editing Text 22

Removing Text with the Delete Key 24

Highlighting and Selecting Text 26

Copying and Pasting Text 28

Cutting and Pasting Text 30

Adding Special Characters 32

Checking Spelling 34

▶ Personal Workbook 36

Chapter 3: Filling Out Forms 38

Selecting One Option from Many 40

Selecting Many Options 42

Selecting from a Pull-Down List 44

Selecting from a Scrolling List 46

Selecting from a Multiple-Choice List 48

Contents

Entering a Password 50

Selecting from a Picture 52

Resetting and Submitting Forms 54

▶ Personal Workbook 56

Part II: Navigating the World Wide Web 58

Chapter 4: Jumping Into the Web 60

Using Web Addresses 62

Moving Between Web Pages Using Hyperlinks 64

Viewing Recently Visited Pages 66

Peeking at Web Page Information 68

Understanding Web Page Security 70

▶ Personal Workbook 72

Chapter 5: Using Favorites 74

Adding a Web Page to Favorites 76

Selecting a Favorite 78

Assigning a Favorite to an F Key 80

Adding a Favorites Folder 82

Removing a Favorites Folder 84

Discarding a Favorite Site 86

Renaming a Site 88

Moving Favorites Between Folders 90

▶ Personal Workbook 92

Chapter 6: Searching the Web 94

Using the Search Key 96

Adding Search Phrases 98

Limiting Searches with Mixed Case 100

Limiting Searches with Quoted Phrases 102

Contents

Limiting Searches with + ... 104

Browsing Categories 106

▶ Personal Workbook 108

Chapter 7: Exploring the Web **110**

Singing with WebTV 112

Playing an Online Game 114

Asking for Advice 116

Watching TV While Surfing the Web 118

▶ Personal Workbook 120

Part III: Mastering Electronic Mail **122**

Chapter 8: Building Basic E-Mail Skills **124**

Reading Electronic Mail 126

Moving Through the Mail List 128

Writing Electronic Mail 130

Sending Mail to Multiple Recipients 132

Replying to Electronic Mail 134

Forwarding Electronic Mail 136

Adding a Picture to Electronic Mail 138

Attaching a Sound Clip 142

Getting Help with E-Mail 146

▶ Personal Workbook 148

Chapter 9: Creating and Maintaining Your Address Book **150**

Adding to the Address Book 152

Adding to the Address Book from E-Mail 154

Addressing a Letter with the Address Book 156

Updating Address Book Entries 158

Removing Names from Your Address Book 160

Finding E-Mail Addresses 162

▶ Personal Workbook 164

Contents

Chapter 10: Building Intermediate E-Mail Skills 166

Using an E-Mail Signature 168

Choosing a Mail List Order 170

Enabling Carbon Copy (cc:) 172

Sending E-Mail Using Carbon Copy 174

Replying to All E-Mail Recipients 176

Enabling E-Mail Inclusion 178

Including the Original Letter 180

Stopping and Continuing E-Mail 182

Erasing an E-Mail in Progress 184

Correcting Misaddressed E-Mail 186

▶ Personal Workbook 188

Chapter 11: Taking Charge of E-Mail Storage 190

Enabling Storage 192

Storing a Letter 194

Discarding a Letter 196

Cleaning Up Storage 198

Discarding a Letter Permanently 200

Retrieving a Discarded Letter 202

Resending a Sent Letter 204

▶ Personal Workbook 206

Chapter 12: Mastering Advanced E-Mail Techniques 208

Checking for E-mail Automatically 210

Sending and Retrieving E-mail Hyperlinks 212

Accepting E-mail Attachments 214

Retrieving Mail from Other Accounts 216

▶ Personal Workbook 220

Chapter 13: Joining E-Mail Lists 222

Finding an E-Mail List with ListServ 224

Joining an E-Mail List with ListServ 226

Contents

Finding an E-Mail List with Liszt 228

Leaving an E-mail List 230

▶ Personal Workbook 232

Part IV: Making the Most of WebTV 234

Chapter 14: Introducing WebTV Centers 236

Using WebTV Centers 238

Using WebTV Entertainment 240

Reading a News Story 242

Customizing WebTV News 244

Customizing Money 246

Customizing Weather 248

Customizing Sports 250

Shopping Online 252

▶ Personal Workbook 254

Chapter 15: Watching TV with WebTV 256

Exploring TV Home 258

Retrieving TV Listings 260

Retrieving TV Listings Automatically 262

Selecting a Television Show 264

Viewing TV Listings by Date and Time 266

Searching TV Program Listings for a Show 268

Searching TV Listings for a Type of Show 270

Setting Up TV Favorites 272

Using TV Favorites 274

Selecting from Recently Viewed TV Shows 276

Exploring Crossover Links 278

Planning Television Viewing 280

Controlling Your VCR with WebTV 284

▶ Personal Workbook 288

Contents

Chapter 16: Building Community **290**

Moving Around Town 292

Finding a Chat 294

Finding a Newsgroup 298

Creating a Web Page 302

▶ Personal Workbook 308

Chapter 17: Administrating Your WebTV Account **310**

Adding a Secondary User 312

Removing a Secondary User 316

Switching Users 318

Checking Your Billing Information 320

Switching Onscreen Keyboard Styles 322

Enjoying Background Music 324

Adjusting Font Sizes 326

Asking WebTV for Help 328

▶ Personal Workbook 330

Personal Workbook Answers **333**

Index 343

Teach Yourself®
WebTV®

PART

I

CHAPTER **1**   Acquiring Basic WebTV Skills

2   Editing Text

3   Filling Out Forms

Introducing WebTV

Before you're ready to run marathons, you may need to learn how to put on your sneakers. Never take basic skills for granted. They provide the strength and flexibility that underlie experience and expertise. This section teaches you to use WebTV's basic equipment. When you finish this section, you will be able to tackle any WebTV or World Wide Web screen you come across.

The first chapter in this section introduces you to the most basic WebTV skills. These skills include using WebTV's yellow box, yellow cursor, and onscreen or physical keyboards. You also learn to power on your WebTV unit and how to sign up for WebTV using either your remote control or optional keyboard. By the time you finish the first chapter, you will be able to sign up for WebTV, move between WebTV screens, and understand how to enter basic information.

The second chapter introduces text-editing techniques. You learn how to correct mistakes, reuse text, move text around, and insert specialty characters. This chapter teaches you a variety of text skills, which you can use to write e-mail, enter chatrooms, post messages in Usenet newsgroups, and so on. Because the Internet is primarily text-based, a good foundation in text-manipulation skills is invaluable.

The final chapter introduces the most common elements of World Wide Web forms. On the Internet, you will need to fill out forms for a variety of reasons. The skills you acquire in this chapter enable you to engage in online shopping, account maintenance, and many other Internet activities.

This section covers the most important fundamental WebTV features. By learning these techniques, you will understand the full range of WebTV's interaction modes. No screen element, whether on a main WebTV screen, or out on the Internet, should come as a complete surprise after mastering the skills in this section.

CHAPTER **1**

MASTER THESE SKILLS

▶ **Powering On WebTV for the First Time**

▶ **Signing Up for WebTV Using Your Remote Control**

▶ **Signing Up for WebTV Using Your Keyboard**

▶ **Introducing the Yellow Box**

▶ **Using the Yellow Cursor**

▶ **Using the Onscreen Keyboard**

▶ **Touring the Keyboard**

Acquiring Basic WebTV Skills

There are certain skills without which you cannot fully enjoy WebTV. These few skills make it possible for you to go anywhere and do anything that WebTV permits. After mastering these skills, you will be able to take full advantage of all of WebTV's features.

First, you learn to power up your WebTV unit and sign up using either the remote control or keyboard. You cannot use your WebTV account until you have finished signing up, giving your name, billing address, and other information. Therefore, it is vital to get this process out of the way at the start so that you can begin your WebTV adventure.

Second, you learn to use WebTV's yellow box. This feature opens the Internet and the World Wide Web to you. When you control the yellow box, you control WebTV.

Finally, you learn about WebTV's yellow cursor. This cursor lets you type text in WebTV. You learn to use either the onscreen or the physical keyboard to enter text where you see the yellow cursor flash.

After finishing this chapter, you will be able to power on your WebTV unit and start to explore the full capabilities of the Web.

Powering On WebTV for the First Time

owering on your WebTV unit for the first time is an exciting experience. You are about to embark on a new adventure that will take you places that you've never been before and that will provide information, services, and experiences that you'll appreciate and come to depend on. All you need to do is turn the WebTV unit on and fill out a few online forms.

Starting WebTV is simple. Once your unit has been set up and connected to your television, phone line, and power, all you have to do is press Power on your remote or keyboard to get started. The unit will begin the registration process.

WebTV automatically knows you are a new customer by checking to see if your billing and account information have been set up. New units will not yet have any information, and reconditioned units have had that information taken off before resale. If you have a reconditioned unit, however, be aware that you will be asked if the WebTV unit has "moved" from the previous phone number. (The answer is "yes," the unit has indeed moved.) In both cases, WebTV will attempt to discern your location and automatically provide you with a local phone number for accessing WebTV services.

WebTV calls a special toll-free number and uses a patented technology to determine your calling area. It ascertains your location from your home phone number via caller identification. WebTV will always try to find a local phone number for your unit to use each time you sign onto the Internet. This is not always possible; using WebTV outside of major metropolitan areas might require a toll call.

Once WebTV has found a local access number for you, it will hang up from the special toll-free service line and dial that number. You are now ready to register.

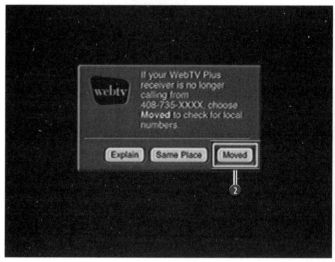

❶ Press Power on your remote or keyboard.

❷ If you have bought a reconditioned (also known as "renewed") unit, WebTV will ask you if your receiver is no longer calling from the previous number. Confirm that you have moved by highlighting Moved. Press Go on the remote or Return on the keyboard.

CROSS-REFERENCE

The next two topics cover signing up with the Remote Control and the Keyboard.

6

❸ *WebTV will call the special toll-free number to determine your location and find a local access number for your unit. It will display the Connecting to WebTV screen.*

❹ *WebTV will hang up from the toll-free number and dial the local access number. The number it is dialing is displayed at the bottom right of the screen.*

▶ *WebTV will tell you if it cannot find a local access number.*

▶ *You are now ready to access the on-ramp to the information highway.*

Signing Up for WebTV Using Your Remote Control

Using the WebTV wireless keyboard is extremely convenient but totally optional. You can complete the entire WebTV signup process using only your remote control. You need never buy a WebTV keyboard unless you wish to do so. Some people prefer to just use the remote.

WebTV provides tools that enable you to surf the World Wide Web, send and receive electronic mail, and perform many other common Internet tasks using the remote control as your sole interaction device. The remote is certainly not as convenient as the keyboard, especially if you have some experience typing. However, WebTV furnishes an onscreen version of a keyboard, which enables you to fill out forms, and so forth. You can read more about using the WebTV onscreen keyboard later in this chapter.

The most important features of the remote control are the Power button, arrow keys, and the Go button. The Power button lets you turn your unit on and off and works more or less the way you would expect it to. The arrow keys enable you to point to things on your TV screen. The Go button selects and activates WebTV features. Your remote control also has a number of other special-purpose buttons, which are discussed elsewhere.

Many people find it a comfort that the included remote control opens up the entire world of WebTV. Most, however, eventually opt to buy the keyboard for its convenience and ease of use.

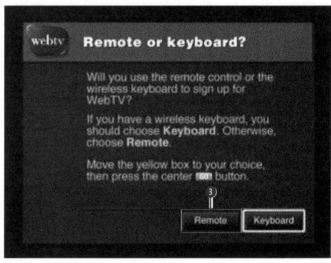

① WebTV introduces the special yellow box, which enables you to select items on your TV screen. You often see this yellow box when you are using WebTV.

② Use the arrow keys on your remote control to move the yellow box to the word **Continue**. Press Go on your remote to activate your selection.

③ It's time to choose whether to use the keyboard or remote control. Press the left arrow key to move the yellow box from Keyboard to Remote.

CROSS-REFERENCE

Want to learn more about the onscreen keyboard? Read further in this chapter.

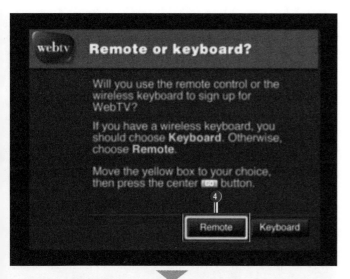

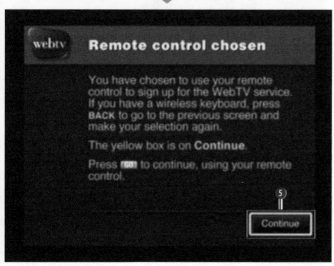

④ With the yellow box surrounding **Remote**, press Go.

⑤ WebTV confirms that you have chosen to use the remote control. The yellow box surrounds Continue. Press Go on your remote to finish signing up for WebTV.

▶ You will be asked for your name, address, and billing information. You learn more about using the onscreen keyboard later in this chapter.

▶ **CONSIDER BUYING A KEYBOARD**

Consider spending the money for a wireless keyboard. It is significantly easier to use than the remote control. Recently, when visiting the Magnavox outlet store in Fort Collins, Colorado, I saw refurbished keyboards being sold with a full warranty for less than twenty dollars.

▶ **PS/2 STYLE KEYBOARDS**

If you have a WebTV Classic unit (as opposed to the WebTV Plus unit), you can plug a personal computer keyboard directly into your unit. Classic has a PS/2-style keyboard jack on the back of the unit. If you have an older keyboard with the round five-wire semicircle arrangement, you can purchase an inexpensive PS/2 adapter. This is not the most convenient way to use a keyboard with WebTV, but it provides a cheap alternative for those people who may have some outdated PC equipment around the home.

▶ **WEBTV CLASSIC**

WebTV Classic supports remote-control interaction, as does WebTV Plus.

FIND IT ONLINE

Visit **http://help.webtv.net/equipment/keyboards. html** to read about WebTV peripherals.

Signing Up for WebTV Using Your Keyboard

WebTV's optional wireless keyboard is extremely convenient and proves well worth its nominal price. The keyboard enables you to enter text quickly and efficiently whether or not you are an experienced typist. There are many situations where you need to type text: filling out forms, searching for information, sending electronic mail, and so forth.

The most important thing to remember about the keyboard is that the Return key on the keyboard is equivalent to the Go button on the remote control. You can use the arrow keys on the keyboard in much the same way that you use the arrow keys on the remote. They enable you to point to things on the WebTV screen. The Return key selects and activates WebTV features.

Another important thing to remember in using your wireless keyboard is to keep the line-of-sight between the top of your keyboard and your WebTV unit clear of obstructions. Although it is convenient to place the keyboard on one's lap, one's knees may block the signal between the keyboard and the unit. If you find your keystrokes are not transmitting well to the WebTV unit, carefully inspect your keyboard line-of-sight.

Finally, remember to occasionally look up at the screen while typing. If you are an especially slow typist, WebTV may occasionally "time out" while you are in the middle of a sentence. If you are timed out, WebTV displays a small box with the "reconnect" rectangle. To reconnect, press Return. When your unit times out, it will ignore any additional keystrokes until you are connected again to the Internet. Peeking up occasionally will help prevent your keystrokes from being ignored.

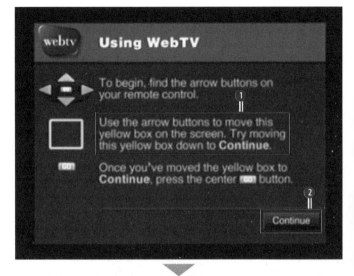

❶ WebTV introduces the special yellow box and directs you to move it to **Continue** using the arrow keys on the remote.

❷ Instead, use the arrow keys on your keyboard to move the yellow box to **Continue**. Press Return on your keyboard to activate your selection.

❸ The word **Keyboard** should be highlighted. If not, use the arrow keys to move the yellow box from **Remote** to **Keyboard**. Press Return on your keyboard.

CROSS-REFERENCE

The previous topic shows you how to sign up for WebTV using only your remote control.

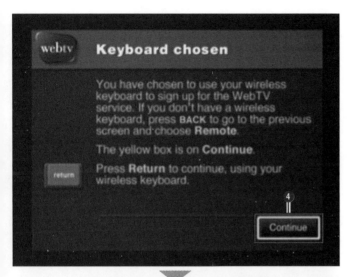

TAKE NOTE

BUILD UP YOUR TYPING SKILLS

If you have touch-typing experience, you may save straining your neck muscles. Some people find it jarring to keep looking down at the keyboard and then up at the screen again and again. The better you type, the easier it is to operate your WebTV remote keyboard.

PS/2-STYLE KEYBOARDS

As mentioned in the previous topic, WebTV Classic units let you plug PS/2-style keyboards directly into your unit. See the previous topic for details.

WEBTV CLASSIC

WebTV Classic supports keyboard interaction as does WebTV Plus. A keyboard from any given manufacturer will work on both its Classic and Plus units. Keyboards may or may not operate correctly on units made by other manufacturers.

④ *WebTV confirms that you chose to use the keyboard. The yellow box surrounds* **Continue**. *Simply press Return on your keyboard.*

⑤ *WebTV provides a review of keyboard skills, similar to step 1 above. Use the arrow keys on your keyboard to move the yellow box to* **Continue**. *Press Return.*

▶ *Complete the sign up process for WebTV. You will be prompted for your name, address, billing information and new Internet name.*

FIND IT ONLINE

Visit WebTV's support page at **http://webtv.net/ subscribers/index.html**.

Introducing the Yellow Box

The yellow box is WebTV's most obvious and outstanding feature. You can move this box around the WebTV screen to highlight different parts of the screen, both text and images.

The arrow keys on your remote control or keyboard control the movement of the yellow box. Use the up and down arrows to move the box vertically. Use the left and right arrows to move it horizontally. WebTV will not permit you to move the box to any place "bad" or "wrong." So, feel free to explore where the yellow box can go.

Whenever the yellow box surrounds a WebTV element, you can "activate" that element by pressing Go on your remote control or Return on your keyboard. This tells WebTV that you wish to *link* to the surrounded item. This is similar to turning the page in a book. The "link" tells WebTV which page to turn to. Of course, instead of book pages, WebTV moves you around the Internet to Web pages and to WebTV special features.

When you perform these actions — moving the yellow box and then pressing Go or Return — you are "activating" a link. In the example on the facing page, you activate **TV Home** to move from the Web Home page to the TV Home page. Throughout this book, you are asked to activate a variety of WebTV features. These features are always visible. That is, you can always visually locate a feature and move the yellow box to it. Also, wherever you are directed to activate a link by pressing Go on the remote, you may also press Return on the keyboard to achieve the same result.

Mastering WebTV's yellow box is the first step toward mastering WebTV itself.

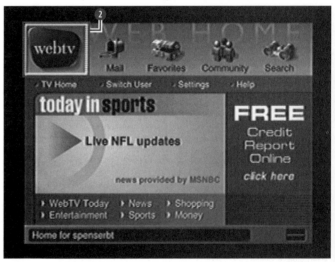

❶ The yellow box surrounds WebTV objects that may be activated with the Go button on your remote or the Return key on your keyboard.

❷ The arrow keys control the yellow box. In this example, the left arrow has been pressed and the yellow box has moved once to the left, from **Mail** to **WebTV Plus**.

CROSS-REFERENCE

Read about the yellow cursor in the next topic.

TAKE NOTE

NOTHING IS "ILLEGAL"

There are no "illegal" operations on WebTV. If you can move your yellow box to any visible feature, you can activate it with Go or Return. WebTV is so well designed that you will never face the same type of "Oh no! What did you do?" situations that face many new users of personal computers. WebTV is an extremely "safe" system. In general, you cannot perform actions that are harmful to your WebTV unit or account.

THE YELLOW CURSOR

Occasionally the yellow box will turn into a yellow blinking vertical line. This line is called the cursor and indicates when you can type and manipulate text. See the next topic for more details.

WEBTV CLASSIC

The yellow box works the same on WebTV Classic and WebTV Plus units. There is, however, no TV Home on the Classic unit as shown in the examples on the facing page.

▶ *A press of the down-arrow key moves the yellow box down to **TV Home**.*

❸ *With the yellow box in place, activate **TV Home** by pressing Go or Return.*

❹ *WebTV senses your actions — in particular the action of pressing Go or Return — and moves you to the TV Home page.*

FIND IT ONLINE

Read more about it. Visit **http://help.webtv.net/ newusers/yellowbox.html.**

Using the Yellow Cursor

The yellow cursor acts as the text-based analogy for the yellow box. Whereas the yellow box enables you to select and activate WebTV features, the yellow cursor enables you to edit words, sentences, and other text.

The yellow cursor is a yellow-colored vertical line that blinks periodically. It indicates the current text-entry location. Any character that you type appears directly before the location of the yellow cursor.

You can change the location of the yellow cursor — and hence the text-entry point — by moving the cursor with the arrow keys. The left and right arrow keys move the cursor horizontally. Wherever the cursor appears, newly typed text is entered to its left. If you wish to add text to the end of a line, move the cursor all the way to the right. If, instead, you want to insert text into an existing line, move the yellow cursor to the desired insertion point.

The up and down arrow keys move the cursor vertically. If the text entry space is a one-line area, as in the example on the facing page, the up and down arrows may move the cursor in another way. If the cursor moves to another text area, you can type in and edit this second text area. If the cursor moves out of the text area and onto a WebTV feature, it transforms from the yellow cursor to the yellow box.

When typing in a multiline text-entry area, such as an e-mail, be sure to use the Return key to move the yellow cursor to a new line and insert a carriage return. Many people become confused when their down-arrow key press moves them to the **Send** button instead of inserting a new line. The Return key on both the physical and onscreen keyboards correctly moves the yellow cursor to a fresh line without leaving the text-edit area.

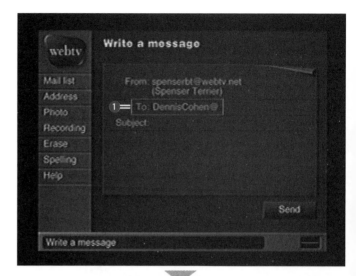

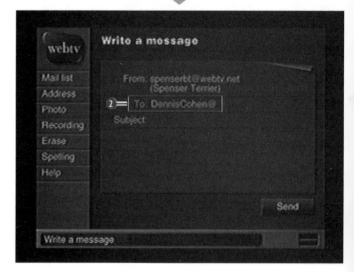

▶ *From your Web Home, activate **Mail**. From the Mail list, activate **Write**. A new Write a message screen appears.*

❶ *When WebTV expects you to enter text, the yellow cursor appears. The yellow cursor is the blinking yellow-colored vertical line.*

❷ *As you type text, the yellow cursor moves to the right, showing the current point of text insertion.*

CROSS-REFERENCE

Read about the yellow box in the previous topic.

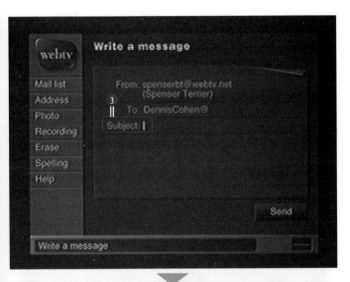

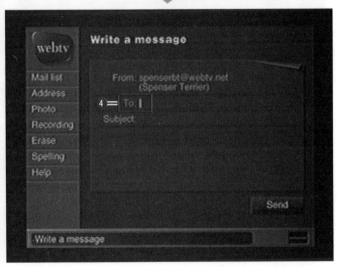

▶ THE EDIT BUTTON

When the yellow box surrounds a text-entry area, but the yellow cursor is not evident, press Edit to activate the text area and its yellow cursor. You can also press Go or Return for identical results.

▶ RETURNING TO THE YELLOW BOX

When you move the cursor outside a text area, it will turn back into the yellow box. The yellow blinking cursor can appear only in areas that support text entry and manipulation. This rule, cursor for text and box for navigating WebTV and the World Wide Web, applies universally when using WebTV.

▶ WEBTV CLASSIC

The yellow cursor works the same on WebTV Classic and WebTV Plus units.

③ The left and right arrow keys enable you to move the yellow cursor to the left or right within a text area. In this example, the yellow cursor has been moved to the left of the @ sign. Any new text typed appears at the location of the cursor, and hence to the left of the sign.

④ Press the up and down arrows to move between lines. In this case, the down arrow has moved the yellow cursor to the next text field, the **Subject:** line.

Using the Onscreen Keyboard

Whether using WebTV's built-in features or exploring the World Wide Web, you need to type text. Many screens contain areas for you to fill in with text. These fill-in forms are recognizable by the presence of a yellow blinking vertical line.

Text entry areas vary widely. They include text slots intended for a single line of text, boxes for paragraphs of text, and large free-form areas, such as those used for writing e-mail. What unifies these different visual elements on your screen is the cursor. The yellow cursor will always alert you to screen areas in which you are expected to enter text.

If you do not own a physical keyboard (whether the optional remote keyboard or, with the Classic unit, a PS/2-style keyboard), you will need to use the onscreen keyboard to enter information in these areas. The onscreen keyboard is certainly not the fastest way to enter text. I highly recommend using a physical keyboard. However, WebTV provides an easy-to-use, if not terribly efficient, alternative with its onscreen keyboard.

You can set up the onscreen keyboard to use either traditional QWERTY or alphabetical ABCDE key layouts (see Chapter 17). Many nontypists find the alphabetical layout easier to use, whereas experienced touch typists prefer the QWERTY keyboard. Typing is a matter of using your remote's arrow keys and the Go button to select keystrokes.

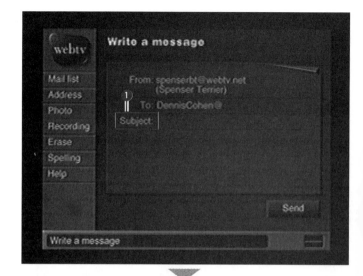

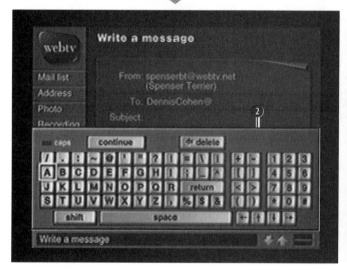

❶ *The blinking yellow cursor indicates that WebTV expects typed text. To bring up the onscreen keyboard, press Go on the remote control when you see the yellow cursor.*

❷ *Use the arrow keys to select individual letters, numbers, and punctuation with the yellow box. After selecting each keystroke, press Go on the remote control. Text appears at the insertion point above.*

CROSS-REFERENCE

Read about special keys on your keyboard in the next topic.

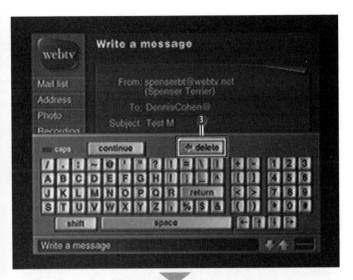

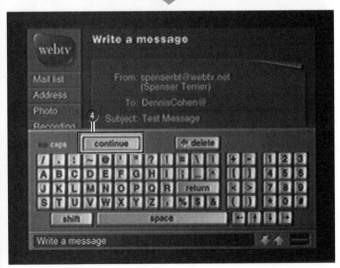

3 *If you make a mistake, move the arrow keys to highlight* **Delete** *and press Go on the remote control.*

4 *When finished, use the arrow keys to highlight* **Continue** *and press Go on the remote control.*

TAKE NOTE

▶ CAPITAL LETTERS

To capitalize a single letter, use the arrow keys to highlight **shift** and press Go. The red **caps** indicator at the upper left of your onscreen keyboard will illuminate. Move the arrow keys to highlight any letter and press Go again. This letter is typed capitalized and the **caps** indicator is turned off, the keyboard reverting to lowercase.

▶ DO NOT WORRY ABOUT LINE WRAPS

WebTV automatically handles line wraps. When you reach the end of a line, keep typing. If you want to leave a space between paragraphs, simply use Return on the onscreen keyboard to end a paragraph or to add extra vertical space.

▶ GET RID OF THE KEYBOARD

If you ever bring up the onscreen keyboard by accident, press Back on your remote or on your (physical) keyboard to hide it again.

▶ THE EDIT KEY

If at any time you believe you are at a text-entry area, but the yellow cursor is not flashing, try pressing Go on your remote control. If this truly is a text-entry space, the yellow box will disappear and be replaced by the yellow cursor within the space.

▶ WEBTV CLASSIC

Onscreen keyboards work the same on WebTV Classic and WebTV Plus units.

FIND IT ONLINE

Read more about the red "shift indicator light." Visit **http://help.webtv.net/keyboards/reddot.html.**

Touring the Keyboard

WebTV's optional remote keyboard has a myriad of buttons and features associated with it, but not all of their uses are intuitive. The keyboard is designed to present you with the most power and options in the least available physical space. In this, WebTV has succeeded. The keyboard is small, light, and portable. It does not, however, sacrifice functionality for size. The keyboard has a vast array of functions despite its diminutive dimensions.

For those people familiar with typewriter keyboards, the center of the WebTV remote keyboard looks like a standard typewriter keyboard. The keys are laid out in the common QWERTY pattern. Many standard functions are replicated here: shift key, caps lock, tab, spacebar, and carriage return. If you have used a normal typewriter, the center of the keyboard does not vary much from your experience.

It is the keys that line the edges that provide the WebTV keyboard with its additional functionality. Many of these keys may be unfamiliar to people without significant personal computing experience.

Keys are labeled fn, cmd, home, and scroll up. You may find the purpose of these keys obscure. To remedy this, take the tour on the facing page. Although experience alone provides comfort and familiarity, a solid tour of the keys acquaints you with the general purpose of the key groups and should smooth your introduction to the keyboard.

① The keyboard's right side has keys for basic navigation.

② The arrow keys move you directionally. The scroll keys move you a page at a time.

③ The back button returns you to your previous task. The recent button presents a list of recently visited pages.

④ The options button lets you access a menu of common WebTV functions.

⑤ The keyboard's bottom left has keys related to keyboard functions. The ctrl and fn keys are rarely used.

⑥ The caps lock and shift keys capitalize typed characters.

⑦ The alt key lets you type foreign language characters.

⑧ Using the cmd key with other keys, you can copy, cut, and paste text, and so forth. Use of this key is addressed elsewhere.

CROSS-REFERENCE

Read about the onscreen keyboard in the previous topic.

MOVING FAST

Pressing cmd and one of the scroll keys zooms you to the top or bottom of the current page.

RELOAD A PAGE

Want to reload a Web page? Press and hold cmd and tap R. This is enormously convenient when you view pages with changing content, such as news features, stock listings, and so on.

ARE YOU SECURE?

Is the Internet page that you are looking at secure? Find out by pressing the info key. If the page is secure, a button labeled Security Details appears and lets you view specifics for this Web page.

ASSIGNED FAVORITES

The F keys on the upper left of the keyboard can be assigned to seven "favorite" pages. To learn how, read more about it in Section II.

WEBTV CLASSIC

Keyboards generally work the same on WebTV Classic and WebTV Plus units. However, there are certain WebTV Plus features (such as TV Home) that cannot be accessed on WebTV Classic, even though the keys or buttons are available on the keyboard.

⑨ The keyboard's top-right contains a hodge-podge of keys. The edit key brings up the yellow cursor for text entry. The find key searches for information on the page.

⑩ The info key provides information about your page, while the goto key lets you bring up another page. Save a page to your favorites or send its address by e-mail.

⑪ The keyboard's top-middle section contains keys devoted to the tasks you most commonly want to access. Favs takes you to your favorite page, home to your home page, and mail to your mailbox. The search key brings you directly to WebTV's Internet search page.

FIND IT ONLINE

Visit **http://www.useit.com/alertbox/9702a.html** for a discussion of the WebTV remote and keyboard.

Personal Workbook

Q&A

1 How do you power on your WebTV unit?

_____

_____

_____

2 Can you use WebTV without buying the optional keyboard?

_____

_____

_____

3 What does the onscreen keyboard do?

_____

_____

_____

4 How do you make the onscreen keyboard display?

_____

_____

_____

5 How do you finish typing with the onscreen keyboard?

_____

_____

_____

6 What does it mean to "activate" a WebTV feature?

_____

_____

_____

7 What does the home key do on the keyboard?

_____

_____

_____

8 If the yellow cursor is not blinking, how do you activate a text-entry space?

_____

_____

_____

ANSWERS: PAGE 333

EXTRA PRACTICE

1 Move the yellow box around the screen and activate some WebTV features.

2 Use the back button after activating a feature to return to the previous page.

3 Type text using the onscreen keyboard.

4 Acquaint yourself with the special keys on the remote keyboard.

5 Practice making the onscreen keyboard appear and disappear.

6 Use the arrow and delete keys to practice editing text.

REAL-WORLD APPLICATIONS

✔ You do not own a WebTV keyboard. You try borrowing one and discover that it makes typing far easier.

✔ From your WebTV home screen, you move the yellow box to the bottom right of your WebTV screen. You activate this corner and you are able to visit My WebTV, which contains the latest news headlines and weather.

✔ From your WebTV home screen, you move the yellow box to **Search** and activate it. You practice entering text into the search text space.

Visual Quiz

How do you make this onscreen keyboard disappear?

_____

_____

_____

_____

_____

_____

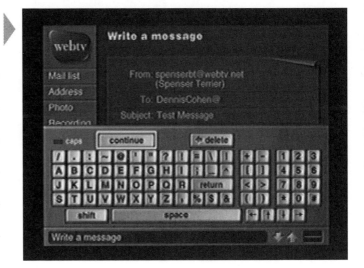

CHAPTER 2

MASTER THESE SKILLS

▶ **Removing Text with the Delete Key**

▶ **Highlighting and Selecting Text**

▶ **Copying and Pasting Text**

▶ **Cutting and Pasting Text**

▶ **Adding Special Characters**

▶ **Checking Spelling**

Editing Text

To be in control of what you write, you need to be able to manipulate text. This chapter introduces you to various methods of taking charge of the text you write, of fixing errors, and of producing special text effects.

First, you master the Delete key. This key lets you quickly correct misspellings and typographic mistakes. The Delete key is a vital part of the basic text editing process.

Second, you learn to highlight and select text. This allows you to mark portions of text for later manipulation. Highlighting text is an important prerequisite to advanced text-manipulation techniques.

Third, you learn to cut, copy, and paste highlighted text. This allows you to remove text, to reposition it, or to duplicate it elsewhere. These three features — cutting, copying, and pasting — form the basis for the most important text-editing techniques.

Finally, you learn to add special characters to your text such as mathematical symbols, including fractions, foreign currency symbols, and letters found in foreign alphabets. You learn how to insert these special characters and add accents to letters.

When you have finished this chapter, you will have mastered a number of techniques related to correcting, editing, and enhancing your text.

Removing Text with the Delete Key

The Delete key is a useful and immediate tool for correcting typographic errors. This key will remove one character to the left of the flashing yellow cursor with each key press. Need to remove one letter? Press it once. Need to remove five letters? Press it five times. Each time you tap Delete, one character is erased.

You may switch between deleting characters, moving the yellow cursor, and typing new characters at any time. For example, if you mistyped "General Washingson," you may move the cursor to just before the *o*, tap Delete to remove the *s*, and tap t to correct the spelling. You do not have to enter a special "delete" mode to correct your mistakes. You can type — and correct — on the fly.

Delete acts as a buffer between you and mistakes. If you catch a typographic error immediately, a single tap will move you back, ready to enter the correct character. If a mistake is found on reviewing already entered text, the arrow keys will move the yellow cursor into place to allow deletion and, possibly, corrective insertion.

Having grown up with traditional typewriters — correction tape, whiteout, and so on — I find it a great relief to be able to correct my spelling on the fly. I do not miss the mechanical labors that were once involved. The electronic age and the Delete key have made proper spelling much more approachable.

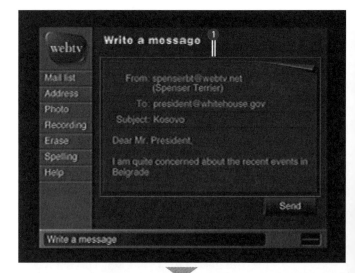

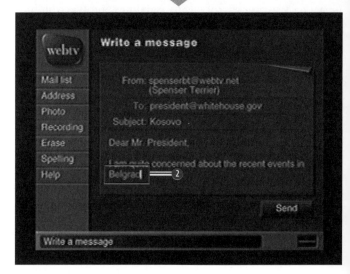

❶ Begin with a new Write a message screen. From your Home Page, activate **Mail**. From your Mail list, activate **Write**. Type any message in the text area.

❷ While typing, press delete once to remove a single character. The character to the left of the yellow cursor is removed.

CROSS-REFERENCE

Read about using the WebTV remote keyboard in the previous chapter.

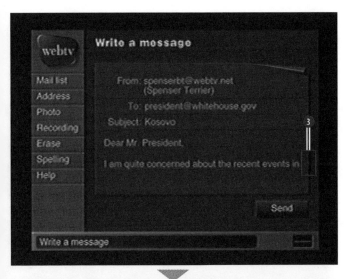

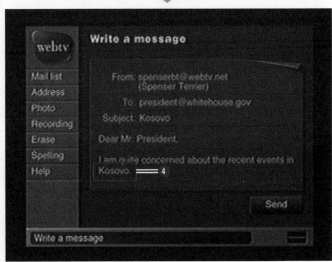

▶ **UNDO**

WebTV does not provide any "undo" mechanism for deleting characters. If you accidentally press delete too many times, you will have to manually retype that text back in.

▶ **INSERTION**

You do not need to take any special actions to insert text. Whatever characters you type will be inserted at the yellow cursor. Contrast this with the behavior of some personal computer programs that require you to press an Insert key. WebTV will never "overwrite" existing text. The designers, who have placed the emphasis on ease-of-use and safety, have saved us enormous headaches with their simple and straightforward design.

▶ **REMOVE AN ENTIRE LINE**

Want a shortcut to remove an entire line at once? Press and hold the cmd button and tap delete. WebTV will delete the whole line. Which line? The line in which the blinking yellow cursor is positioned.

▶ **WEBTV CLASSIC**

WebTV Classic supports delete functions just like WebTV Plus.

❸ *To remove additional characters, press delete again — once for each character to be removed. When all undesired characters have been eliminated, start typing the corrected text.*

❹ *After the correction has been made, continue with your typing task.*

FIND IT ONLINE

Visit an online dictionary at
http://www.dictionary.com.

Highlighting and Selecting Text

WebTV lets you select an entire section of text at a single time. This selection process is called "highlighting." Text within the selection is colored with a green background. Selected text can be changed, reused, altered, and so on. With selections, you can work with a word, a line, or even multiple paragraphs at one time, rather than focusing on single characters.

There are several ways to select text. The simplest involves holding down the Shift key while tapping the arrow keys. The arrow keys move the yellow cursor. The characters between the original location of the yellow cursor and its new location become selected.

If you tap the left or right arrows while creating a selection, you increase your selection by a single character at a time. If you tap the up and down arrows while holding down the Shift key, your selection will grow by an entire line at a time. To deselect highlighted text, continue holding down the Shift key and tap the opposite arrow.

You can select the entire text by pressing the cmd key while tapping A. This shortcut, called "select all," highlights the entire text.

Highlighted text can be manipulated in many ways, which you will read about further in the following topics.

The best way to explore text manipulation is to practice creating an e-mail message. Press the Mail button to move to your mailbox and activate **Write**. Use the arrow keys to move the yellow cursor to the blank space just below the word "Subject:." Type some sample text into this area and you are ready to practice highlighting and selecting skills. Practice using the Shift and cmd keys to exercise precise control over your selection.

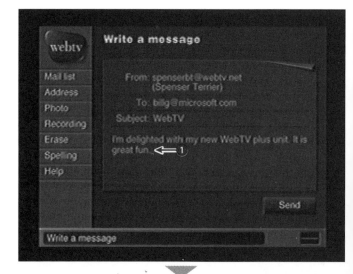

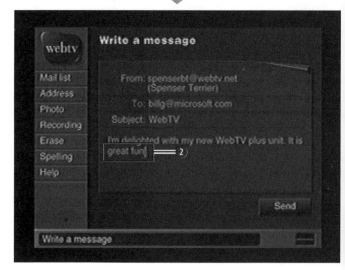

❶ To highlight a single character, press and hold Shift and tap the left arrow. In this example, the period will be selected.

❷ To expand the selection, continue to press Shift and tap the left arrow several more times. This example highlights "great fun."

CROSS-REFERENCE

Read how to use highlighted text in the next few topics.

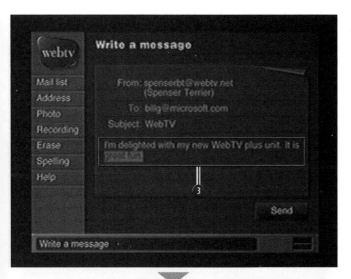

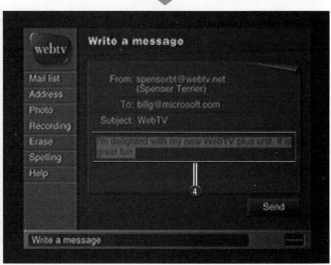

③ To add a whole line to the selection, tap the up arrow while pressing Shift .

④ As you can see, WebTV added an entire line to the selection. Everything is selected and highlighted.

FIND IT ONLINE

Read more about it. Visit **http://help.webtv.net/mail/ cutpaste/selecttext.html**.

Copying and Pasting Text

Sometimes you find a turn of phrase that sparks your fancy or strikes you as being misplaced. In either case, you may want to copy that text and reuse it elsewhere. You can tell WebTV to "remember" some text by highlighting it and "copying" it to memory.

To copy any highlighted text, simply press and hold the cmd key and tap C. This tells WebTV to remember that text in its special memory. You can place this text anywhere you move the yellow cursor. To paste the remembered text, press and hold the cmd key and tap V.

WebTV can only "remember" one thing at a time. If you copy one selection and then copy a second selection, WebTV will "forget" the first, replacing it in its memory with the second. Remember this when you have a number of things that you wish to paste. You may have to use the recent button to move back and forth between the information you are interested in copying and the page where you are pasting the text.

Some people ask, "Why C?" and, "Why V?" The answers are not terribly complex. "C" is short for the word "Copy" and "V" looks like the caret mark that publishers use for inserting text. These conventions of "C" for copy, "V" for paste, and "X" for cut, have been used on computers for decades and are considered "standard" abbreviations.

Most often, you will use copy and paste while composing letters. You may copy from one part of the letter to another. You may copy from an old letter to a new one. You may also copy information from a Web site or other Internet location and insert it into your letter. You can leave mail with a letter in progress and return to it later. WebTV stores your in-progress letter until you return to finish it or erase it. (See Chapter 10 for more information.)

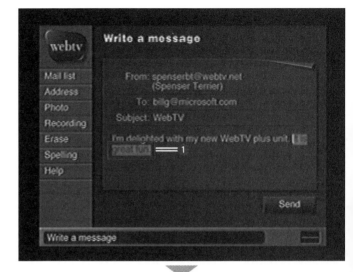

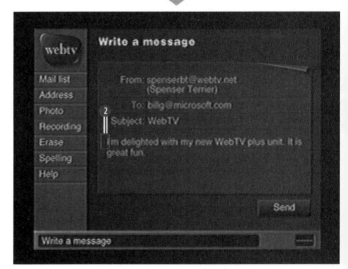

1 This example shows how to copy selected text and reuse it elsewhere. Start by highlighting some text. Copy it by pressing the cmd key and tapping C.

2 Move the yellow cursor to the position where you wish to insert the copied text. In this case we're moving it to the beginning of the message.

CROSS-REFERENCE

Read how to use cut text in the next topic.

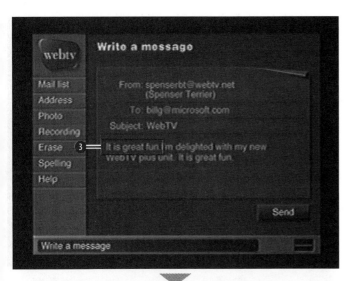

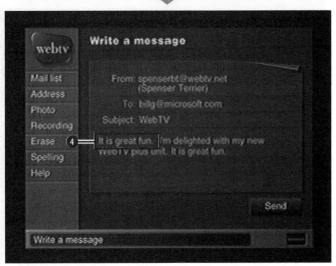

❸ *Press and hold the cmd key and tap V to paste the copied text at the location of the yellow cursor.*

▶ *Because we have not pasted spaces after the period, press the spacebar a couple of times to insert the proper spacing.*

❹ *The newly copied and pasted text appears before the original text.*

Cutting and Pasting Text

Sometimes a phrase is misplaced. If you are editing some text, you can cut a phrase from one place and paste it where it better belongs.

To cut any highlighted text, press and hold the cmd key and tap X. This tells WebTV to remove that text but store it in its temporary memory. You can place this text anywhere you move the yellow cursor. To paste the remembered text, press and hold the cmd key and tap V.

When cutting text, it is not necessary that you paste it anywhere. You can choose to cut some text out of your work and never reuse it. While copying lends itself automatically to pasting, cutting does not. Only paste cut text if you wish to reuse it; otherwise, forget it.

Although "copy and paste" and "cut and paste" operate in a similar fashion, they are used for different reasons. Copy and paste is used when you need to retain a copy of the original text in its original location. Cut and paste is used when you want to move a piece of text to a new physical location. However, as with copying and pasting, you can create several new locations for that text.

As with the previous task of highlighting and selecting, the best way to practice these skills is to create a practice e-mail message and manipulate its text. To work on a practice e-mail, press the Mail key and then activate **Write**. Then move the yellow cursor to the blank space just below the line labeled "Subject:." This area lets you type, highlight, cut, copy, and paste text. You do not need to address the letter or ever send it. To start a fresh letter and remove your changes, activate **Erase**.

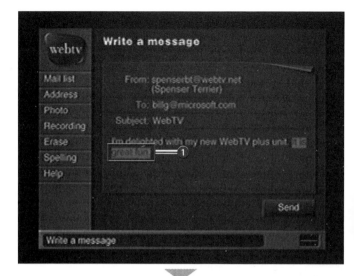

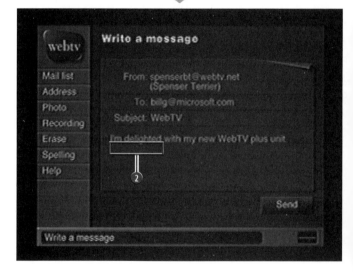

❶ This example shows how to cut the selected text and reuse it elsewhere. Start by selecting some text.

❷ Cut the text by pressing and holding the cmd key while tapping X.

CROSS-REFERENCE

Read how to use copied text in the previous topic.

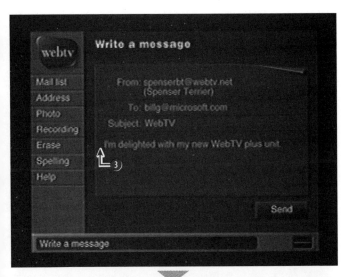

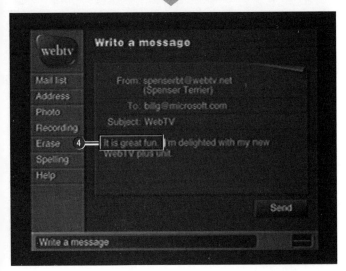

PASTING SEVERAL COPIES

After cutting or copying, you can, if you wish, paste the copied text in several places. WebTV does not "forget" the cut or copied text until you have powered the unit off or cut or copied a different selection.

PASTING IN DIFFERENT LOCATIONS

You do not have to perform all paste operations in a single e-mail or other text area. Once information has been copied to WebTV's memory, it can be used again and again throughout numerous tasks. You can paste a joke or a story in several e-mails at different times. You can paste personal information on a number of Web pages. So long as your WebTV unit is not powered off and no new information has been copied or cut, WebTV retains the text selection in memory.

WEBTV CLASSIC

WebTV Classic allows cutting and pasting in the same way as WebTV Plus.

❸ *Move the yellow cursor to the position you wish to insert the cut text. In this case we moved to the beginning of the text.*

❹ *Press and hold the cmd key and tap V. This pastes the cut text at the location of the yellow cursor.*

▶ *Because we have not pasted spaces after the period, press the spacebar a couple of times to insert the proper spacing.*

FIND IT ONLINE

Read more about it. Visit **http://help.webtv.net/mail/ cutpaste/paste.html.**

Adding Special Characters

WebTV includes a key on your keyboard labeled Alt, which is short for alternate. This key lets you type special characters. When you press and hold Alt and tap other characters, WebTV produces a variety of special numbers and punctuation, as well as a fair number of foreign characters.

These characters include fractions, foreign currency symbols, accented characters (including grave, acute, tilde, circumflex, dieresis, cedillas, and such), and others. This expanded character set lets you communicate more effectively with foreign correspondents, mathematicians, and other people who use special characters.

To create an accented character, first type the special key combination for that accent. For example, to add an acute accent, press and hold Alt and tap the apostrophe or single quote key ('). Next, tap the character you wish to accent, for example, A. This produces an Á with the acute accent. This combination — first producing the accent and then the affected character — will correctly create whichever special character you need. However, you can create certain accented characters simply by pressing Alt and the letter. For instance, press Alt and type E to create an acute accented é.

If you are typing nonaccented characters — that is special characters that are not associated with a base character — simply type the Alt combination. For example, to type the Greek character mu (μ), press and hold Alt and tap M. You need not type additional keys to produce the character.

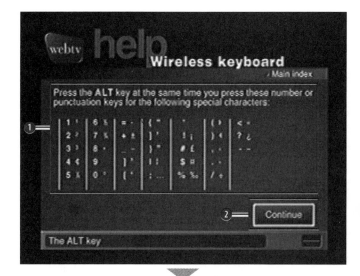

❶ To reach this table and the ones that follow, type *http://help.webtv.net/keyboards/specialchar.html* and then activate *Alt Command List*. The table lists the special characters that you can produce with Alt and numbers and punctuation marks.

❷ Activate *Continue* to move to the next reference page.

❸ This table lists the alphabetic combinations you can produce using Alt.

❹ Activate *Continue twice* to move to the next reference page.

CROSS-REFERENCE

Read more about the keyboard in Chapter 1.

Not every accent is available for every character. For example, you can add an acute accent to e, but not to x.

Similarly, not every accented or foreign character has been mapped to an intuitively obvious key. For example, the copyright symbol © is connected to the letter g. The lowercase letter l is used to create the mathematical symbol for Boolean negation, again a big stretch.

WebTV has access to a limited number of keystrokes. Clearly, they had to use the available keystrokes as efficiently as possible. Some keystroke combinations are mysterious at best, but are still easily found on the keystroke charts.

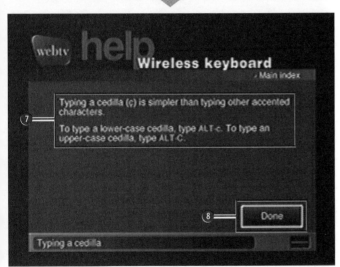

TAKE NOTE

▶ **SHORTCUT YOUR CEDILLA**

The combination Alt+C produces a C-cedilla — as in the word façade — without having to use the more complex accent methodology. Note that the cedilla only affects the letter c. Need an uppercase C-cedilla? Press Shift in combination with the other keys (Shift+Alt+C).

▶ **WEBTV CLASSIC**

WebTV Classic allows typing of special characters, as does WebTV Plus.

⑤ This table lists the accent shortcuts. Note for which letters each accent is available.

⑥ Activate **Continue** to move to the next reference page.

⑦ This page tells you how to add cedillas to your letters.

⑧ Press **Done** or the Home key to leave these help pages.

FIND IT ONLINE

Read more about it. Visit **http://help.webtv.net/keyboards/specialchar.html**.

Checking Spelling

A re you a poor speller or typist? Do you get ahead of yourself when you're composing a message? Finally, do you really hate it when people criticize your spelling errors?

WebTV's e-mail system offers you a little peace of mind. There is a spelling checker that can check your email for you before you send the message.

At any time during your message composition you can invoke the spell-checker by moving the yellow box to **Spelling** and pressing either Go or Return. The spell-checker even has Help screens associated with it.

Once you've invoked the spell-checker, it will go through your message a word at a time, highlighting any word it doesn't recognize. It will offer you a list of alternative words.

If you're sure that you have the word spelled correctly (maybe it's an acronym that the spell-checker would not know or a company name) you can tell the spell-checker to skip this word and go on to the next suspected misspelling.

If you see the word you really meant to type in the list of suggestions, select it with the yellow box and press Go. The spell-checker will make the replacement and proceed to the next questionable spelling.

At any point in the process you may back up to the previous word (maybe you skipped and didn't mean to or decided that you wanted a different suggestion than the one you chose) by selecting **Previous** and pressing Go.

Maybe you just don't like any of the suggestions that WebTV is offering but do know the correct spelling (or just want to use a different word). Select the text in the **Possible Misspelling** box, change it as described earlier in this chapter, select the **Change** button, and press Go.

When you're done, select **Done** and press Go to see your message redisplayed with all the changes made.

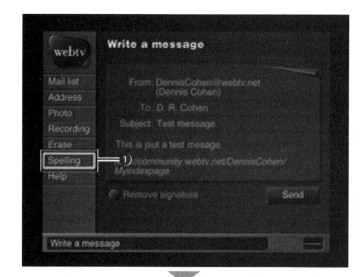

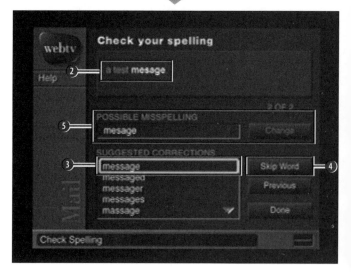

❶ *After you have created the text of your email message, select **Spelling** and press Go.*

❷ *When the spellchecker encounters a misspelling, it displays the word in context.*

❸ *Select the correct spelling from the list of suggestions and press Go.*

❹ *If you don't wish to change the spelling, select **Skip Word** and press Go, or*

❺ *Correct the word in the Possible Misspelling box, then select **Change**.*

CROSS-REFERENCE

Learn more about e-mail in Part III.

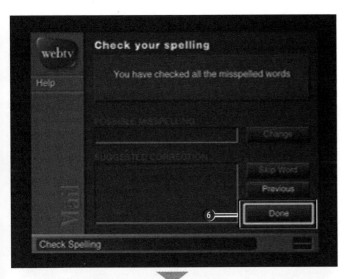

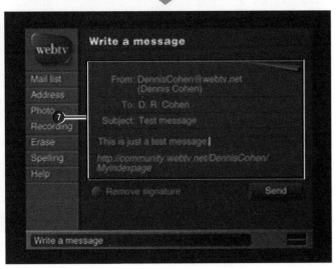

TAKE NOTE

FALSE SECURITY

Spellchecking only guarantees that the words you typed are really words, not that they are the right words. There is no context-checking to ascertain that you really want "there" rather than "their" or "they're." Similarly, if you have a typo and produce "field" when you meant to type "filed," the spell-checker won't catch the error. Don't get a false sense of security — recheck what you've typed even after spell-checking.

INFLEXIBLE DICTIONARY

Unlike the spell-checking software in personal computer word processors, you are limited to the words in WebTV's dictionary. This means that you will be questioned about technical terms, names, and acronyms each time they are encountered.

WEBTV CLASSIC

WebTV Classic supports spell-checking the same as WebTV Plus.

⑥ Select **Done** and press Go when you have finished checking the spelling of your message.

⑦ WebTV will return you to your email message with all of the spelling changes implemented.

FIND IT ONLINE

Learn about HTML at **http://www.utoronto.ca/ webdocs/HTMLdocs/NewHTML/index.html.**

Personal Workbook

Q&A

1 When you press Delete, which character is removed?

_____

_____

_____

2 What happens if you press Delete while the yellow cursor is positioned before the entirety of your text?

_____

_____

_____

3 How do you highlight text with the arrow keys?

_____

_____

_____

4 How do you cut highlighted text?

_____

_____

_____

5 What is the difference between cutting and copying text?

_____

_____

_____

6 What does cmd+A do?

_____

_____

_____

7 What happens if you type cmd+A several times in sequence?

_____

_____

_____

8 Do you execute the command to add an accent before or after the letter it will be attached to?

_____

_____

_____

ANSWERS: PAGE 333

EXTRA PRACTICE

1 Type some text and delete it.

2 Highlight some text.

3 Copy some text.

4 Cut some text.

5 Paste some text.

6 Type some special characters.

REAL-WORLD APPLICATIONS

✔ You try writing to a friend in a foreign country. You include special characters unique to the language of that country.

✔ You write a letter to a friend and copy the body of the text. Then you send the letter to several other friends by pasting the text, but editing the recipients' names and addresses.

✔ You write a "puzzle" letter. You cut out every other line and paste the lines in a second letter. You send both copies to a correspondent and let him or her puzzle out your meaning.

Visual Quiz

How do you type the one-half character?

_____

_____

_____

_____

_____

_____

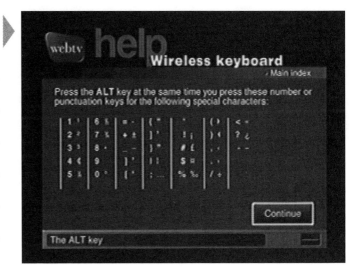

CHAPTER 3

MASTER THESE SKILLS

▶ Selecting One Option from Many

▶ Selecting Many Options

▶ Selecting from a Pull-Down List

▶ Selecting from a Scrolling List

▶ Selecting from a Multiple-Choice List

▶ Entering a Password

▶ Selecting from a Picture

▶ Resetting and Submitting Forms

Filling Out Forms

O n the Web, as in life, forms abound. Just as we have job applications, sales slips, and tax forms in the real world, there are various forms to fill out while on the Internet. With online forms, you may have to type information on lines and in boxes, or make check marks, or select an item from a list.

This chapter introduces you to some of the most common form elements on the Web. If you are unsure how to make a selection, these lessons show you how.

The Internet provides a range of interaction styles, allowing you to select information in many ways. Some form elements let you select a single choice out of a field of many. Other form elements let you choose as many or as few options as you wish. Still others reset the form to the default values, or submit the form to a Web page's owner.

Although a thorough survey of all form elements could make up a whole book, this chapter introduces you to the most common — and most confusing — types of form entry on the World Wide Web. By the time you finish this chapter, you will be familiar enough with these form techniques to be able to handle the majority of forms that you encounter while on the Web.

Selecting One Option from Many

You can quickly recognize a "one-of-many" choice when filling out forms. This type of form element looks like a list. A column of circles appears to the left of the list, one on each line. These circles are called radio buttons. The name derives from the fact that people can only listen to one radio station at a time.

When you push a station button on a real radio, you can no longer listen to your original station. The "radio button" list operates the same way. When you select a choice with the yellow box and activate it with Go or Return, any previous selection is superceded by your new choice.

Why do people include one-of-many choices in forms? To limit your selection to a single option. For example, you may wish to receive your newspaper on Sundays, on weekdays, on weekends, or daily. It is unlikely you would choose both daily (seven days a week) and Sunday delivery — unless you wish to receive two editions each Sunday. The designers of a form who wish to reasonably limit your choice to only one of a selection of options, will present a radio buttons list to you.

The red dot

WebTV displays all radio button selections the same way. It shows a column of circles to the left of each option. Options that have been chosen appear with a bright red dot. This consistency of presentation ensures that you can recognize a one-of-many choice in any form you fill out.

Some radio button choices appear as a line of options rather than a column. The circle always appears to the left of each option. Be sure to recognize that circles indicate one-of-many choices regardless of the physical configuration of the list.

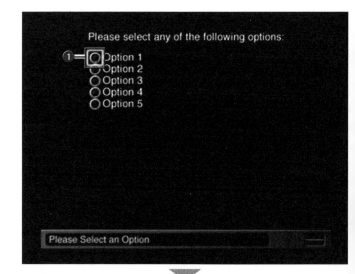

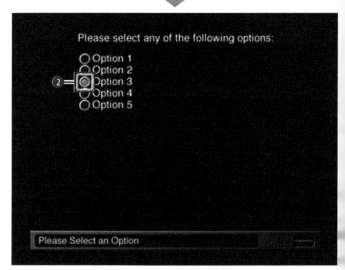

▶ *This example uses a screen created by me to demonstrate the use of the one-of-many choice.*

❶ *To select an option from a one-of-many list, move the yellow box to the related radio button and activate it. In this example, there is no default option, so no circles have yet been highlighted with a red dot.*

❷ *Once you move the yellow box to an empty radio button and activate it, a red dot will appear within the button. In this example, I chose Option 3.*

CROSS-REFERENCE

Learn to select several options at once in the next topic.

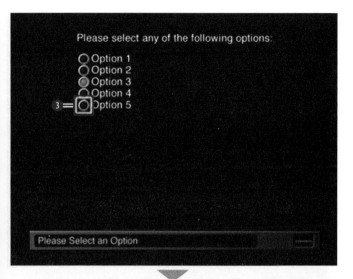

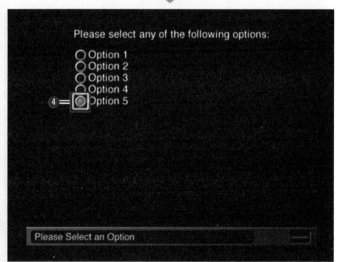

TAKE NOTE

YOU CANNOT PICK TWO

There is no way to select two options on a radio button list. If you are permitted to select more than one option, you will see checkboxes instead. This is detailed further in the next topic.

DEFAULT SELECTIONS

In the example on the facing page, there is no default selection. The list appears initially without a predetermined choice. This varies by form. Some forms appear with one option already selected. Others do not. A predetermined selection is called the "default." The designer of the form has picked this option as the one you are most likely to choose.

MULTIPLE ONE-OF-MANY CHOICES

A single form can contain many radio button choice lists. A well-designed form, however, makes it clear where one list begins and another ends.

WEBTV CLASSIC

Forms appear the same on WebTV Classic and WebTV Plus.

③ After an option is chosen, you may move the yellow box to another selection. Only one option can be selected at a time.

④ When you activate the new option, the selection moves. In this case, Option 5 is selected and Option 3 is deactivated.

FIND IT ONLINE

Find out about Talk Radio. Visit **http://www.talkradioguide.com/**.

Selecting Many Options

To recognize a "pick any options" choice, look for square boxes. Each square box appears before an option. These choices may appear as a list, as a row, or as a series of columns of choices.

To pick an option, move the yellow box to the square box that appears to its left. Check the box by activating it with Go or Return. Want to uncheck the box? Press Go or Return again.

When you encounter this form element, you may select as many options as you want. You can select as few as zero options or as many as all. Whereas a one-of-many choice might ask you to choose your job title, a pick any options choice might ask you to list your job responsibilities. Perhaps you might pick marketing, correspondence, sales calls, or something else. This form element lets you select all those options that best fit your answer.

WebTV makes it easy to identify a pick any options choice. The square boxes and check marks provide a quick visual cue. When you see these visual elements in a form, you will recognize that you may select any of several choices.

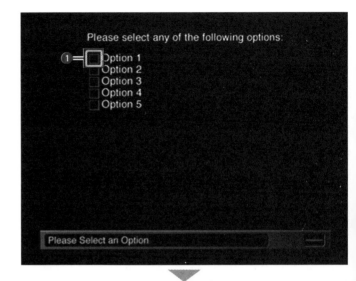

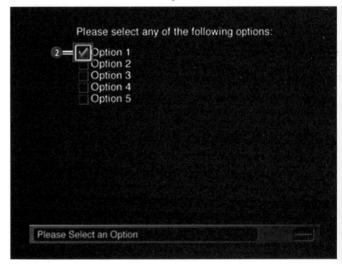

▶ This example uses a mocked-up screen that I created to demonstrate the use of the select-many choice.

❶ To select any option from the select-many list, move the yellow box and activate it with Go or Return.

❷ Checkmarks appear in the options that you select.

CROSS-REFERENCE

Learn to select a one-of many option in the previous topic.

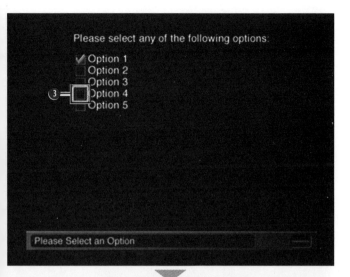

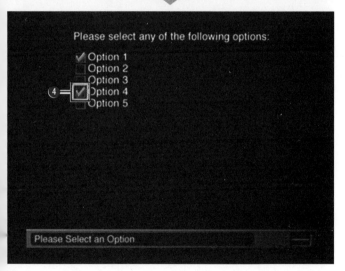

TAKE NOTE

DEFAULT SELECTIONS

Occasionally, you find forms with preexisting checks, which are called default selections. The person who designed the form felt it likely that these options apply to most people. If you do not wish to accept these defaults, uncheck those options.

THE CHECK MARK

WebTV displays all checkbox selections the same way. It shows a column of squares corresponding to a list of options. Options that have been chosen appear with a check mark. You should be able to recognize an any-of-many choice in any form you are filling out.

ROWS VERSUS COLUMNS

Some checkbox choices appear as a line of options rather than a column. The corresponding checkbox always appears to the left of each option. Be sure to recognize that squares and checks indicate any-of-many choices. You should easily identify them regardless of the physical configuration of the list.

WEBTV CLASSIC

WebTV Classic and WebTV Plus both utilize check box option forms.

③ *After an option is selected, you may move the yellow box to another selection.*

④ *You may select any number of boxes to check — from none to all.*

▶ *You may remove checks by moving the yellow box to the selected option and pressing Go or Return.*

FIND IT ONLINE

See checkboxes in action. Visit **http://wecare.webtv. net/mail/receive/extras.html.**

Selecting from a Pull-Down List

To recognize a pull-down list, look for a gray, rounded rectangle with a down-facing triangle. When you activate this rectangle, the list of options will appear. Select an option with the yellow box and press Go or Return.

The gray, rounded rectangle always shows the current selection. Only one option can be selected at a time. When you select a new option, it replaces the previous option.

Sometimes more options exist than can be displayed on the screen at once. When this occurs, you can move up and down through the options using either the arrow or scroll keys. Gray triangles pointing up or down indicate when more options exist.

You will find pull-down lists in many places on WebTV. For example, WebTV uses these lists to let you select times for checking e-mail or downloading TV listings and for setting the default presentation font size.

Pull-down lists function in much the same way as radio buttons. Both provide one-of-many selections. So why does WebTV offer both features? The answer, in a nutshell, is screen space. Radio button choices show you every option at once, but they take up a lot of room on your screen. Pull-down lists, in contrast, show only your current choice unless the list is opened. This allows the information to be "packed away" until you are ready to make your selection, saving a great deal of room on the screen.

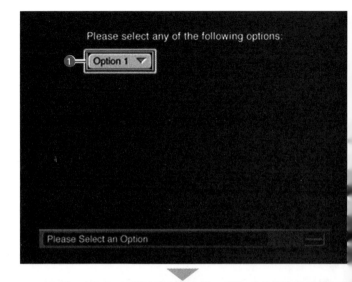

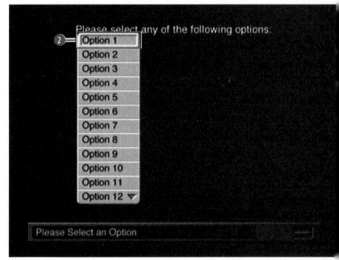

▶ This example uses a mocked up screen that I created to demonstrate the use of the pull-down choice.

❶ To select an option from the pull-down list, start by highlighting the button with the yellow box and pressing Go or Return.

❷ The list appears. Use the arrow keys to move the yellow box to your selection.

CROSS-REFERENCE

Learn how to select an option from a scrolling list in the next topic.

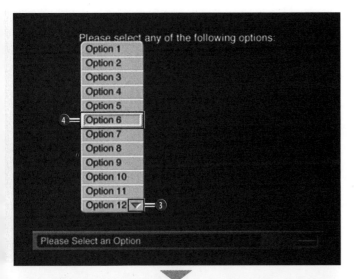

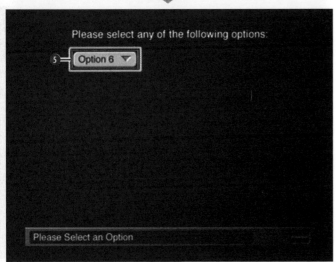

PULL-DOWN LISTS SAVE SPACE

Many form designers use pull-down lists to save screen space. When an option is selected, it is easily seen and the other choices are conveniently hidden. This enables the designer to better use the remaining space on the screen.

DEFAULT SELECTIONS

Any option initially displayed on the rounded gray rectangle is considered the default. Sometimes the gray rectangle starts out blank (except for the downward triangle). This indicates that the form designer has not selected a default choice.

THE ROUNDED GRAY BOX

WebTV displays all pull-down lists the same way. It shows a rounded gray rectangle with a downward-facing triangle.

MULTIPLE PULL-DOWN LISTS

A single form can contain many pull-down lists.

WEBTV CLASSIC

WebTV Classic and WebTV Plus forms function the same way.

---

③ The triangle indicates that additional options exist. To see more options, use the scroll keys.

④ Confirm your choice by pressing Go or Return.

⑤ The list closes and your choice appears as the current selection.

FIND IT ONLINE

Read about issues in user interface design at http://www.useit.com/alerbox/990124.html.

Selecting from a Scrolling List

Scrolling lists appear as a column of options on a gray, rectangular background. Squares are drawn to the left of each option. Up- or down-facing triangles indicate when the list may be scrolled down or up.

To select an option from a scrolling list, you must first activate the list with Go or Return. This lets you "enter" the list area and make your choice.

Once "inside" the list, use the arrow and scroll keys to move up and down. When you spot the choice you wish to select, activate it with Go or Return. A check mark will appear before your choice and the yellow box will return to the outside of the entire list.

If you wish to change your selection, repeat the process. Enter the list, select another choice, and activate it.

When you encounter this form element, you may select only one option at a time. The next topic discusses multiple-choice scrolling lists. The single-choice behavior helps you recognize a simple scrolling list. Once a choice is made, the yellow box snaps back to the outside of the box. You are not given the chance to select a second choice. This helps you to distinguish a basic scrolling list from a multiple-choice scrolling list.

This form element acts as a compromise design, falling somewhere between radio buttons and the pull-down list. As with those screen elements, you can select only one choice from many. However, with scrolling lists, you are able to see more choices than with pull-down lists while it occupies less screen space than a full radio list.

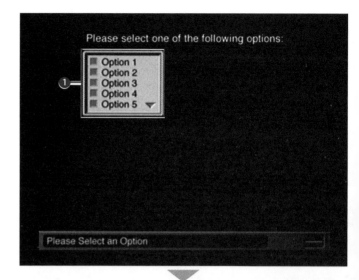

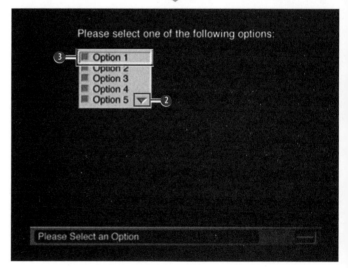

▶ This example uses a mocked up screen to demonstrate the use of the scrolling list.

❶ To select an option from the list, activate the list with Go or Return. The yellow box will move from outside the list to within it.

❷ Triangles indicate that you may scroll up and down through the list.

❸ Move the yellow box to the selection you wish to make.

CROSS-REFERENCE

Learn how to select from a pull-down list in the previous topic.

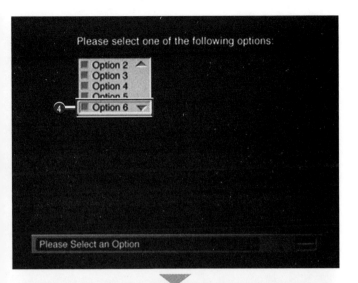

TAKE NOTE

DEFAULT SELECTIONS

Occasionally, you find a scrolling list with a preexisting check. This check is called a "default selection." When designing this form, someone felt it likely that this option applied to most people. If you do not wish to accept the default, select another option.

WEBTV CLASSIC

Scrolling lists look the same on WebTV Classic and WebTV Plus.

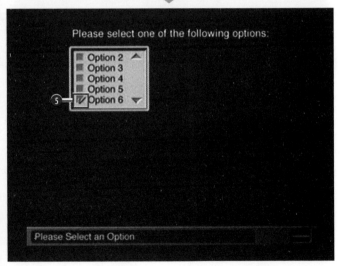

④ When you have found the option that you want, activate it with Go or Return.

⑤ After the option has been selected, a check mark appears next to the choice and the yellow box returns to the outside of the list.

FIND IT ONLINE

Visit the tooth fairy at **http://www.toothfairy.org.**

Selecting from a Multiple-Choice List

Multiple choice scrolling lists and basic scrolling lists are distinguished by one feature: the number of options that may be selected. Basic scrolling lists let you select only one option. In contrast, multiple-choice scrolling lists let you select any number of options. Please refer to the previous topic before reading this one.

To select an option from a scrolling list, you must first activate the list with Go or Return. This lets you "enter" the list area and select your choice.

Once "inside" the list, you can navigate by using the arrow and scroll keys to move up and down through the choices. When the yellow box surrounds a choice that you wish to select, activate it with Go or Return. A check mark appears before each choice you make.

If you selected an option by accident, repeat the process. Pressing Go or Return a second time turns off the check mark.

When you encounter this form element, you may select many options at a time. Unlike a single-choice scrolling list, the yellow box will not "snap back" after a choice is made. You may move to other choices and select them before finishing.

To "leave" the multiple-choice scrolling list, use the left or right arrows to move elsewhere in the form. You cannot use the scroll keys, up and down arrows, or Go or Return buttons, as they only move you within the list or select more choices.

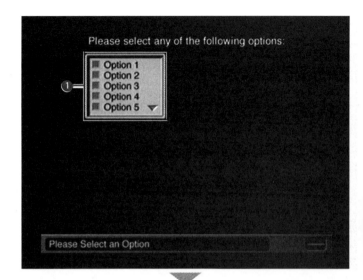

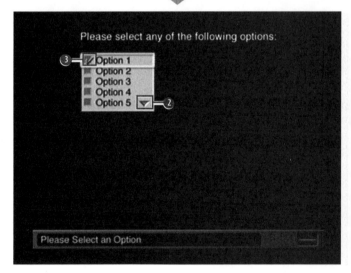

▶ This example uses a screen that I mocked up to demonstrate the use of the scrolling list.

❶ To select options from the list, move the yellow box to surround the list and activate it with Go or Return. The yellow box will move from outside the list to the first choice within it.

❷ Triangles indicate that you may scroll up and down through the list.

❸ Move the yellow box to any selection you wish. When you have found the option you want, activate it with Go or Return.

CROSS-REFERENCE

Learn to select from a basic scrolling list in the previous topic.

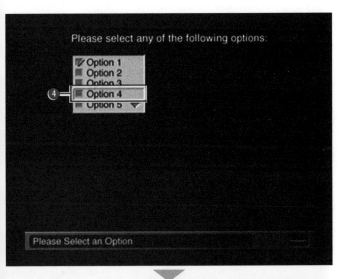

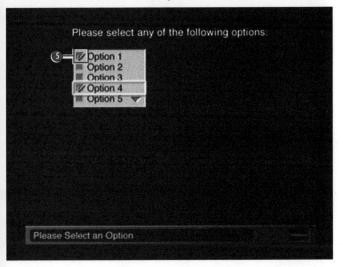

TAKE NOTE

▶ YOU CAN PICK ZERO TO ALL

When using multiple-choice scrolling lists, you may select as few as zero or as many as all of the options.

▶ THE CHECK MARK

WebTV displays all list selections the same way. It shows a column of squares to the left of each option. Options that have been chosen appear with a check mark.

▶ WEBTV CLASSIC

WebTV Classic and WebTV Plus both utilize scrolling multiple choice lists.

④ *You may now move to another selection. When you have found the option you want, activate it with Go or Return.*

⑤ *When you have finished selecting your options, press the left or right arrow key to conclude and to move elsewhere in the form.*

FIND IT ONLINE

Where is the Web going? Visit **http://www.useit.com/ alertbox/981227.html.**

Entering a Password

Areas that allow you to enter passwords initially appear indistinguishable from text-entry spaces. Only by typing into the field can you detect the difference. When you enter text in a password field, the normal text does not appear. Instead, WebTV displays a series of dots. This "hides" your passwords from casual observers who might be in the room with you.

Exercise extreme care when typing a password. Because you will not receive the normal feedback (only dots), you must use extra precision while typing. If at any time you believe you have made a mistake, start from scratch. Erase the entire password and begin again. This helps ensure the greatest accuracy when typing passwords.

You may wonder from whence this paranoia springs. Since the very early days of computing, protecting passwords has been a critical component of computer security. In the 1950s and 1960s, few people might have visualized a day when you used a computer in your living room or bedroom.

Unfortunately, WebTV does not provide an option to turn off password security and make visible the contents of password fields. This leaves you with the unfortunate responsibility for filling out the occasional password field without helpful visual feedback.

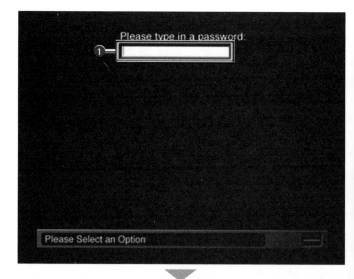

▶ This screen was mocked up to demonstrate the use of the password field.

❶ Password fields initially appear indistinguishable from those spaces intended for normal text.

❷ When you type in a password field, your text is "hidden." Each character is replaced by a large dot.

CROSS-REFERENCE

Learn to assign a password to a user account in Section IV.

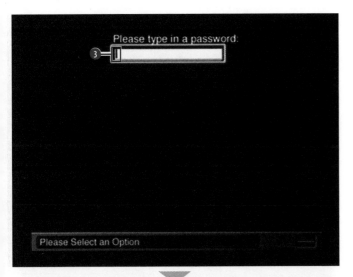

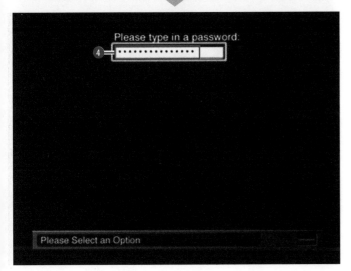

KEEP IT SHORT

If you must use passwords with your WebTV unit, I suggest that you keep them short and easy to type.

SELECTING PASSWORDS

At times, on various Web pages, you will be asked to select a new password. A good rule of thumb for creating a new password is to combine two short words together. These word combination passwords are usually easy to remember and hard for others to guess. For example, you could pick "jump-sofa," "heartfoot," "chairfork," and so forth. Each of these passwords uses a combination of common, and hopefully memorable, words. Try picking words that have little to do with each other.

UTILITY PASSWORDS

Some people find it convenient to use a single password for all but the most secure of their World Wide Web dealings. By using a single, memorable password, you limit the number of phrases you must memorize or write down and make it less likely you will misplace or forget a password when you most need it.

WEBTV CLASSIC

Password forms appear the same on WebTV Classic and WebTV Plus.

③ *Exercise extreme caution when typing a password. If you believe you made a mistake, erase the entire field and start over. Precision in typing passwords is critical. Enter each character carefully. You will not receive the normal feedback while typing, only dots.*

④ *When you believe you have correctly entered a password, use the arrow keys to move to another part of the form.*

FIND IT ONLINE

Learn more about password authentication. Visit **http://jafar.stanford.edu/srp**.

Selecting from a Picture

An image map is a special Web feature that lets you pick a selection from a picture rather than a list. You can recognize image maps because when the yellow box surrounds it, a small yellow arrow appears at the bottom right.

To activate an image map, press Go or Return. The yellow box disappears and is replaced with a light-blue box. A yellow arrow appears in the middle of the image.

Once the yellow arrow appears within the image, you can move it around with the arrow keys. Navigate the arrow to the part of the image you wish to "select" and activate your selection by pressing Go or Return a second time.

A white starburst "click" will appear around the yellow arrow and WebTV will link to the Web page with the coordinates of your selection.

Image maps have become very popular in recent years. They provide an elegant way to visually design a selection scheme. Visual choices help to internationalize a Web site. It's easier for a user to "point" to a book than to have to read through a list like "Book * Libro * Livre * Buch" and so on.

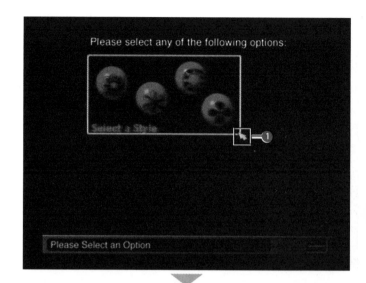

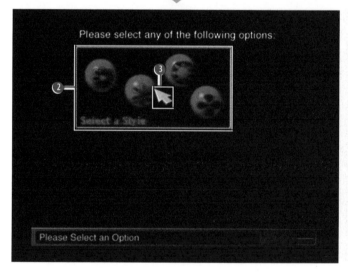

▶ This example uses a mocked up screen that I created to demonstrate the use of image maps.

① The yellow arrow on the bottom right of the image map indicates that you can activate it with Go or Return.

② The image's bounding rectangle turns light blue.

③ A yellow arrow appears in the middle of the image.

CROSS-REFERENCE

Learn about "resetting" and "submitting" forms in the next topic.

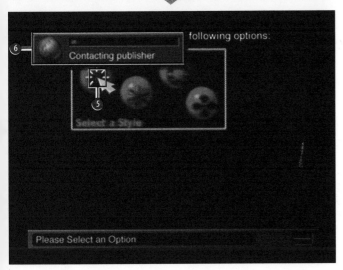

④ Use the arrow keys to move the arrow within the box. When the arrow points to the object you wish to select, press Go or Return.

⑤ The activation produces a white-starburst "click" around the point of the arrow.

⑥ WebTV will attempt to contact the publisher of the Web page whose link you selected.

TAKE NOTE

▶ YOU CAN PICK ONE LOCATION

When using image maps, you may select only one part of the image. The location you select corresponds to the position of the point of the yellow arrow.

▶ SLOW-MOVING YELLOW ARROW

Does the yellow arrow move too slowly? If you hold down the arrow key, the onscreen arrow will move more rapidly in any given direction than if you were to repeatedly press the arrow key.

▶ MOVING OFF THE END

When the yellow arrow hits the border of the image map, WebTV will leave the image map and move the yellow box to the next hyperlink. Use extra care when trying to select image elements that lie near the borders of image maps.

▶ SCROLLING

When an image map exceeds the size of the WebTV screen, you can use the arrow keys to move the yellow arrow "off" the current display and cause automatic scrolling. Do not press the scroll keys, thinking that the image map and arrow will automatically scroll. Pressing the scroll keys deselects the image map and removes the yellow arrow.

▶ WEBTV CLASSIC

WebTV Classic and WebTV Plus are both enabled to use image maps.

FIND IT ONLINE

Try out an image map. Visit **http://www.eng.auburn. edu/alabama/map.html.**

Resetting and Submitting Forms

When using forms, you will discover two special items: Reset Form and Submit Form. These items do more or less what you would expect them to. Reset will reset the form to its initial configuration, erasing any changes you made. Submit sends current form data to the Web page provider. Each of these items typically appears as a rounded rectangle somewhere near the bottom of the form.

While these items are usually labeled Reset and Submit, the label can vary. Sometimes you will see items that say "submit form" or "reset to default," "send my feedback" or "oops!," "mail information" or "erase information," or similar. Be at ease, these are simply Reset and Submit masquerading with different text. Submit always sends a form's information to the Web page's publisher. Reset, no matter how labeled, returns the form's contents to the default.

These two items usually appear side-by-side at the bottom of Web forms. Because submission is usually the last step in filling out a form, it is logical that they appear last. These items are often found on forms intended for collecting orders or feedback. These forms enable you to purchase goods or services and provide personal opinions about a site or situation.

Always think before you submit a form. Consider to whom the form will be sent and what information you are disclosing. Prudence should dictate when and when not to activate submit.

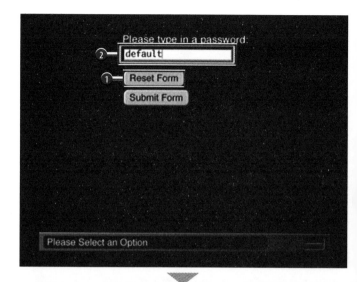

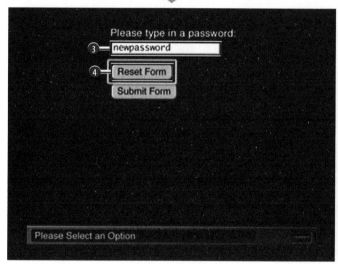

▶ This example uses a mocked up screen that I created to demonstrate the use of submitting and resetting forms.

❶ Many forms contain Reset and Submit buttons.

❷ Some text spaces initially appear with default text.

❸ In this example, we type new text.

❹ Next, we activate the Reset button.

CROSS-REFERENCE

Learn about using image maps in the previous topic.

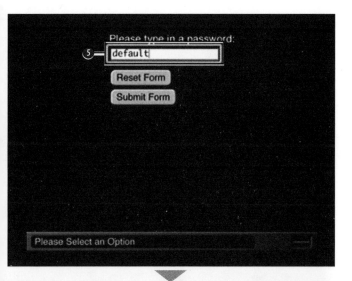

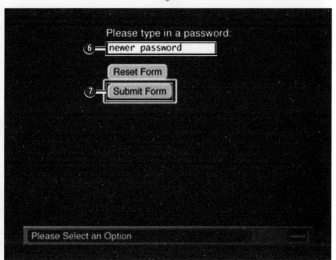

⑤ *When the Reset button is activated, WebTV returns the text space to its default value.*

⑥ *The user may reenter information or may choose to type new or changed information.*

⑦ *When finished with the form, activating Submit instructs WebTV to send the form contents to the Web page provider.*

TAKE NOTE

▶ SECURITY

Always take care when submitting personal information over the Internet. If you want to know whether your form information is secure, press the Info button on your keyboard. If the security information rounded rectangle appears, you can be reasonably sure that submitting the form is secure.

▶ PRIVACY

If at any time you worry about someone looking over your shoulder as you fill out a form, consider activating Reset. Although the information you have entered will be lost, you may retain some peace of mind and, more importantly, your privacy.

▶ HOW INFORMATION IS SENT

When you activate Submit, WebTV contacts the publisher of the Web page on which the form resides. WebTV sends the information you have typed in one of two ways. First, it may send this information via e-mail, creating an electronic letter with your information attached. This method is most common when sending feedback. Second, it may use the CGI (Common Gateway Interface) protocol to directly contact a computer program to process the form data. This method prevails when placing orders. In either case, the information you provide moves through the Internet.

▶ WEBTV CLASSIC

WebTV Classic and WebTV Plus forms work indistinguishably from one another.

FIND IT ONLINE

Try out a form with reset and submit options. Visit
http://users.neca.com/opinion3/ff970301.htm.

Personal Workbook

Q&A

1 When you encounter a list in which a radio button precedes each item, how many items may you select at once?

_____

_____

2 When you encounter a list in which a square box precedes each item, how many items may you select at once?

_____

_____

3 What does a rounded gray rectangle with a downward pointing triangle indicate?

_____

_____

_____

4 How many items may you select from a pull-down list at once?

_____

_____

5 How do you identify a scrolling list?

_____

_____

_____

6 How do you move through a scrolling list?

_____

_____

_____

7 What do you see when entering information into a password field?

_____

_____

_____

8 What happens when you activate the Reset button in a form?

_____

_____

_____

_____

ANSWERS: PAGE 334

Filling Out Forms

1. Try selecting a choice from a radio button list.

2. Try selecting several choices from a checkbox list.

3. Practice entering information and then resetting a form.

4. Try using an image map.

5. Practice using both single-choice and multiple-choice scrolling lists.

6. Practice typing into a password field, making sure to type accurately!

7. Try making a selection from a pull-down list.

✔ You want to try shopping online. You pick a likely site and get ready to purchase. You fill out those forms necessary to submit your order and billing information.

✔ You enter an online contest in an attempt to win a free computer or all-expense-paid vacation. As most contests require you to fill out extensive demographic forms to compete, you use your newly acquired form skills to handily complete your submission.

✔ You're visiting a new Web site and want to let the site's designers know you enjoyed the experience. Many Web sites include a feedback page to collect information about the site's appeal and usefulness. You fill out a form about what you thought of the site.

Visual Quiz

What does the yellow arrow on the right-bottom corner of this box mean?

_____

_____

_____

_____

_____

_____

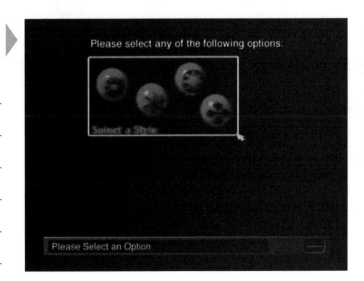

PART

II

CHAPTER

4 Jumping Into the Web

5 Using Favorites

6 Searching the Web

7 Exploring the Web

Contents of 'Desktop'

Name

My Computer

Network Neigh

Internet Explore

Microsoft Outlook

Recycle Bin

My Briefcase

3252-9

3259-6

3261-8

3262-6

3281-2

3286-3

DE Phone List

Device Manager

In

Iomega Tools

Navigating the World Wide Web

What a rich treasure is the World Wide Web! The Web offers a tremendous variety of knowledge and services. If you are looking for information, chances are that it can be found somewhere on the Web. This section teaches you the skills you need to find and use any site on the World Wide Web.

The first chapter in this section introduces you to the most basic Web skills. These skills include using Web Addresses, moving back and forth between Web pages, peeking at page information and security details, and sending a Web address through e-mail. By the time you finish the first chapter, you will understand how to visit any page on the World Wide Web.

The second chapter introduces WebTV's "favorites." This WebTV feature enables you to save and organize your favorite World Wide Web pages. Never again will you "lose" a favorite Web page. You learn to add a Web page to your Favorites and recover it again later, or even assign it to one of the special F keys on your keyboard. You learn to create and remove Favorites folders and how to remove and move pages between these folders. You also learn how to specialize the way WebTV displays your favorites and how to rename the way favorites are listed.

The third chapter teaches you how to search the World Wide Web for any information that you could dream of. By the time you finish this chapter, you will know how to use the Search key and how to limit searches by using extra phrases, mixed-case, and quoted phrases. You will also learn how best to use the special + and – characters to get exactly the results you want.

The final chapter gives you a tour of some of the Web's richness and character. In this chapter, you learn to use WebTV's Explore feature, MIDI Karaoke, Yahoo's Picks of the Week, online games, and free advice sites. No book can give a full idea of the Web's scope and depth, but these sites will give a taste of the variety of Web sites available for exploration.

This section covers the basic skills involved in surfing the World Wide Web with WebTV. By learning these techniques, you will be able to explore the entire Internet and all of its extraordinary wealth of information.

CHAPTER 4

MASTER
THESE
SKILLS

▶ Using Web Addresses

▶ Moving Between Web Pages Using Hyperlinks

▶ Viewing Recently Visited Pages

▶ Peeking at Web Page Information

▶ Understanding Web Page Security

Jumping Into the Web

The World Wide Web offers an immense range of resources. Any topic that you can think of, any hobby, any occupation, any sphere of human activity, probably has a Web site associated with it. The World Wide Web is like an enormous electronic library. If you have the skills and a Web address, you can visit any site on the entire Internet. In this chapter, you will learn how to navigate World Wide Web sites.

First, you learn about Web addresses. These addresses tell WebTV how to find sites on the World Wide Web. You learn to use WebTV's Go To key to enter addresses and visit Web sites.

Second, you learn to move between Web pages using hyperlinks. These links, which act like "live" footnotes, let you jump between Web documents and explore Web pages in further detail.

Third, you learn to review those pages you recently visited. You learn to jump between recent pages using WebTV's Recent button. With only a few key presses, you can move back and forth between recent Web pages.

Fourth, you learn to peek at secret Web page information. This might not be a hugely important skill to acquire, but it is neat to know how to do this and to show it off to your friends.

Fifth, you learn to check the security of a Web page. This skill is vital if you intend to engage in online shopping or sending personal information across the Internet. Always determine a page's level of security before revealing any sensitive information.

Finally, you learn to send a Web page to a friend, family member, or colleague. This skill lets you share important information or curious pages with others.

By the time you have completed this chapter, you will be comfortable both going to World Wide Web pages and moving between those pages. You will have "jumped into" the Web and gained some Web surfing experience.

Using Web Addresses

Every page on the World Wide Web has an address. Just as we can find a real building by its street address, WebTV can find a Web page by its Web address. The address tells WebTV how to locate the computer that hosts the Web page and specifies the page on that computer to be displayed.

The Web mirrors our protocol of street address, city, state, and Zip code. Web addresses have a formal structure, too. This structure is called a uniform resource locator, or URL. URLs tell WebTV how to locate Web pages. Fortunately, the phrase URL is somewhat dropping out of use, being replaced by the more reasonable "Web address" or "Web page address."

Today, you will find Web addresses everywhere: in commercials, newspapers, product literature, business cards, junk mail, and so on. Often you will see something along the lines of, "Visit our Web site at http://www.somecompany.com." This latter bit, starting with http://, is the Web address. You can type this into your WebTV unit and visit that Web site. The screens on the facing page demonstrate how to type in a Web address.

To save time when you press the Go To key, WebTV will type http:// for you. This cryptic bit stands for hypertext transfer protocol, which is the language that computers on the World Wide Web use to establish connections across the Internet. Almost every Web address starts with this acronym. When you hear about "anycompany.com," it is assumed that you know to begin the address with http:// before adding anycompany.com.

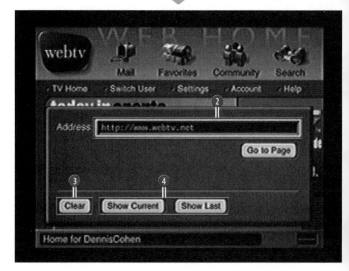

❶ To access a Web page directly, start by pressing Go To on your keyboard or Options on your remote and then activating Go To. The address box appears with http:// already typed in.

❷ Type the Web page's address (or URL) in the line that says **Address.**

❸ (Optional) If you make a typing error, activate **Clear** to clear the Address line.

❹ (Optional) Activate **Show Current** or **Show Last** to bring up recent addresses.

CROSS-REFERENCE

The next topic discusses using hyperlinks, teaching you another way to move between Web pages.

Sometimes addresses contain specific page references. For example, you may see a Web address that looks like http://www.somecompany.com/index.html. In this case, WebTV knows to look for a page called index.html on the Some Company Web site. Some Web addresses are more complex than this, while some are less. Always type in the entire Web address. This helps ensure that WebTV will find and load the correct page.

TAKE NOTE

▶ BE PRECISE

When typing in Web address, be precise. Even a small typographic mistake will leave WebTV unable to load your desired Web page.

▶ UPPER- AND LOWERCASE

Web addresses are, for the most part, case insensitive. However, you should make sure to carefully reproduce all case changes. For example, "http://www.somecompany.com/MyPage.html" is not the same address as "http://www.somecompany.com/mypage.html." Always match the case of the Web address you have been given.

▶ WEBTV CLASSIC

Access the World Wide Web identically on WebTV Classic and WebTV Plus.

⑤ *Activate **Go to Page**.*

⑥ *WebTV will take you to the new page. You may press Back to return to the previous page.*

FIND IT ONLINE

Looking for the right word? Visit **http://www. thesaurus.com**.

Moving Between Web Pages Using Hyperlinks

The World Wide Web provides two ways to move to a Web page. First, you can enter an address as discussed in the previous topic. Second, you can activate a *hyperlink.*

Hyperlinks, better known as "links," let you access additional Web pages by activating a word or picture. Page authors and designers build these links directly into Web pages. When you encounter one, you can activate it with Go or Return, and WebTV will automatically take you to that new page.

You can detect links on a Web page because they are usually displayed in a different color or design. A sure way to confirm that you have found a link is that you can surround it with WebTV's yellow box. According to the official documentation, "On WebTV, any word or image you can highlight with the yellow cursor box is a hyperlink."

Image maps are a special type of hyperlink. As you discovered in Chapter 3, image maps are surrounded with the yellow box, but when you activate them, a yellow arrow appears. Each visual part of an image map picture corresponds to a link. When you activate the yellow arrow somewhere on the image, you are actually selecting a link.

Links work very much like footnotes in books. When reading a book, you may come across a footnoted reference to "Arky Malarky's Official Guide to Whatever." To check out this reference, you would have to find a copy of the book and search for the correct chapter and page.

❶ When the yellow box surrounds words or pictures, you have found a hyperlink.

❷ Use the arrow keys to move between hyperlinks.

CROSS-REFERENCE

Read about image maps in Chapter 3.

On the Internet you can avoid this labor. To view any linked reference, you need only activate it with Go or Return. The name "World Wide Web" reflects this philosophy. Designers envisioned the Web as a world-spanning collection of documents, each of which referenced others, forming an enormous web of information links. Well-designed links let you scan a reference and return to the main Web page to continue your browsing experience.

TAKE NOTE

▶ TAKE A PEEK

You can "peek" at the Web address that lies behind a hyperlink. Press the cmd key and the Ctrl key at the same time. The hyperlink address appears in the lower left-hand corner of your WebTV screen.

▶ GO BACK

If you activate a hyperlink by accident, you may press Back at any time. You do not need to wait for the page to finish loading. Pressing Back stops the page loading and returns you to the page you were originally browsing.

▶ WEBTV CLASSIC

Access the World Wide Web identically on WebTV Classic and WebTV Plus.

③ *If you press Ctrl and cmd at the same time while the yellow box surrounds a hyperlink, you can see the secret Web address of that hyperlink.*

④ *Activating a hyperlink with Go or Return takes you to the Web page pointed to by that link.*

FIND IT ONLINE

Stop by the Dilbert Zone. Visit **http://www.dilbert.com**.

Viewing Recently Visited Pages

WebTV provides an easy way to revisit pages. Just press the recent key on the keyboard and select from among up to 12 of the most recently visited pages. These recent pages help you re-trace your steps without having to use Back to move a page at a time. You can return to an interesting page. You can "back up" from a recent digression of hyper-links. You can also move back and forth between two interesting pages.

The recent list of pages appears as a large gray rectangular dialog box. A snapshot and an abbreviated title summarize each page. Use the arrow keys to choose a recent page and activate your selection with Go or Return.

WebTV lays out the recent pages in a three-rows-by-four-columns configuration. Older pages appear in the upper-left of the box. Newer pages appear at the bottom and right. When you visit more than 12 pages in a single session, older pages will "timeout." WebTV always shows the 12 most recent pages, whether they are Web pages or your own WebTV home pages.

Of course, you can always use Back to return to older pages, but be careful. WebTV does not provide a forward key. Hit Back one too many times and you may accidentally pass by the page you wanted. Using the recently visited list ensures greater control over your Web surfing. Perhaps WebTV and the manufacturers of its components (Sony, Philips-Magnavox, and so on) will include a forward key on future WebTV hardware. However, to maintain backward compatibility, it's unlikely that any future design changes will displace existing and essential keys.

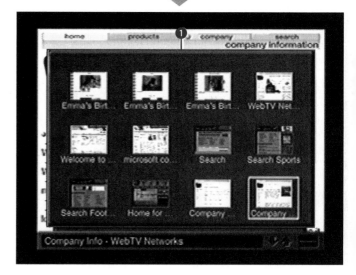

▶ To visit a recently viewed page, start by pressing Recent on your remote control or keyboard.

❶ WebTV displays all recent pages as snapshots.

CROSS-REFERENCE

Learn about the secret information behind Web pages in the next topic.

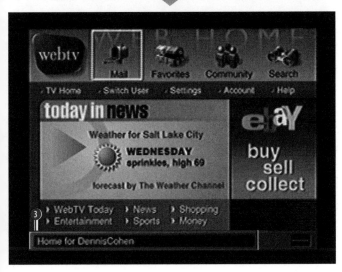

② Use the arrow keys to select a recent page. Activate it with Go or Return. In this example, we choose to visit the Home page.

③ WebTV moves you to the recently visited page you chose. In this example, you switch to the Home page.

Peeking at Web Page Information

Are you the curious type? Would you like to know more about the Web pages you visit? WebTV provides two ways of peeking at Web page information. You can sneak looks at both general page information and at hyperlinks.

To view further page information, press Info on your keyboard. This button tells WebTV to show you some interesting data about the Web page. You may see the page's Web address, the date it last changed, and, sometimes, page security information. This page security information is of particular interest when you intend to submit personal or confidential information in a form on this Web page.

To peek at hyperlinks, move the yellow box to a link. Press Ctrl and cmd on your keyboard at the same time. The "real address" of the hyperlink will appear in the lower-left corner of your WebTV screen.

With these tricks, you can easily uncover Web addresses and page information. I'm not entirely sure how you might use this data, but it's fun to show these tricks to other friends who use WebTV.

If you have trouble accessing a Web page, WebTV asks that you send them the address. The Info button may be useful in such a case.

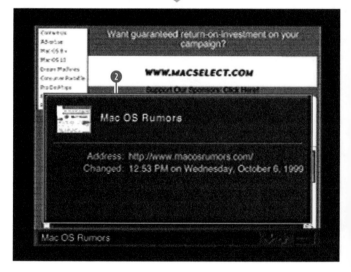

① To start your Web page peeking, select an interesting Web page and press Info on your keyboard. On your remote, press Options and then highlight and activate Info.

② WebTV displays information about the Web page you are viewing. Press Back to return to the Web page.

CROSS-REFERENCE

The previous topic teaches you to use the Recent button.

③ Use the arrow keys to select a hyperlink at which you wish to peek.

④ Press Ctrl and cmd on your keyboard at the same time. WebTV displays the hyperlink information in the lower left-hand corner of the screen.

TAKE NOTE

GETTING RID OF THE INFO BOX

You can dismiss the information box by pressing Info a second time or by pressing Back.

CHECK THE DOMAIN

Some domains are commercial and end with .com. Others are organizations, ending with .org, or belong to the government and end with .gov. In an infamous case, people eager to catch sight of pictures from NASA's Pathfinder mission mistakenly typed nasa.com rather than nasa.gov. They were shocked to discover an adult-themed Web site. This site, thankfully, seems to have disappeared.

RELATIVE VERSUS ABSOLUTE ADDRESSES

When you peek at a hyperlink address, you sometimes see a complete (or "absolute") address such as http://help.webtv.net/surfing/trouble.html. At other times, you see only a short (or "relative") address such as surfing/trouble.html or simply trouble.html. In this latter case, the site is always assumed to be the same as that of the referring Web page. To find the complete address, you may need to move to that page and press Info on your keyboard rather than rely on the cmd+Ctrl keyboard shortcut.

WEBTV CLASSIC

Access the World Wide Web identically on WebTV Classic and WebTV Plus.

FIND IT ONLINE

One use of the "peek" feature is discussed at **http://help.webtv.net/surfing/trouble.html.**

Understanding Web Page Security

WebTV provides an easy way to check for page security. When you press Info, look for a gray, rounded rectangle labeled Security Details. Any page information lacking this Security Details option is **not secure**. Do not type any personal information on this site.

Check security before you ever type personal information on the Internet. Before you enter your social security number or credit card information ensure that your information will be transmitted securely.

Even when Security Details appears, make sure to activate it with Go or Return. Read these details carefully. Make sure that WebTV rates the page as having at least a "high level of security."

And remember that not every page on a secure Web site is secure. Many Web sites have both "secure" and "unsecure" ordering forms. Check for security on the exact page on which you intend to enter information!

Secure sites offer a variety of services that mandate a certain level of privacy. You may wish to place an order for goods or services online and will need to enter shipping and credit card information. You may use an online banking service and will need a high level of assurance that no one else will be able to see, let alone manipulate, your online account information. You may want to engage in online stock trades and need to ensure that your buy or sell order is transmitted safely and accurately.

WebTV supports the secure socket layer, or SSL, protocol. According to WebTV, this protocol "encrypts data, so that the transmission of confidential information over the Internet is safe. WebTV Networks supports this

❶ Many commercial Web sites offer secure ordering pages.

▶ To view security information from a "secure" page, start by pressing the info button on your keyboard. On your remote, press the Options button then activate Info.

❷ When the page info box displays, activate **Security Details** to view further security information.

CROSS-REFERENCE

The previous topic teaches you other uses for the Info button.

standard allowing you to conduct online banking, shopping, and trading." SSL encryption "protects the transmission of confidential information over the Internet by coding it in a way that is difficult to intercept."

This means that after checking a page's security, and ensuring that SSL protection is in place, you can feel fairly confident that WebTV will protect your personal information and that you can submit confidential data with a reasonable expectation that it will stay confidential.

3 *WebTV confirms that this site uses a high level of security.*

4 *When you have finished inspecting the Security information, activate **Done**.*

5 *Many Web sites offer additional information about their security.*

TAKE NOTE

▶ **SECURITY PROTOCOLS DIFFER**

Different secure Web pages may use different security protocols. Only enter personal information on pages that WebTV reports as having "high level(s) of security." Most secure pages use the secure sockets layer (SSL) protocol and are rated with a "high level of security." Future releases of WebTV hardware and software may support additional security protocols.

▶ **WEBTV CLASSIC**

The Security Details option is accessed identically on WebTV Classic and WebTV Plus.

FIND IT ONLINE

Read more about it. Visit **http://wecare.webtv.net/ surfing/shopping.html**.

Personal Workbook

Q&A

1 What is *URL* an acronym for?

_____

_____

_____

2 What is a more common name for URL?

_____

_____

_____

3 What does http:// mean?

_____

_____

_____

4 What is a *hyperlink?*

_____

_____

_____

_____

5 How do you detect hyperlinks?

_____

_____

_____

_____

6 What is the difference between the Back and Recent buttons?

_____

_____

_____

_____

7 How do you know when a Web page is unsecure?

_____

_____

_____

_____

ANSWERS: PAGE 335

EXTRA PRACTICE

1. Visit some Web sites.

2. Use Back to return from a Web site.

3. Activate some hyperlinks.

4. Use Info to peek at Web information.

5. Practice jumping between two Web pages using the Recent button.

REAL-WORLD APPLICATIONS

✔ You're visiting a shopping site and decide to place an order. First, you confirm the security of their ordering pages before submitting any personal information.

✔ You pick up a newspaper or magazine. You notice that a lot of the articles and advertisements have Web sites listed. You visit some of them to see what they are about.

Visual Quiz

Is this Web page secure?

_____

_____

_____

_____

_____

_____

amazon.com

Completing Your Order Is Easy

We encourage you to enter your credit card number online [why this is safe]. However, you also have the option of phoning us with the number after completing the order form. If you have any problems or questions, see the bottom of the page for details on our toll-free (800) customer support number.

1. Welcome.

Please enter your e-mail address:

Please **check** your e-mail address for accuracy; one small typo and we won't be able to communicate with you about your order.

Secure Page Amazon.com Order Form - ...

CHAPTER **5**

MASTER
THESE
SKILLS

▶ **Adding a Web Page to Favorites**

▶ **Selecting a Favorite**

▶ **Assigning a Favorite to an F Key**

▶ **Adding a Favorites Folder**

▶ **Removing a Favorites Folder**

▶ **Discarding a Favorite Site**

▶ **Viewing Site Snapshots**

▶ **Renaming a Site**

▶ **Moving Favorites Between Folders**

Using Favorites

Memory is fleeting. WebTV knows this. Thus, it allows you to collect lists of favorite World Wide Web sites without having to remember their addresses. In this way, you can build a collection of favorite Web sites that you return to again and again. You need never remember the exact Web address for each site. WebTV will do that for you.

In this chapter, you learn a number of skills related to creating, maintaining, and using your WebTV Web site favorites.

First, you learn to save a Web page to your favorites list. Use this skill to mark out and collect those pages that you find particularly interesting, novel, or useful. Then you learn to proceed in reverse: selecting a Web page already in your favorites list. You learn to return to a favorite Web page without having to type in the full Web address.

You learn to assign a favorite Web site to one of the special keys on your WebTV keyboard. These keys, which are marked F1 through F7 can be associated with seven of your most important sites. You learn to access these Web sites by a single key press.

Next, you learn to add and remove Favorites folders. These folders enable you to organize your WebTV favorites by associating them with similarly themed sites. For example, you can create a folder for mountain-climbing sites, another for online shopping, and so on.

You also learn to clean up and organize your favorites. WebTV permits you to remove old, outdated, or undesired Web sites from your Favorites. You can also move a site from one folder to a more appropriate one. Some sites have unusual or confusing names. You can change these names to more sensible or enlightening titles. You can also specify how WebTV displays your favorite sites. Use these techniques to keep your favorites well-structured and easy to use.

By the time you finish this chapter, you will have mastered all the necessary skills associated with creating, maintaining, and using WebTV favorites.

Adding a Web Page to Favorites

Have you come across a particularly interesting or informative Web page? You can save a Web page and visit it later. WebTV lets you store the address of a Web page in your Favorites folder and return to that page at a later time.

You can easily save a Web page. Press the Save key, select a Favorites folder to save it to, and activate **Save Page**. WebTV will place a reference to the Web page in the folder you specify.

WebTV allows you to have a number of Favorites folders. You may have one for News, another for Family, and yet another for Hobby. When you save a Web page, select the folder that best matches the site. WebTV creates a Recommended and a Personal folder by default. However, first you must go to the Favorites screen and activate them. WebTV fills up the Recommended folder with a number of commercial sites it believes you will find interesting. If you have not defined any other folders, save your page to the Personal folder.

Although you may initially save a Web page to your Personal folder, you can create additional folders later. WebTV also lets you move favorites between folders. You may use the Personal folder as a catch-all for saving favorite sites until you have time to file them more appropriately.

Always err on the side of caution. If you think you may wish to revisit a site in a later WebTV session, save it. It's easy enough to remove an unwanted favorite — much easier, typically, than refinding a particularly interesting site. As a rule, save first, sort later.

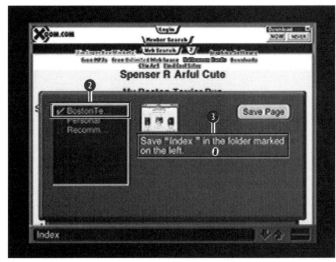

❶ Go to the Web page you wish to save in your Favorites folder. Press Save on your keyboard. On your remote, press Options and then activate save.

❷ From the list at the right of the Save Page dialog box, select the Favorites folder in which you want to save the Web page.

❸ WebTV displays the name of the page being saved in the message.

CROSS-REFERENCE

You can read about sending a Web address by e-mail in the previous chapter.

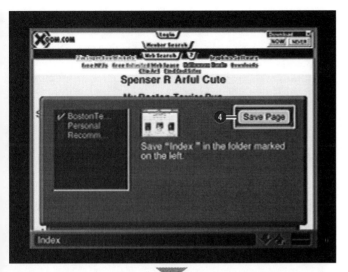

④ Activate **Save Page.**

⑤ *WebTV displays this message as it stores the page as one of your Favorites.*

▶ WHEN NOT TO SAVE

There are some pages that you really ought not to save. News articles and order confirmation pages are rarely kept on Web servers for longer than a day or week. In some cases, these pages "disappear" in a matter of hours. Save pages that you are sure will persist and that others can refer to later. In the case of breaking news stories, consider sending the Web address rather than saving it. The immediacy of electronic mail helps promote rapid viewing of the article.

▶ LIMITS OF FAVORITES

WebTV lets you create up to 20 Favorites folders. This means that you can readily organize your favorites in a well-structured and sensible way. Each folder can hold up to 32 individual favorites. Keep in mind, though, that 32 favorites in a folder can prove to be overly cluttered. You may want to consider leaving your Favorites folders sparse and easy to navigate.

▶ WEBTV CLASSIC

Both WebTV Classic and WebTV Plus allow you to create Favorites folders and save favorite Web sites.

FIND IT ONLINE

Read more about it. Visit **help.webtv.net/favorites/ howmany.html.**

Selecting a Favorite

WebTV enables you to store Web addresses in the various Favorites folders. Each page is stored with a screen snapshot and a title to better help you recognize the page. You can access Favorites by pressing the favs key on your keyboard or by activating **Favorites** from your WebTV home page.

When you arrive at the Favorites page, select the folder that you wish to browse and activate it with Go or Return. Because WebTV lets you manage up to 20 folders, you may find quite a list of folders to select from.

Once you have activated a folder, you can select a page to visit with the yellow box. Use the arrow and scroll keys to navigate through the folder. WebTV lets you store up to 32 favorites per folder. This may take up several screens. Check for the green arrows at the bottom of the display. They indicate when you may use the scroll keys to move up and down a page at a time.

When you have moved the yellow box to a Web page, you may activate it with Go or Return. WebTV moves you to the Web address associated with that favorite.

People save favorite sites for all sorts of reasons. Some pages contain vital information; some pages provide convenient reference material; and some pages are amusing. Others provide up-to-date news or services. The key to choosing which pages to save lies in avoiding losing track of any pages that truly interest you and those that prove important to you.

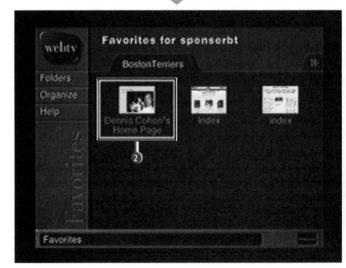

▶ *Go to the Favorite folders page by pressing favs on the keyboard.*

❶ *Select a folder and activate it with either Go or Return.*

❷ *Use the arrow and scroll keys to move through the folder.*

CROSS-REFERENCE

You can read about saving a Web address in the previous topic.

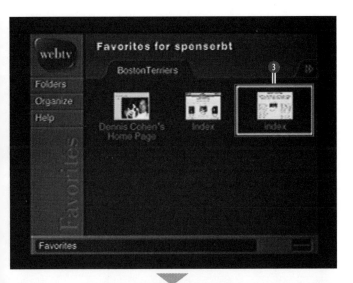

My favorites contain all sorts of Web sites — sites I think my family will find interesting or useful, news sites, sites about some of my ongoing projects, entertaining sites, and so forth. Some people save sites they are in the middle of scanning. They later return and fully read the pages and then remove them from their Favorites folders.

The times you visit a saved page may vary. You may frequently visit some pages, but others, only occasionally. Whether or not you return to a page often, the secret to favorites is organizing your favorites logically so you may easily revisit your most used pages, as well as quickly find the important but less visited ones.

TAKE NOTE

▶ **OOPS, WRONG FAVORITE**

If you have activated the wrong favorite, just press back. This will stop WebTV from loading that page and return you to the Favorites folder. You need not wait for WebTV to finish loading the Web page before pressing the back key.

▶ **WEBTV CLASSIC**

Access Favorites folders in the same way on WebTV Classic and WebTV Plus

③ *When you have found a page you wish to visit, select it with the yellow box and activate it with either Go or Return.*

④ *WebTV moves you to the Web page you selected.*

FIND IT ONLINE

Read more about it. Visit **http://help.webtv.net/ favorites/viewsite.html.**

Assigning a Favorite to an F Key

Imagine jumping to a favorite Web page by pressing a single key. WebTV lets you pick seven of your favorite Web pages and do just that. The WebTV keyboard has seven special keys that you can associate with seven of your favorite Web sites. These keys are labeled F1 to F7. You can find them on the upper-left of your keyboard, just to the right of the Esc key.

To assign a key, the Web site must already reside in your Favorites folders. Start by moving to the folder that houses the Web page and activate **Organize**. Choose **Shortcuts** and move the yellow box to the "key" to the right of the Web page you wish to assign. Activate the "key" with Go or Return and select an F key. Confirm your choice with **Done** or bypass it with **No Shortcut**.

Once you have assigned a Web page to an F key shortcut, you can go to that page instantly. Just press the appropriate F key and WebTV automatically moves you to that page. WebTV remembers the shortcuts between sessions. Once you have assigned a page to an F key, it stays assigned until you change assignments.

Pick Web pages you expect to visit a lot. To help you remember which keys correspond to which Web page, you may wish to keep a list by your keyboard or paste a thin strip of masking tape above the F keys and write informative labels on the tape. If at any time you forget which keys are assigned to which favorites, visit the WebTV Favorites folders. As you can see in step 3 on the facing page, you can scan down the list of favorites and immediately detect which are assigned to F keys.

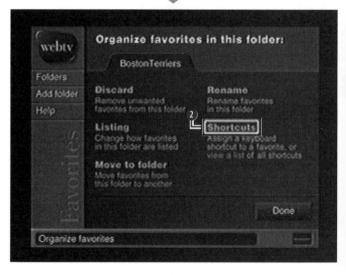

❶ *While viewing a Favorites folder, activate* **Organize**.

❷ *WebTV displays an Organize favorites in this folder screen, showing several options for the current folder. Activate* **Shortcuts**.

CROSS-REFERENCE

You can read about discarding Favorites later in this chapter.

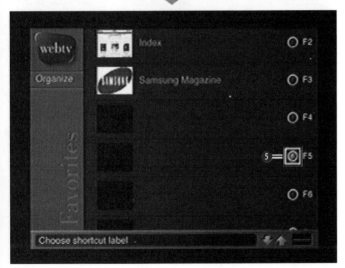

I've found it particularly useful to assign one F key to **http://askwebtv.webtv.net**. This adds a "help" key to your keyboard, a feature that WebTV sadly did not initially include in the keyboard design. Press this key whenever you have a question about how to use your WebTV unit, wait for the Ask WebTV screen to load, and then type your question in the box provided. WebTV will search through its help files to match your question to a WebTV answer.

TAKE NOTE

▶ **UNASSIGNING A FAVORITE**

To unassign a favorite, follow steps 1 through 5 on the facing page — as if you were assigning the favorite in the first place. Then activate **No Shortcut** to remove the assignment from that key. WebTV will release the F key. You can now use that key for another page if you wish.

▶ **WEBTV CLASSIC**

Use favorite Web sites identically on WebTV Classic and WebTV Plus.

---

③ *WebTV displays an Assign shortcut to favorite screen, with all of the favorites in the folder listed. In this example, a favorite has already been assigned to the F2 key.*

④ *Select an unassigned favorite and activate the gray "key" to its right.*

⑤ *Select an F key from the list of radio buttons provided by WebTV.*

▶ *(Optional) You can leave this key unassigned by activating No Shortcut. Scroll down to find this option.*

▶ *To finish assigning the favorite to an F key, activate Done, at the bottom of the page.*

FIND IT ONLINE

Read more about it. Visit **http://help.webtv.net/favorites/P8617.htm**.

Adding a Favorites Folder

WebTV allows you to create named "folders" for your favorite sites. In this way, you can keep your favorite news sites distinct from your favorite entertainment or family sites, and so on. Folders keep your favorites organized and easy-to-find.

By default, WebTV provides two folders: Recommended and Personal. The Recommended folder contains a number of WebTV's favorite sites. I suspect that there were a number of comarketing agreements signed before this folder was put in place. These Web sites include the Discovery Channel, PBS, Barnes and Noble, Amazon, and Warner Brothers, among others.

In addition to the Recommended folder, WebTV supplies five other prebuilt folders: Fun, Money, Reference, News, and Movies. To create one of these folders, activate **Samples** instead of proceeding to step 2 on the facing page. Select the folders you desire and activate **Add**. WebTV will create these prefabricated folders for you.

Until you create other folders, you can store your own favorite Web sites in the Personal folder. This folder acts as a catch-all, allowing you to save Web addresses without sorting through them. You can save up to 32 Web addresses this way. The Personal folder starts empty, allowing you to save new Web sites as needed.

Of course, you need never create additional folders if you are happy with the universal Personal one. Many people will use WebTV for years without ever desiring extra folders. However, if you tend to collect a lot of Web addresses and want to avoid clutter, folders may be right for you.

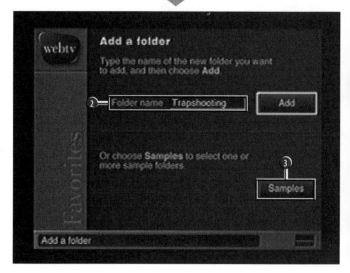

❶ Press favs and then activate **Add folder**.

❷ Type in the name of a new folder. Keep the name short and easy to remember.

❸ (Optional) You can activate **Samples** to add one of WebTV's predefined folders.

CROSS-REFERENCE

You can read about removing a Favorites folder later in this chapter.

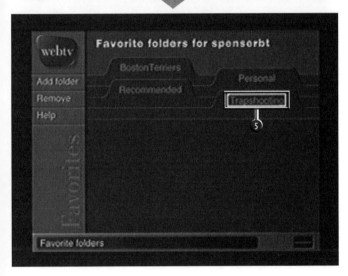

Some people will save Web sites directly in appropriate folders. They will put, for example, gardening-sites directly in their Gardening folder. Others choose to save everything in Personal and later sort through them. Moving favorite sites between folders is discussed later in this chapter.

TAKE NOTE

▶ **LIMITS**

WebTV lets you create a total of 20 Favorites folders. You can assign up to 32 favorites per folder.

▶ **REMOVING FOLDERS**

If you add a folder and later find you do not wish to use it, you can always remove it. Details follow in the next topic.

▶ **WEBTV CLASSIC**

Create new folders for your favorite Web sites the same way on WebTV Classic and WebTV Plus.

④ Activate **Add**.

⑤ WebTV adds the new folder to your Favorites.

FIND IT ONLINE

Read more about it. Visit **http://help.webtv.net/ favorites/createfolders.html.**

Removing a Favorites Folder

Sometimes, well-intended folders do not work out. Some may remain empty, while others may contain only one or two favorites. When cleaning your favorites, you may choose to discard a folder. Fortunately, you can remove a Favorites folder as easily as you can create it.

Whenever a Favorites folder is not empty, WebTV will ask you to confirm your request. This way, you cannot remove a favorite Web site by accident. Consider moving all the items out of a folder before removing it. You can learn how to move favorites between folders later in this chapter.

Once you have removed a folder, you cannot "undo" your action, although you can later manually recreate the folder and its contents. Consider carefully before removing folders — especially folders that contain personal Web sites that may be unlisted with the major Internet Web site search services. These sites may prove extremely difficult to refind.

Before removing a folder, you may want to carefully review its contents. When there are any favorite sites you wish to keep, consider transferring them to another Favorites folder or writing their names and Web site addresses on a piece of paper for later reference.

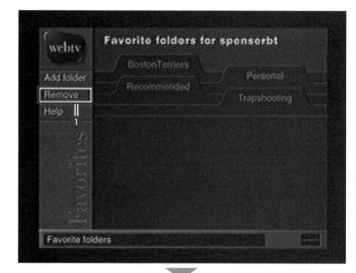

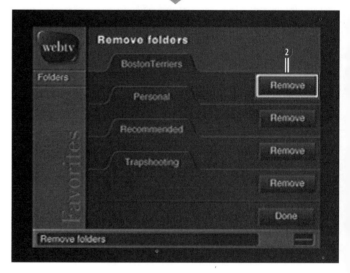

❶ Press favs and then activate **Remove**.

❷ Choose which folder to remove and then activate the **Remove** to its right.

CROSS-REFERENCE

You can read about adding a Favorites folder in the previous topic.

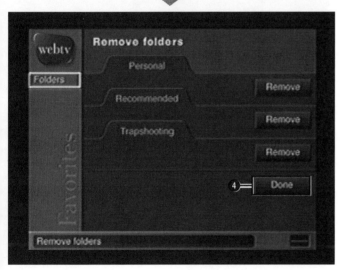

③ If the folder contains any favorites, WebTV will ask you to confirm. Activate **Remove**.

④ WebTV removes the folder. From here, you may continue to remove folders or activate **Done** to finish.

TAKE NOTE

▶ REMOVING RECOMMENDED

Do not fear to remove WebTV's Recommended folder or any of the other sample folders. WebTV can instantly recreate Recommended and the other sample folders for you from the Samples screen. Follow the directions in the previous topic to re-create the sample folders.

▶ YOU CANNOT AFFECT SECONDARY USERS

Any folder removal you do to your user account will not affect other primary or secondary user accounts. For example, say both you and another user have a News Favorites folder. When you remove yours, the other user's Favorites folder remains un-affected. Similarly, if one of your secondary users accidentally removes one of his or her Favorites folders, there is nothing you can do as primary user to retrieve it. Caution your secondary users about using care before removing any Favorites folder.

▶ WEBTV CLASSIC

Remove Favorites folders identically on WebTV Classic and WebTV Plus.

FIND IT ONLINE

Read more about it. Visit **http://help.webtv.net/ favorites/removingfolders.html**.

Discarding a Favorite Site

Every now and then, consider giving your Favorites folder a spring-cleaning. Weed out sites that you believe you will never revisit. Reorganize your folders to better match the way you use Favorites. Determine which Web addresses no longer point to valid Web sites and give them the boot.

A few steps are all it takes to discard a Web site from your Favorites folder. Start in any of your Favorites folders and activate **Organize** and then **Discard**. WebTV will present you with the list of Web sites saved in the folder, with each followed by a Discard button. Use the arrow and scroll keys to navigate through this list. To remove a site, activate the **Discard** button to the right of the site.

Take care when discarding sites. WebTV will not, I repeat *not*, ask you to confirm removing a site. And once the site is discarded, it is gone. Choose carefully and with full premeditation. You may wish to write down the Web addresses of the sites that you discard to protect against disaster or a later change of mind.

On the positive side, removing old and unused favorites can bring new life to your Favorites folders. Useful favorites become easier to find and, hence, easier to use. You can more readily scan visually through the remaining favorites and detect both sites that you are actually searching for and sites that may tickle your interest for a revisit. Visiting those interesting but infrequently used sites can prove both entertaining and rewarding, as you remember why you saved them as favorites in the first place.

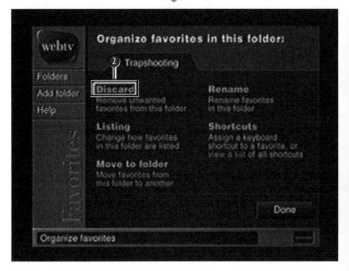

❶ From any Favorites folder, activate **Organize**. | ❷ Activate **Discard**.

CROSS-REFERENCE

You can read about adding a favorite in the first topic of this chapter.

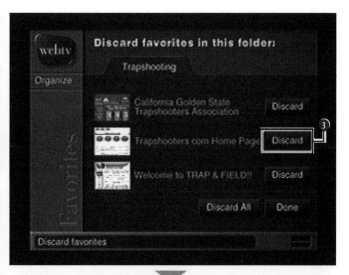

UNDOING

There is no way to undo removing a favorite, other than going back to that site and saving it again. Have you lost track of a site? Consider searching for it using the Search key. Once you find it, save it again.

AVOIDING "OOPS"

Before removing a favorite, you may want to first visit the site and then return to the Favorites folder. This allows you to change your mind by seeing how the site excited you in the first place and it gives you a way to undo an accidental deletion. When you have recently visited a site you accidentally discarded, you can use the Recent key to move back to that site and save it again.

WEBTV CLASSIC

Use favorite Web sites identically on WebTV Classic and WebTV Plus.

3 Use the arrow and scroll keys to select a Web site and activate the **Discard** to its right. In this case, we discard Trapshooters.com.

4 WebTV discards the site and lets you select additional sites to remove.

5 To finish, scroll to the bottom of the page (if it isn't visible) and activate **Done**.

FIND IT ONLINE

Read more about it. Visit **http://help.webtv.net/ favorites/removing.html.**

Renaming a Site

Some of the names that are associated with Web sites are simply unhelpful. Feel free to change these names and replace them with something more expressive. For example, you may wish to change a site labeled "FamTree" to "Helpful Genealogical Site."

WebTV enables you to edit the names associated with a Web address. This allows you to better manage your Favorites folder and identify favorite Web sites. From any folder, activate **Organize** and then **Rename**. Scroll through the list of names and edit them to your liking. When finished, activate **Done**.

Do be careful when editing names. WebTV does not have an undo feature. If you do not pay attention, you may accidentally erase a site name and be unable to remember what that site was about. If this occurs, just revisit the site. Still, it's better to avoid the waste of time and not get distracted while editing site names.

One of the best ways to decide a new name for a site is to revisit it. Read through the pages and spend time thinking about what the site does. In particular, consider how you are going to use the site. Although a site might primarily provide news headlines, you may use it solely to recover weather forecast information. If so, a name reflecting forecasts will work better for you than one about news headlines. Thinking about what the site does for you will help you come up with a useful and descriptive name.

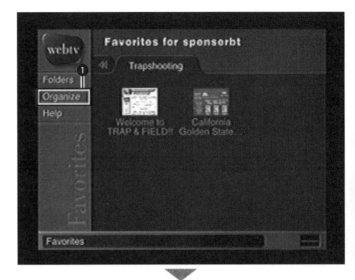

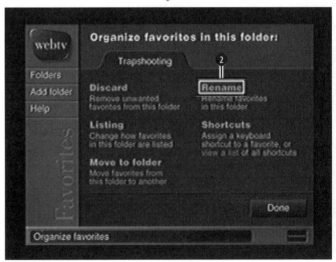

① *From any Favorites folder, activate* **Organize**.

② *Activate* **Rename**.

CROSS-REFERENCE

Want to move a favorite site from one folder to another? Read the next topic.

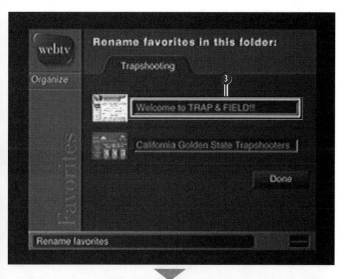

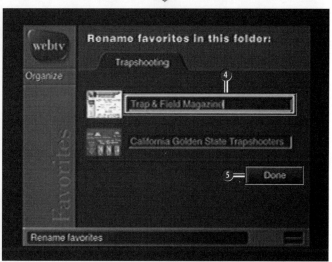

When a site's use or purpose changes for you over time, do not hesitate to update the name to reflect this. Feel free to include the former name in the description too. For example, you may wish to name a site "Great Cartoons (was: 'Dr. Lunacy')." This lets you maintain context while keeping the listing current and updated.

TAKE NOTE

▶ PROVIDE INSURANCE

Before changing a site's name, you may want to copy the name to WebTV's memory. Do this by first ensuring that the yellow cursor is blinking in the line with the old name and selecting the name with cmd +A. Copy the name with cmd+C. If you are unhappy with the new text that you have typed, you can always restore the old text. Paste it back by selecting the new, undesired name with cmd+A. Then paste the old name with cmd+V.

▶ WEBTV CLASSIC

Use favorite Web sites identically on WebTV Classic and WebTV Plus.

③ *Move the yellow box to the site that you wish to rename and press edit on your keyboard.*

④ *Edit the name as desired.*

⑤ *When finished, use the arrow or scroll keys to select another site or activate **Done** at the bottom of the page.*

FIND IT ONLINE

Read more about favorites. Visit **http://help.webtv. net/favorites/whatis.html.**

Moving Favorites Between Folders

Sometimes a favorite Web site does not seem to match the other sites listed in a folder. Some folders may have accumulated unrelated favorites. Other folders may grow to be large enough to merit a split. WebTV enables people to organize their favorites folders, moving favorites from one folder to another. This permits you to regain the order and philosophy you designed when you created the various folders.

Some people prefer to save all their favorites by default to the Personal folder created by WebTV. Later, they sort through these sites, assigning each to the folder they deem most appropriate. This method enables you to delay organizing your sites until the mood strikes.

Moving a favorite site between folders is nondestructive. WebTV will not let you overwrite another favorite. You cannot move a favorite site to a nonexistent folder. If at any time a favorite site seems to have "disappeared," look through the other folders. You may have moved it by accident or moved it deliberately and forgotten.

Moving favorites allows you to cluster favorite sites with sites of a similar theme. Take advantage of this functionality to make your Favorites folders easier to navigate, and to make your favorite sites easier to find.

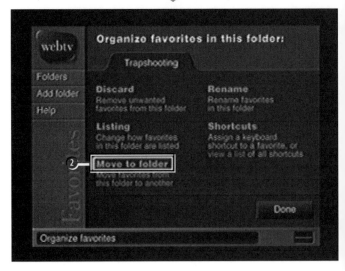

❶ From any Favorites folder, activate **Organize**.

❷ Activate **Move to folder**.

CROSS-REFERENCE

Learn about adding new favorite Web sites earlier in this chapter.

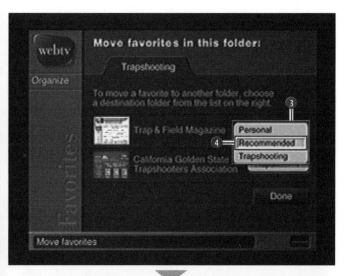

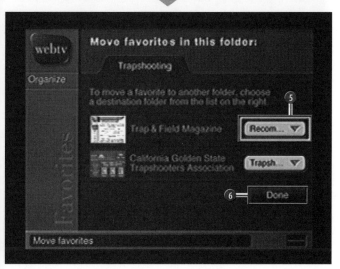

▶ UNDOING A MOVE

WebTV does not confirm your changes until you have activated **Done**. If you have selected a folder change by accident, you can change your mind before proceeding. If you do move a site and later wish to change your mind, repeat the moving procedure. Simply move the favorite back to the original folder.

▶ CREATE NEW CLUSTERS

You will occasionally find that a favorite from one folder and several from another seem to match each other well, but not match either of the existing folders. In this case, consider creating a new folder and moving these favorites to it. WebTV permits you to create up to 20 favorites folders and it may prove useful to you to take advantage of this organizational opportunity. Keep favorites clustered in ways that make sense to you and that facilitate quick retrieval when you are searching for a Web site.

▶ WEBTV CLASSIC

Use favorite Web sites identically on WebTV Classic and WebTV Plus.

③ Move the yellow box to the pull-down menu (the gray, rounded rectangle) to the right of site you wish to move. Activate it with Go or Return.

④ After you have activated the pull-down menu, a list of your current folders appears. Select a new folder with the yellow box and press Go or Return.

⑤ The gray, rounded rectangle now shows the new folder assignment for the favorite Web site.

⑥ When finished, use the arrow or scroll keys to select another site or activate **Done** at the bottom of the page.

FIND IT ONLINE

Read more about it. Visit **http://help.webtv.net/ favorites/moving.html**.

Personal Workbook

Q&A

1 What is the difference between a Web address and a Web page?

_____

_____

_____

2 How do you add a Web address to your Favorites?

_____

_____

_____

3 What are _F keys?_

_____

_____

_____

4 How many Favorite folders does WebTV let you maintain?

_____

_____

5 How many favorites may you store in a single folder?

_____

_____

_____

6 If you rename a Web site favorite and later wish to resume the former name, what can you do?

_____

_____

_____

7 Why might some people prefer to omit site snapshots?

_____

_____

_____

8 If several sites seem to have a common theme, what is a way to organize them?

_____

_____

ANSWERS: PAGE 335

EXTRA PRACTICE

1 Visit some Web sites and save them to your favorites.

2 Use favorites to return to your saved Web sites

3 Assign a favorite to an F key.

4 Add a Sample Favorites folder and save some sites to that folder.

REAL-WORLD APPLICATIONS

✔ You are a real news junkie. You love to keep on top of the latest headlines. You visit some of the more famous News sites (newspapers, network news, and so on) and create a Favorites folder devoted to getting the breaking news as it happens.

✔ You are an amateur, but enthusiastic, golfer. You search the Internet for sites related to the best putters available and the best putting techniques. You save those sites to a putting-themed Favorites folder.

Visual Quiz

Which site is assigned to an F key? Which F key?

_____

_____

_____

_____

_____

_____

CHAPTER 6

MASTER THESE SKILLS

▶ Using the Search Key

▶ Adding Search Phrases

▶ Limiting Searches with Mixed Case

▶ Limiting Searches with Quoted Phrases

▶ Limiting Searches with +

▶ Browsing Categories

Searching the Web

The World Wide Web holds information on almost any topic you can conceive of. No matter what your hobby, your job, or your special interests, it is likely that you will find relevant information, articles, and special-interest groups on the Web. These are published on Web sites, scattered around the country and around the world.

The key to finding these sites is knowing how to search the World Wide Web. With the power of searching, you can find Web sites relating to practically any topic that you can imagine.

By the time you finish this chapter, you will have learned how to search skillfully and effectively. You should be able to find information on practically any topic that you choose.

You start by learning to use the Search key. This key brings you to WebTV's special search page. On this page, you learn to submit a search request to the WebTV/Infoseek database. You also learn to narrow your search by adding extra phrases to your search terms. In this way, you learn to perform basic Web searches.

Next, you learn to limit your searches by using mixed case and quoted search terms. These techniques permit you to narrow your searches further to produce the best possible matches to your queries.

Finally, you learn to use the + and − symbols to require or disallow terms within a Web page. With these prefixes, you can either force a phrase to appear within a Web page or reject all pages that include that phrase.

When you have mastered all of these skills, you will be able to create well-defined specific searches that produce the pages that you truly desire and exclude those that are irrelevant.

Using the Search Key

Imagine, if you will, standing in the largest library in the universe. Books, magazines, and various other media surround you. Imagine the effort of searching for a book or doing research if someone has not cataloged the collection. In many ways, the World Wide Web is the library of our example. Fortunately for us, however, a number of people have made it their business to create partial catalogs of the Internet. Special programs called search engines have created these catalogs.

Search engines automatically scan Web pages on the Internet. They look at a Web page and collect all the hyperlinks on that page. These links are added to the list of sites to explore. The program adds the page to its database, picks a hyperlink from the unexplored site list and collects all the links on that page.

This process works in much the same way as the game "six degrees of separation." In this game, players attempt to create a web of connection between two people. For example, if two people share a common friend but do not know each other, they are considered to share one degree of separation. Similarly, one person might have a friend who has a friend who has a friend who knows the second person. Mathematicians have estimated that each person on earth can be associated with any other person on earth using no more than six links.

World Wide Web search engines work on the same hypothesis. They assume that if you explore each link on a Web page, and each link on the pages that those links represent, and on and on, you will eventually find every page on the Internet that has ever been published.

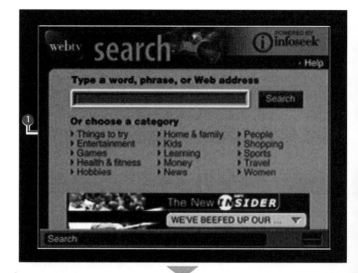

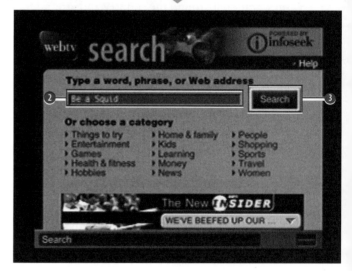

➊ Press Search on your keyboard. You will enter WebTV's Search the Web screen.

➋ Type in a word, a phrase, or several words that relate to your topic in the box below What are you looking for?

➌ Activate **Search**.

CROSS-REFERENCE

Learn more about hyperlinks and URLs in Chapter 4.

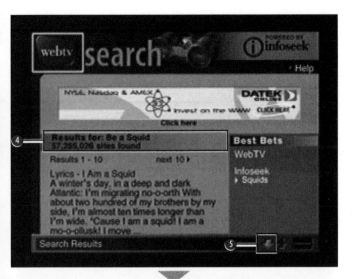

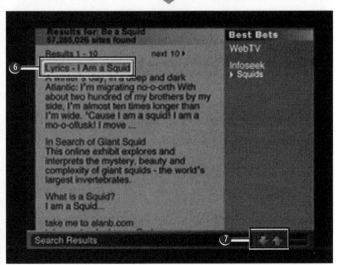

For your convenience, WebTV offers built-in access to let you search the World Wide Web. The popular Infoseek search engine powers this Internet search facility. You can search the Web by pressing Search on your keyboard. Type in a search phrase and let WebTV and Infoseek do the rest.

▶ *WebTV searches the Internet for your topic.*

④ *A banner above the results will remind you of your topic and tell you how many matches were found.*

⑤ *Scroll down to see the first page of results. WebTV lists the results with the closest matches first.*

⑥ *To visit any site, move the yellow box to its title and activate it with Go or Return.*

⑦ *Use the arrow or scroll keys to see the entire page of search results. WebTV displays links to ten sites at a time. Activate the down arrow to view additional Web sites.*

FIND IT ONLINE

Visit my father's favorite search engine at
http://www.dogpile.com.

Adding Search Phrases

The goal of an effective search is to produce a few high-quality sites that match your search phrases well. Adding extra search phrases can help narrow your search and focus on more specific topics.

In general, when you type search phrases, WebTV and Infoseek attempt to find sites that match as many of the phrases as possible. Those sites that best match your phrases are listed first in the search results.

Add extra phrases one at a time. The goal of adding a phrase is to help define your search more exactly. After you add a phrase, scan the results. When the sites found move closer to your expectations, feel free to add another limiting phrase. If, however, you add a word that seems to change the nature or flavor of your search, step back and try searching with another phrase instead.

Avoid adding a lot of extra phrases at once, as this may dilute your search. It may also inadvertently change the focus of your query. Instead, start small and slowly add phrases.

When the page of results seems to closely match your desired search, stop adding new phrases. Explore the pages that you have found or activate **next 10** to see additional sites that matched your search query. Adding extra phrases at this point will hurt rather than help you.

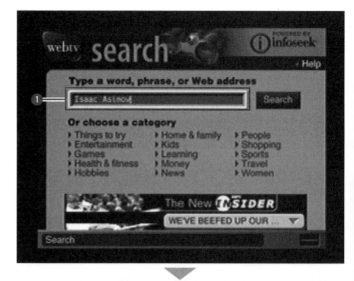

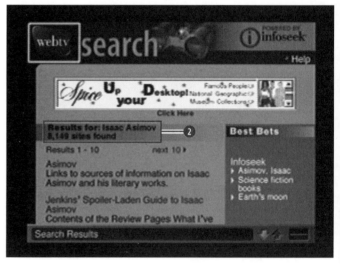

▶ In this example, we will search for mysteries by Isaac Asimov.

▶ Call up the search page by pressing Search on the keyboard or by activating **Search** from your WebTV home screen.

❶ Type in your search phrase and activate **Search**.

❷ WebTV and Infoseek found over eight thousand pages related to his work. Clearly, the most popular pages are related to his science fiction.

CROSS-REFERENCE

The previous topic discusses the basic nature of search engines.

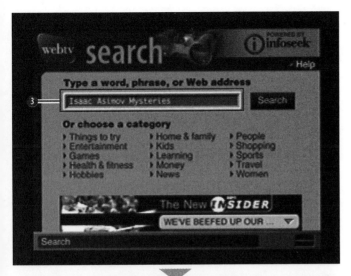

MORE PHRASES CAN ALSO HURT

When you add an extra phrase to a search, make sure to use a word that helps limit — rather than expand — the search. Common words may inadvertently add undesired sites to your search results. For example, consider searching for *Niagara*. You may find pages about the famous falls, and others about the starch product. If you expand your search to *Niagara Falls*, you may add sites about waterfalls and lawsuits rather than remove sites about starch. See the next few topics for better ways to add precision when needed.

FIRST IS USUALLY BEST

When scanning through search results, the best matches to your query are usually found on the first few pages, and on those, the earliest listed often provide the closest matches. Although the search engine attempts to list best matches first, you still may find it valuable to read through the next few pages to find some gems.

WEBTV CLASSIC

Search the Web identically on WebTV Classic and WebTV Plus.

③ *You may wish to further limit your search by adding phrases. Next, we search again, but this time adding the extra word Mysteries. After calling up the search page again, type in the modified search phrase and activate **Search**.*

④ *WebTV and Infoseek found less than 50 pages relating to Asimov's mysteries. Contrast this with having to browse more than 8,000!*

Limiting Searches with Mixed Case

WebTV's search facility considers "WebTV," "Webtv," and "webtv" as entirely different entities. When you search using a phrase with mixed upper- and lowercase, WebTV attempts to match that phrase exactly. "WebTV" will match "WebTV" but not "Webtv."

In contrast, when you search using lowercase only, you match phrases using any case combinations. Searching for "webtv" will match "WebTV," "webTV," "Webtv," and son on.

So why use mixed case at all? Using mixed case lets you limit your search and produce more focused results. For example, searching for "Champagne France" excludes many of the more common uses related to drinking the sparkling wine and helps narrow your search to the region of France.

Use mixed case to specify proper names. Names such as "Bill" or "Newt" are spelled like common English words. Capitalizing these names helps restrict your search to the people involved, rather than legislative agendas or small lizards.

Some corporations also use common words as their names. Consider NeXT, Apple, Sprint, and Be — all are common words used for corporate names. Using mixed case helps assure that you find the right site.

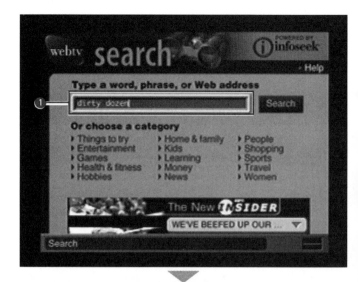

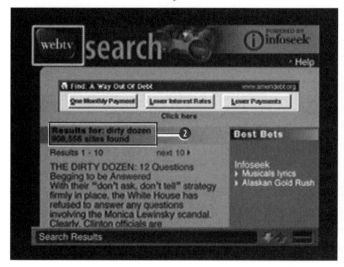

▶ Call up the Search the Web screen by pressing Search on your keyboard or by activating **Search** from your WebTV home screen.

❶ In this example, we search for dirty dozen. Type this phrase in and activate **Search**.

❷ WebTV and Infoseek have found almost 1 million sites with this search phrase.

CROSS-REFERENCE

Learn to limit searches using quoted phrases in the next topic.

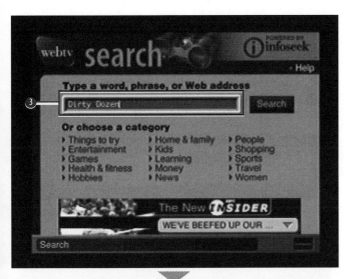

WHEN TO AVOID MIXING CASE

When you are unsure of the exact upper- and lowercase spelling of a word, always use lowercase. This enables WebTV and Infoseek to search more broadly and avoid missing important sites. The computer company NeXT springs to mind as an excellent example of confusing case usage. This rule applies even when you are sure of the case usage but believe that information publishers (such as reviewers, retailers, and so on) may be using the capitalization incorrectly.

CAPITALIZE KEYWORDS CAUTIOUSLY

In some cases, you may be unsure as to which words to capitalize. Always select those that are most unambiguous. Place names and institutions are almost always capitalized, whereas product names may not be. Err first on the side of caution. You can always return to the search page and refine your search if additional words prove most commonly capitalized.

WEBTV CLASSIC

Use Infoseek to search the Web on both WebTV Classic and WebTV Plus.

▶ *Return to the search screen by pressing Search on your keyboard or by using Back to return to Search the Web.*

❸ *Next, we search again, but this time using mixed case: Dirty Dozen.*

❹ *This time, WebTV and Infoseek have found only 3,245 sites, although the first is not nearly so good a match as the other top sites.*

FIND IT ONLINE

Visit the home of Infoseek at **http://www.infoseek.com**.

Limiting Searches with Quoted Phrases

When you include a quoted phrase in your search query, you tell WebTV to find the words of the phrase in the exact order you have given them. When you search for "William Rehnquist," for example, you will find exact uses of this name. If you were to omit the quote, your search would return all sites that contained both *William* and *Rehnquist* although not necessarily next to each other.

Employee, personnel, or faculty lists are the chief offenders when it comes to name searches. You may be looking for *Jane Doe* and find a company that employs both *Jane Public* and *William Doe*. In a situation such as this, quoting your strings works best.

WebTV and Infoseek can and will find ordered subsets of your search string. A recent search for "I want to be a squid" quickly found a "Be a Squid" Web site. This can prove helpful when you have overquoted and included extraneous information. Similarly, this can prove harmful when a common phrase appears within your search phrase and causes Infoseek to return with excessive and useless sites.

Infoseek may also take liberties with verb case, and plurals. A search for "I had a dream" resulted in numerous Martin Luther King "I have a dream" sites. Similarly, "United State" returned hundreds of "United States" Web sites.

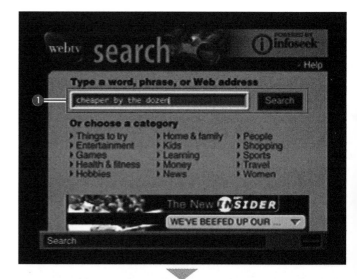

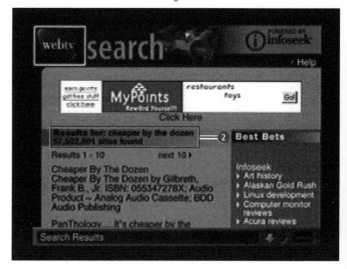

▶ Call up the Search the Web screen by pressing Search on your keyboard or by activating **Search** from your WebTV home screen.

❶ In this example, we search for cheaper by the dozen. Type this phrase in and activate **Search**.

❷ WebTV and Infoseek have found over 57 million sites with this search phrase.

CROSS-REFERENCE

Learn to limit searches using mixed case in the previous topic.

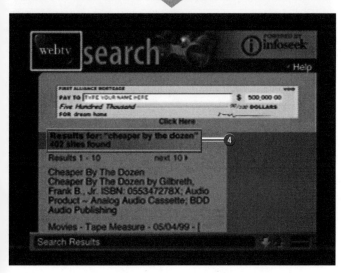

TAKE NOTE

LOOKING FOR NAMES

Remember when searching for names that a person may be listed as "William Roe" or "Roe, William." You may also want to search for "Will Roe" or "Bill Roe" to find less formal Web sites associated with this person.

MIDDLE INITIALS AND NICKNAMES

Middle initials and nicknames may help — or may hinder — your search. Some people may use their nicknames in person but their proper names on official Web sites. When faced with a hundred John Does, knowing the middle initial Q for Quincy may help limit your search.

WHEN NOT TO QUOTE

When you find yourself unsure of an exact quote, avoid this technique. Do not search for "Hell hath no fury like a woman scorned." The actual quote is "Heaven has no rage like love to hatred turned, Nor hell a fury like a woman scorned." Instead, to find the quote, you might search for *hell fury woman scorned* without using quotes.

WEBTV CLASSIC

Use the same techniques to limit searches on both WebTV Classic and WebTV Plus.

▶ *Return to the search screen by pressing Search on your keyboard or by using Back to return to Search the Web.*

❸ *We search again, but this time we use the quoted string, "cheaper by the dozen". Infoseek looks for the complete phrase rather than the individual words.*

❹ *This time, WebTV and Infoseek found 402 excellent matches to the phrase.*

FIND IT ONLINE

Visit Infoseek's home at **http://www.infoseek.com**.

Limiting Searches with +

When you need to find a site that contains a number of search phrases, consider using + to limit your search. Any phrase preceded by + tells WebTV and Infoseek that it *must* appear in each site found. Normally Infoseek will attempt to find as many search phrases as possible within each Web page. When you place a + before a search phrase, it changes that phrase from being desirable to required.

Naturally, if you include too many required phrases, you may not find any Web pages that match your search. Use the + delimiter with restraint unless you are sure that all the phrases do occur on at least one Web page.

When using +, be sure to use exact phrasing. If you are unsure whether to search for "furniture," "ottomans," or "foot stools," avoid +. When performing general searches, keep your phrases more flexible. Use + only when you are certain a search term must be included.

The + delimiter can help cut down enormously on irrelevant sites. In the example on the facing page, the number of "hits," that is pages that matched the search phrase, was reduced from the several millions to 17. When you are sure that each phrase can and will occur on relevant pages, use the + to weed out extraneous pages and to focus your search on those pages that are truly relevant.

When deciding which phrases to prefix, consider how relevant each word will be to your search. Brand names and model numbers are good examples of search phrases that will always prove exact. Feel free to require them when you know they are the precise objects of your search.

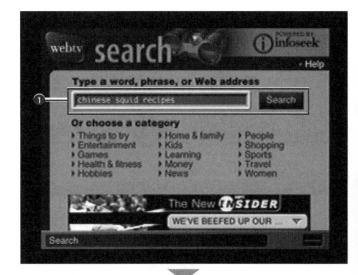

▶ Call up the Search the Web screen by pressing Search on your keyboard or by activating **Search** from your WebTV home screen.

❶ In this example, we search for chinese squid recipes. Type this phrase in and activate **Search**.

❷ WebTV and Infoseek have found almost 1 million sites with this search phrase.

❸ Some of the suggested "Best Bets" are poor matches. Consider "Chinese restaurants" and "Squids"!

CROSS-REFERENCE

Learn to browse categories in the next topic.

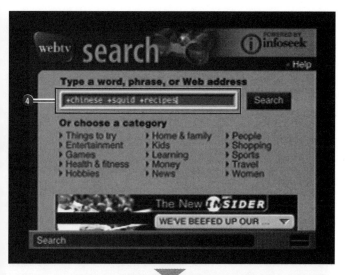

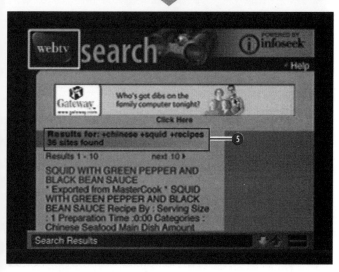

TAKE NOTE

CHECK YOUR SPELLING

Using + to require a search phrase makes your searches even more vulnerable to misspellings. For example, if your search includes +*Wahsington*, you will likely find few matching sites. Check your search phrases carefully for misspellings before activating **Search**.

BEST BETS

When you find a "best bet" that matches your interest, feel free to activate it. In this way, you can find entire categories of related Web pages.

LIMIT YOUR SEARCH USING "–"

Using – in a search phrase tells WebTV and Infoseek to disregard any matches to the key phrase that also include the words preceded by a minus sign. This is another excellent way to limit a search. For example, if you asked for Planet Saturn, you would also get matches for any of the Saturn automobile models. By asking for Planet Saturn -car -auto, you will remove all of those matches.

WEBTV CLASSIC

Use the + sign to limit searches on both WebTV Classic and WebTV Plus.

▶ Return to the search screen by pressing Search on your keyboard or by using Back to return to Search the Web.

④ We search again, but this time we precede each word with the plus sign: +chinese +squid +recipes. Infoseek looks for sites that contain all three words.

⑤ This time, WebTV and Infoseek found 36 excellent matches to the phrase.

FIND IT ONLINE

Search for best buys. Visit **http://www.mysimon.com**.

Browsing Categories

WebTV also provides a number of predefined categories where you can significantly narrow your search. Each category limits the scope of your search until you are left with just those sites that fall within your area of interest. This type of search is called *browsing*.

The subcategories allow you to incrementally refine your browsing criteria until you've narrowed it down to a list of interesting sites. When you select a category and press Go, you are presented with a list of subcategories near the top of the screen and a list of featured sites below them — you might have to scroll down to see the list of sites.

Assuming that you don't see a site of interest in the list provided, look for a subcategory that more closely describes the information you're seeking. As you move past the first level, you are presented with Web sites particular to that subcategory.

Eventually, you'll reach a point where there are no more subcategories — just sites. When you've gotten to this state, you've narrowed things down as far as browsing will allow.

Occasionally, you will find that the Web site is no longer reachable. This is because search engines create these lists of millions of sites, but sites can move to new locations, be removed from the Web by their creators, or the Web server where it resides is temporarily offline. Because all of this information is extracted by software, the information given is only as accurate as the Web page designer made it in the Description tag (see Chapter 16 for more information).

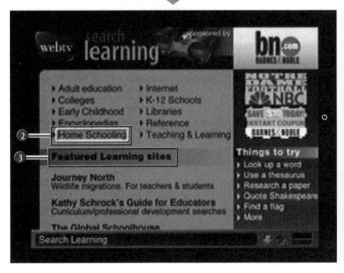

❶ Choose a category through which you'd like to browse. We're using **Learning** in this example.

❷ Select a subcategory of Learning that interests you. Here we're going to investigate **Home Schooling**.

❸ (Optional) You could choose to investigate one of the Featured Learning Sites instead. If so, scroll down and pick one.

CROSS-REFERENCE

Learn how to shop with WebTV in Chapter 14.

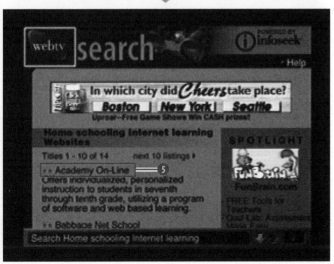

④ You further refine your search to look for **Internet learning programs**.

⑤ We've reached the end of the line. Find a site of interest and press Go.

Personal Workbook

Q&A

1 How do you tell WebTV that you wish to begin searching the World Wide Web?

_____

_____

_____

2 Why do you find Web pages that include only subsets of the search phrases you used?

_____

_____

_____

3 Which will produce more Web pages: a search for *burgundy* or a search for *Burgundy*?

_____

_____

4 What is the difference between searching for *top cat* and *"top cat"*?

_____

_____

_____

5 How might you search for the Gettysburg Address, if you are unsure how to spell Gettysburg?

_____

_____

_____

6 What's a good way to search for song lyrics by Gilbert and Sullivan?

_____

_____

_____

7 If you wish to find information about the Golden Gate Bridge, which query should you use: *San Francisco attraction +golden +gate +bridge* or *+San +Francisco +attraction golden gate bridge*?

_____

_____

8 How might you search for information about camels but exclude pages that talk about the cigarettes?

_____

_____

ANSWERS: PAGE 336

EXTRA PRACTICE

1. Practice using the Search key.

2. Add extra phrases to your search terms and see how the results vary.

3. Use mixed case to limit your searches.

4. Use quoted phrases to limit your searches.

5. Combine the various techniques to produce a complex search query.

REAL-WORLD APPLICATIONS

✔ You search the World Wide Web for information about your various friends and relatives. You find yourself surprised who is, and who is not, represented on the Web.

✔ You search for information about your favorite author or musician. You find numerous reviews and/or excerpts.

✔ You have a medical condition and want to get some help. You search the Web to find information about your condition.

Visual Quiz

How could you view sites about pasta recipes?

_____

_____

_____

_____

_____

_____

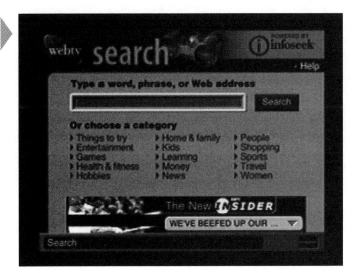

CHAPTER 7

MASTER
THESE
SKILLS

▶ Singing with WebTV

▶ Playing an Online Game

▶ Asking for Advice

▶ Watching TV While Surfing the Web

Exploring the Web

The Internet can be fun. Interesting and unusual Web sites abound. This chapter introduces you to some of the more interesting and unusual ways to explore and enjoy the Internet.

First, you learn to use WebTV's MIDI Karaoke feature. This astonishing innovation lets you sing along with your WebTV unit as the music plays and the words stream in front of your eyes.

Next, you learn about online games: how to find them and how to play them. In this topic, you also learn how to master online Battleship.

Next, you discover the treasure of free, online expertise. Expert sites have begun to spring up on the Internet, offering free access to experts on a wide variety of subjects. You learn to submit a question to a specialist.

And finally, you will learn how to use WebTV's built in "picture-in-picture" capability to watch television and surf the Web at the same time.

By the time you complete this chapter, you will have seen some of the variety of World Wide Web services that exist both to help and entertain you.

Singing with WebTV

Every time you think you've discovered the limits of the WebTV service, another delightful surprise springs up. I was very pleased to discover that WebTV supports MIDI Karaoke on both WebTV Plus and WebTV Classic units. Karaoke, as you might know, is a popular sing-along style of enjoying music that originated in Japan. The phrase apparently means "empty orchestra" and refers to the prerecorded soundtrack that accompanies each song. You provide the vocals. As the song progresses, the Karaoke system prompts singers with lyrics. In short, Karaoke is an updated version of the "follow-the-dancing-ball" sing-alongs of days gone by. If you like singing in the shower, and wouldn't mind an orchestrated accompaniment, WebTV's MIDI Karaoke system may be for you.

MIDI refers to a way that a computer stores and performs music. The phrase stands for Musical Instruments Digital Interface. MIDI files provide a compact and effective means for computers to provide musical presentations. MIDI Karaoke is a special type of MIDI. It allows lyrics to be attached to MIDI files and to have those lyrics timed to specific phrases within a song. WebTV furnishes you with a powerful MIDI Karaoke player as part of its standard software.

With WebTV's MIDI Karaoke player you can fine-tune many features. A tempo bar permits you to accelerate or slow down playback so that you can choose the pace that suits you best. If the song is out of range, the pitch bar lets you adjust the key to better fit your register. In addition, pause, rewind, and forward buttons move the music to where you need to be.

MIDI Karaoke can become an addictive hobby, especially when enjoyed with friends.

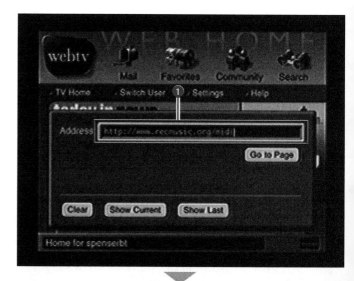

1 *Here's an example to get you started with WebTV MIDI. If you have a keyboard, press Go To. If not, press Options on your remote, select **Goto** with the arrow keys, and then press Go. After **http://** type **www.recmusic.org/midi/** and press Go on the remote or Return on the keyboard.*

2 *Once you have arrived at the Classical Midi with Words page, use the Scroll Down key or button to move down the list until you reach "Largo al Factotum" by Rossini in the Italian section.*

CROSS-REFERENCE

Learn more about sending a Web page in the mail in Chapter 4.

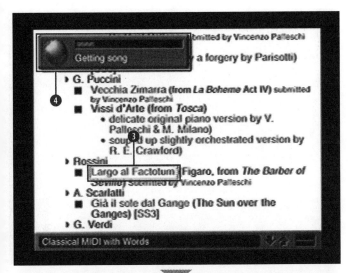

RESPECTING COPYRIGHT ISSUES

Many MIDI Karaoke songs have been published on the Internet in violation of international copyright law. Those sites that are compliant with the law will say so clearly and forcefully. Make sure to check for this. As a general rule, the music at sites that cover traditional and classical music is the music most likely to be in the public domain.

WAITING FOR THE WORDS

Many MIDI Karaoke songs have extensive introductions. Wait a bit and you will be rewarded with the sing-along.

GETTING BACK

After you are done with your MIDI experience, simply press Home or Back to leave the MIDI Karaoke player.

WEBTV CLASSIC

WebTV Plus offers many more MIDI Karaoke features than does WebTV Classic. The Classic MIDI Karaoke player offers only the minimum of controls. Your Classic player will look very different from the pictures on the facing page.

③ Use the arrow keys to move the yellow box around this piece and press Go on the remote or Return on the keyboard.

④ Wait for WebTV to load the song to your unit. WebTV displays a progress box.

⑤ Sing along. The words turn from white to yellow to prompt you. You can fine-tune any of the following features.

⑥ Rewind the song completely.

⑦ This button pauses the song.

⑧ These buttons adjust the tempo.

⑨ These move the pitch higher or lower to match your voice.

FIND IT ONLINE

Visit **http://www.recmusic.org** for a superb list of MIDI Karaoke files.

Playing an Online Game

The World Wide Web isn't just about information and gossip — it's also about fun. You may find playing an online game to be the perfect remedy for stress.

You can find games by using WebTV's search feature or by visiting a listing site like Yahoo. Use the keyword "game" to start your exploration. You will be surprised how many games — of varying quality and enjoyment — can be found on the World Wide Web.

Some Web games involve multiple players. Others, such as the Battleship game shown on the facing page, enable you to play directly against a computer. Whether playing with others or alone, you will find a vast wealth of game-playing options.

Online diversions include strategy, board, card, and gambling games among others. Some allow you to enter shared worlds, called "MUSH"es, "MUD"s or "MOO"s. Others let you play chess by e-mail. If you spend a little time searching for entertaining sites, you are sure to be rewarded.

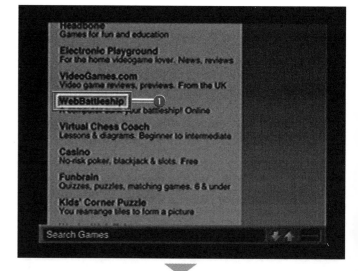

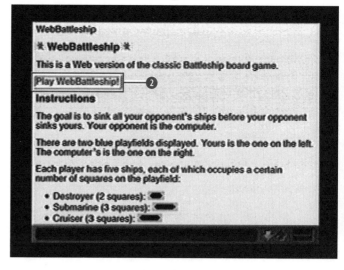

① Activate **WebBattleship** from WebTV's Search page in the Games category.

② Read the instructions and then activate **Play WebBattleship**.

CROSS-REFERENCE

Learn to ask for advice in the next topic.

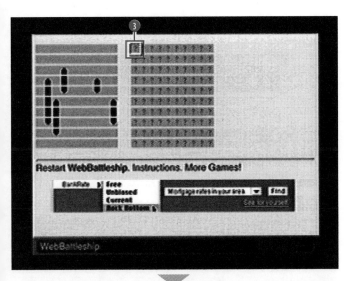

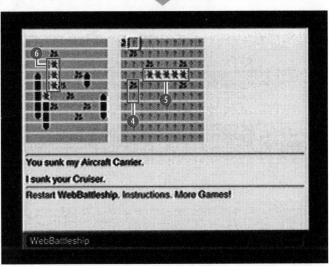

TAKE NOTE

▶ **DON'T OVERDO**

Keep an eye on the clock when indulging in game playing. Some people liken online games to the addictive qualities of Skinner boxes.

▶ **WEBTV CLASSIC**

Internet access works identically on WebTV Classic and WebTV Plus.

③ *Move the yellow box to any square on the right-side, blue rectangle. Press Go or Return to "bomb."*

④ *Little blue "splashes" indicate a miss.*

⑤ *Red and yellow "bangs" indicate a hit.*

⑥ *Oh no! The computer sank my cruiser, but I got his aircraft carrier.*

FIND IT ONLINE

Visit Battleship at http://info.gte.com/ cgi-bin/battle.cgi.

115

Asking for Advice

With online advice services you need never be at a complete loss. Whether your question is medical, personal, or scholarly, there may be someone out there on the World Wide Web to help you. When you consider the millions of people who are now connected to the Internet, it is not surprising that so many provide such a wide expanse of expertise. What is surprising, however, is that so many are willing to volunteer that expertise to help others.

Some experts are trying to make a name for themselves. By volunteering as an information provider, they hope to get their names and expertise known so that it may lead to consulting or to the lecture circuit.

Others volunteer for the sheer goodness of it. Priests, ministers, and rabbis stand ready to answer theological dilemmas that may be plaguing you. These clerics consider these services part of their outreach programs. Still others, such as lawyers and doctors, consider this service part of their pro bono work for the general good of the community.

So how does it work? Why can these sites exist? The general answer is advertising. Site owners sell advertising space on their Web sites to subsidize the service and underwrite the Web pages and the associated services.

In the end, I believe everyone wins. Although the answers you receive may be worth exactly what you paid for them, you may also find valuable and helpful information as well.

After submitting the request on the following page, I received a helpful and informative reply about the nature of manifolds. This went far to help me understand the obscure mathematical research that is performed routinely by my brother-in-law.

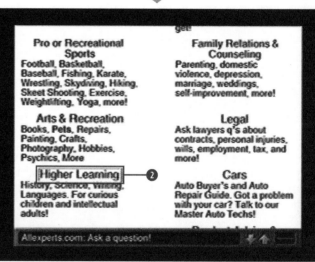

1 To find AllExperts.com, press Go To, type **http://www. allexperts.com**, and activate **Go to Page**.

2 Scroll down until you find a topic of interest and then activate it with Go or Return. In this example, I selected Higher Learning.

CROSS-REFERENCE

Learn to play an online game in the previous topic.

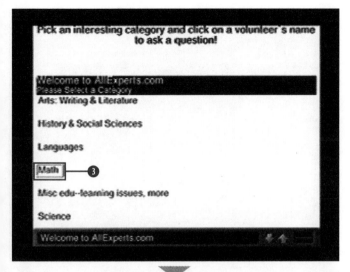

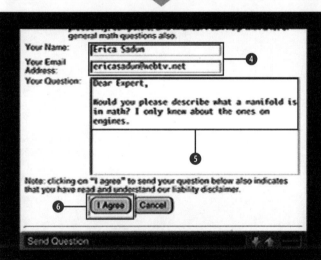

❸ Select appropriate subtopics and activate with Go or Return. You may have to move through several screens until you are ready to ask your question. In the example, I selected Math.

▶ You'll need to also select Advanced Math and then select an expert from their list to determine who you'll ask.

❹ Enter your address.

❺ Type your question.

❻ Read the terms and conditions on the page and then activate **I agree**. An answer is sent to you within a few days.

FIND IT ONLINE

Get advice at **http://www.allexperts.com**.

Watching TV While Surfing the Web

I t wasn't all that long ago when "picture in picture" was a hot selling point for new TV sets. WebTV gives you part of that power regardless of your TV's capabilities. Whenever you are cruising around the Internet, you can continue watching TV on the same screen.

If you're looking at anything on the Web, just press the Option button on your remote control or the Option key on your keyboard. This will display the Options control panel. Move the yellow box to the bottom-leftmost item, "tv window," and press Go or Return. A picture-in-picture box will show up on your screen, displaying whatever you have tuned in on the TV side.

By default, the box shows up in the lower-right part of the screen. This could hide something you want to see on the Web. If you wish to move the TV window to the lower-left (or back), just press the Enter button on your remote control or ⌘+M on your keyboard.

When you wish to remove the TV window from your Web screen, just bring up the Options control panel again and reselect "tv window" and press Go. You will also see a little green light on the TV window button when you have it turned on.

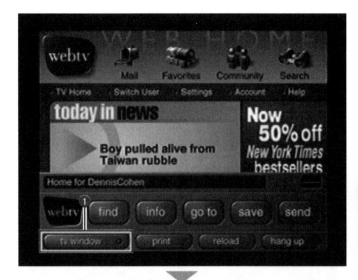

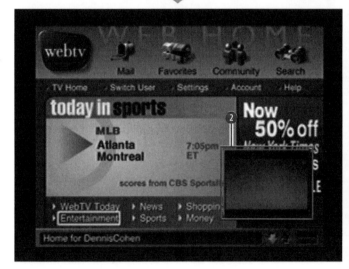

▶ Bring up the Options control panel by pressing the Option button while displaying a Web page.

❶ Move the yellow box to the control panel's tv window button.

❷ The current TV picture is displayed in a miniature screen at the lower right. Press Enter on your remote control or ⌘+M on your keyboard.

CROSS-REFERENCE

Learn to get current TV listings in Chapter 15.

FIND IT ONLINE

Visit Nickelodeon's home at **http://www.nickatnite.com**.

TAKE NOTE

CHANGING CHANNELS

Remember that what is being displayed in your small TV window is just a reflection of what you have selected in your TV Home. Any channel changes, TV listings lookups, and so forth are done by switching to your TV Home.

WEBTV CLASSIC

WebTV Classic and WebTV Plus both support TV picture-in-picture while surfing the Web.

③ The TV window has moved to the left-hand side of the screen.

④ Press the Option button and select the control panel's tv window button. Note that it currently has a green light displayed. Activate Go to remove the TV picture.

Personal Workbook

Q&A

1 What is *Karaoke?*

_____

_____

_____

2 What is the difference between MIDI and MIDI Karaoke?

_____

_____

_____

3 What's a good way to search for MIDI Karaoke songs?

_____

_____

_____

4 What sorts of free expertise can you find on the Internet?

_____

_____

_____

5 How reliable is the free expertise that you find on the Internet?

_____

_____

_____

6 What button on the Options panel will call up the television "picture-in-picture" feature?

_____

_____

_____

ANSWERS: PAGE 336

EXTRA PRACTICE

1. Sing along with MIDI Karaoke.

2. Explore the tempo and other Karaoke playback options.

3. Search for an online game and play it.

4. Ask for advice using online expertise.

REAL-WORLD APPLICATIONS

✔ Do you have an ethical dilemma? Consider asking a religious expert for insight about it.

✔ You invite friends over for an evening of Karaoke. Surprisingly, they remain your friends.

Visual Quiz

How can you change the pitch on this song?

_____

_____

_____

_____

_____

_____

PART

III

CHAPTER **8** Building Basic E-mail Skills

9 Creating and Maintaining Your Address Book

10 Building Intermediate E-mail Skills

11 Taking Charge of E-mail Storage

12 Mastering Advanced E-mail Techniques

13 Joining E-mail Lists

Contents of 'Desktop'

Name

My Computer

Network Neigh

Internet Explore

Microsoft Outlook

Recycle Bin

My Briefcase

3252-9

3259-6

3261-8

3252-6

3281-2

3286-3

DE Phone List

Device Manager

In

Iomega Tools

Mastering Electronic Mail

This part introduces you to electronic mail — what it is and how to use it. It discusses both basic and advanced skills. You learn about address books, mailing lists, and how to maintain your mailbox. By the time you finish this section, you will be able to use electronic mail efficiently and judiciously.

I start by surveying basic electronic mail skills such as sending, receiving, and replying to e-mail. You learn to create a letter, to edit it, and to send it out, as well as to navigate through incoming letters.

Next, you learn to create and maintain an address book. You learn to add to and remove names from your book, as well as update entries when information changes.

You learn about storing mail and weeding through old letters, saving those that are important to you and discarding those that are not. You learn to look at copies of outgoing mail and to store those letters that are precious to you.

Next, you learn a variety of advanced e-mail skills that will make your mail more interesting and exciting.

Finally, you learn how mailing lists work, how to find a list, and how to join discussion groups to get involved with those with whom you share common interests. You learn how to join and leave a list, and how to handle list traffic when you go away on vacations.

CHAPTER 8

MASTER THESE SKILLS

▶ Reading Electronic Mail

▶ Moving Through the Mail List

▶ Writing Electronic Mail

▶ Sending Mail to Multiple Recipients

▶ Replying to Electronic Mail

▶ Forwarding Electronic Mail

▶ Adding a Picture to Electronic Mail

▶ Attaching a Sound Clip

▶ Getting Help with E-Mail

Building Basic E-Mail Skills

It seems like everyone is using electronic mail for his or her most basic communication. Parents keep in touch with their kids, and grandparents with their grandkids, by e-mail. Friends drop a note to each other. Businesses, especially the "need-it-yesterday-thank-you" types, are increasingly operating electronically and less and less by traditional paper. Although it is debated whether electronic mail actually saves paper or uses up more of it, people are finding e-mail to be fast, effective, and reliable for a vast array of needs.

WebTV arrives complete with electronic mail support. You can put most of your immediate family on your WebTV account, each with their own e-mail address, for no additional cost. With just a push of a button, you can send a message across a state, across a country, or to the other end of the world. Most letters arrive in only a minute or two via a network of dedicated Internet phone lines — no more expensive overseas airmail postage needed!

Some letters take a little longer to arrive for a variety of reasons. Because electronic mail travels across a network of phone lines, it may occasionally encounter a busy center and have to be rerouted. Some mailing computers "go to sleep" for the night. Others might be overwhelmed with mail volume. For these reasons, your e-mail may occasionally take as long as an hour or even a few days to arrive!

Electronic mail can open new worlds for you. You can write your congressman. You can keep in touch with your kid's teacher. You can write away for information — and get that information .almost immediately! You can contribute to and receive newsletters. You can join a specialty discussion group, such as those for seniors, new moms, medical-issue support, or gardening. Many people enjoy play-by-e-mail games of chess.

In short, electronic mail is a new avenue of human communication and the limitations to human communication have not yet been discovered.

In this chapter, I introduce the most basic electronic mail skills that will allow you to send, read, and reply to electronic mail effectively.

Reading Electronic Mail

The glowing red light on the front of your WebTV unit tells you when you've received new mail. Any time that red Message light goes on, you can expect a new letter or two. My niece, who is a certified e-mail addict, points out that we are likely to become trained to respond to that red light just as Pavlov's dogs were to the bell. I know I certainly am.

Sometimes you'll notice that the Message light has begun to glow after you've been away from your unit for some time. WebTV may occasionally check for mail even though you haven't turned the unit on yourself. This can happen in several ways. First, you can set it up to check for you at a certain time each day. (This is discussed more fully later in this chapter.) Second, WebTV may have called in to update its TV listings and/or to pick up some advertisements to show you during the connection process. While WebTV is making these outgoing phone calls, as a courtesy it also checks your e-mail.

WebTV provides you several ways to get to your electronic mailbox. From your home page, you can move the yellow box to **Mail** and press Go on your remote control or Return on your keyboard. There are also Mail buttons on most keyboards and remotes. You can press these buttons at any time for access to your mailbox.

New mail listings always look brighter and larger than mail that has already been read. To read a letter, move the yellow box to the e-mail you wish to read and press Go or Return.

After reading a letter, you can return to your mailbox. Move the yellow box to **Mail list** and press Go or Return. Alternatively, you can press Back on your keyboard or remote. If, instead, you want to read the next letter, highlight **Next** with the yellow box and press Go or Return.

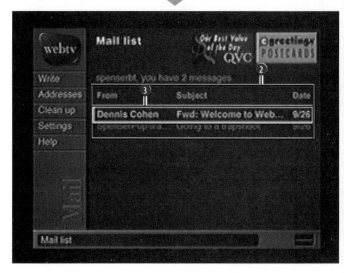

❶ From your home page, you can move the yellow box to **Mail** and press Go on your remote control or Return on your keyboard.

❷ Your Mail list appears as a list of messages. Each message is shown with the sender's address or name (to the left), a subject, and the date the letter was sent.

❸ New mail looks brighter and larger than old mail. Move the yellow box to a new letter. Press Go or Return to display it.

CROSS-REFERENCE

Need to reply to electronic mail? Find it later in this chapter.

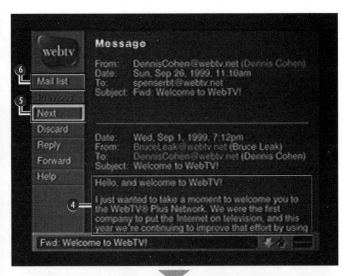

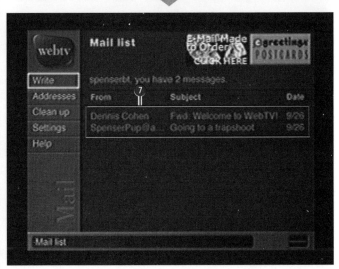

TAKE NOTE

SAVE AN ADDRESS

WebTV provides a handy address book to store important names and e-mail addresses. To add a name to your address book, move the yellow box to the blue-colored address in the **From:** line of the e-mail. Press Go on your remote and WebTV will lead you through the process of saving this address in your address book.

CHAIN LETTERS

Occasionally, some people may send you a chain letter or a petition through electronic mail. The rule of thumb for these sorts of letters is to *Ignore Them and Discard Them*. I know of no legitimate petitions that are distributed through electronic mail, and chain letters are as much a problem in the electronic world as they are in the real one.

WEBTV CLASSIC

Read electronic mail on WebTV Classic exactly as you would on WebTV Plus.

④ You may read the letter as WebTV displays it in the Message screen.

⑤ By default, WebTV highlights the **Next** option. Activate this option to move to the next letter in your Mail list.

⑥ Move the yellow box to **Mail list** and press Go or Return.

⑦ After you have read a letter, the mail listing appears dimmer and slightly thinner than new mail. (Compare with the second figure.)

FIND IT ONLINE

Receiving unwanted e-mail? Visit **http://help.webtv. net/abuse/avoidemail.html.**

Moving Through the Mail List

When reading e-mail, you have the option to move forward or backward through the list of messages as it appears in your Mail list. This is tremendously convenient when you wish to read through incoming mail one after another or back up to review a letter you just read.

Start from the main Mail list and activate the first e-mail by pressing Go on the remote or Return on the keyboard. WebTV automatically highlights the **Next** option with the yellow box — ready for you to activate to move you through your incoming mail.

At any time, if you wish to back up one letter, simply activate **Previous**. Of course, if you are at the first letter of the list, you will not be able to do so. Nor will you be able to go to the **Next** letter if you are at the end of your Mail list.

When you are done viewing individual letters you can activate **Mail list** or press Mail on your remote to return to your mailbox. You can also move on to other things, such as Search, Favorites, or Home. You do not need to return to the Mail list before going on to other tasks.

Remember that the Mail button always takes you directly to your Mail list. If the red light on the WebTV unit goes on while you are in the middle of a task, you can usually take a break and visit your mailbox. After you read your new letters, use the Back key to return to your task.

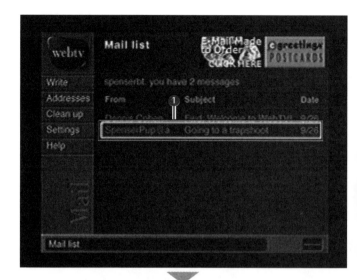

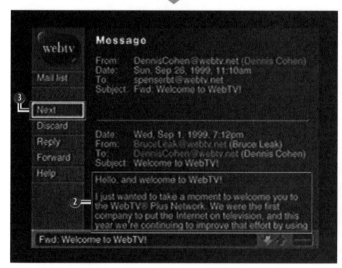

❶ Move the yellow box to any item in your Mail list and press Go on the remote or Return on the keyboard.

❷ WebTV displays the letter for you to read.

❸ The **Next** option is highlighted by default (as long as you're not on the last message). To view the next e-mail in your Mail list, press Go or Return.

CROSS-REFERENCE

Read about ways to store and delete mail in Chapter 11.

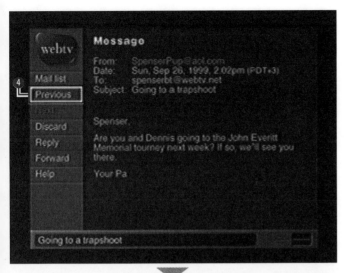

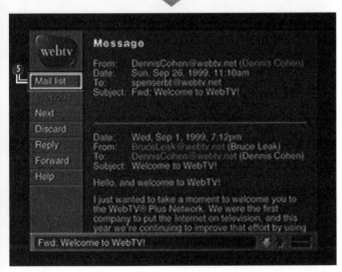

4 Move the yellow box to **Previous** and press Go to move back one letter in your mail list.

5 After reading all the letters, activate **Mail list** to return to your Mailbox.

▶ DIM OPTIONS

When the words **Previous** or **Next** turn from yellow to dark blue, it means that you have reached, respectively, the first or the last letter in your Mail list.

▶ ADDITIONAL OPTIONS

When looking at e-mail, WebTV presents a number of handling options in addition to the navigation options. You can choose to **Discard** a letter, **Forward** it to another party, or **Reply** to the person who sent it.

▶ HELP

Help is available from both the Mail list and from the display of individual letters. Move the yellow box to **Help** and activate it by pressing Go on your remote control or Return on your keyboard.

▶ USING WEBTV CLASSIC

Navigate through WebTV Classic mail as you would with WebTV Plus.

FIND IT ONLINE

Want to learn how kids can check their mail? Visit
http://help.webtv.net/kids/checkmail.html.

Writing Electronic Mail

In electronic mail, as in the usual physical mail, a correct address is necessary to ensure that the mail goes to its intended recipient. Just as letters delivered by the postal service require a street address, city, and zip code, electronic letters also have a formal structure to which you must adhere.

An electronic address looks like this: internet-name@domain. For example, addresses might look like somename@webtv.net, president@whitehouse.gov, or billg@microsoft.com. The at-sign (@) separates the Internet name assigned to a particular person from the information about that person's Internet provider. You were assigned an Internet name when you signed up for WebTV service. Typical Internet names are made up of people's first and/or last names and nicknames, sometimes with initials or numbers attached to them, but this is by no means a firm rule. Internet names can be as creative and strange as the people who choose them.

Once you know an electronic address, you are ready to send a letter. Start at your Mail list. From your home page, move the yellow box to **Mail** and press Go on your remote. Alternatively, press the Mail buttons on your keyboard or remote. Move the yellow box to **Write** and press Go. This tells WebTV that you want to create a new letter. Wait a few seconds for the Write a message screen to load.

Use your arrow keys to move the yellow box to the line that starts with **To:**. The blinking yellow cursor lets you know where to type text. Carefully type in the e-mail address of the person to send mail to. Use the arrow keys to move down to the **Subject:** line and type a one- or two-word summary of the message you are about to write. Keep the subject line short and to the point. You do not have to type any subject at all.

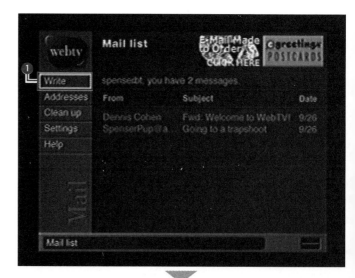

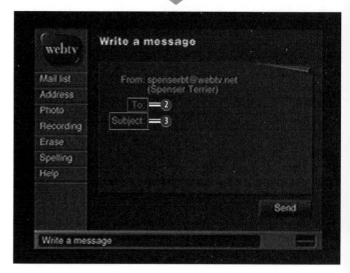

❶ From your Mail list, move the yellow box to **Write** and press Go on your remote control or Return on your keyboard.

▶ WebTV moves you to the Write a message screen, where you can compose a new e-mail message.

❷ Use the arrow keys to move the yellow cursor to the line that starts with **To:**. Carefully type the address of the mail recipient.

❸ Move the cursor to the **Subject:** line and type in the subject of your message.

CROSS-REFERENCE

Read up on finding an e-mail address in Chapter 10.

Next, use the arrow keys or tab to move down to the main message area just below the Subject line. Here you can type your letter. After you have written it to your satisfaction, use the arrow keys to move the yellow box to **Send** and press Go or Return.

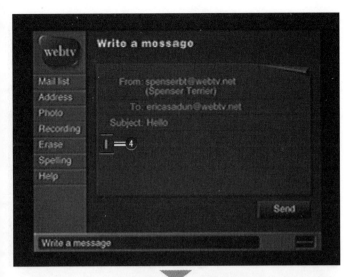

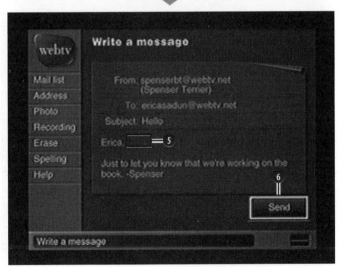

TAKE NOTE

▶ **BE BRIEF**

Brevity is the soul of electronic mail. Keep your e-mail short and to the point. This makes it easier for people to respond to your letter and helps focus your message.

▶ **USING WEBTV CLASSIC**

There are fewer options on the WebTV Classic Write a message screen. For example, you cannot use WebTV Classic to attach Photos or Recordings to your electronic mail.

④ *Move the cursor to the blank area under the subject line and type your message.*

⑤ *Use the **Return** key on either the onscreen or physical keyboard to add carriage returns and blank lines in your letter.*

⑥ *After completing your letter use the arrow keys or Tab to highlight **Send**. Press Go on your remote control or Return on your keyboard to send the letter.*

FIND IT ONLINE

Want more tips on writing e-mail? Visit **http://help.webtv.net/mail/compose/write.html**.

Sending Mail to Multiple Recipients

You can send a letter to several people as easily as to one. The only difference between sending an e-mail to multiple recipients and sending it to one recipient is that you must specify several addresses rather than one.

Begin as you would for sending a letter to one person by selecting **Write** on your main Mail list page. After you have typed the first address on the line that starts with **To:**, type a comma and a space followed by the second address. More addresses? Add a comma and space before each one.

Don't worry about running out of space on the **To:** line. WebTV automatically wraps your addresses. Thus, they may appear on multiple lines as in the pictures on the facing page. Because using the Return key does not move to the next line, as it does in the body of a letter, let WebTV worry about the formatting for you.

Once you've specified the addresses, continue with the letter as usual. Fill in the **Subject:** line if you wish, and move down to the main message area to type your letter. Finish by using the arrow keys to move to **Send** and press Go on your remote or Return on your keyboard.

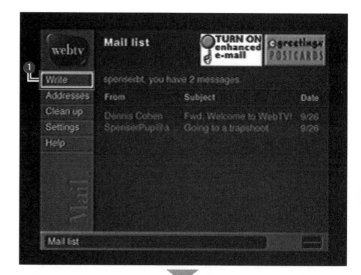

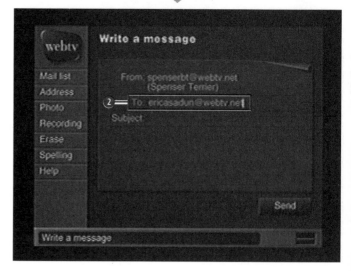

❶ From your Mail list, move the yellow box to **Write** and press Go.

▶ WebTV moves you to the Write a message screen. This screen enables you to compose new e-mail messages.

❷ Move the yellow cursor to the right of **To:** and type in the first address.

CROSS-REFERENCE

You can reply to multiple recipients at once. Learn about it in Chapter 10.

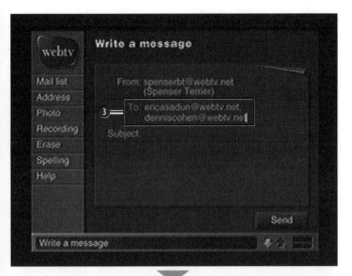

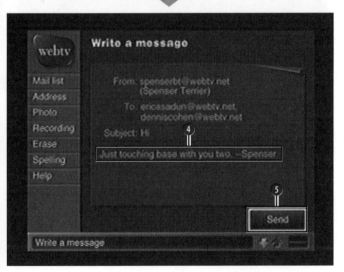

REMEMBER THE COMMA

The most common mistake in sending a letter to several people is forgetting the comma between addresses. Always include a comma and a space between successive e-mail addresses. And remember not to put a comma after the last address.

WEBTV TAKES CARE OF CARRIAGE RETURNS

When you seem to reach the end of a line, keep typing. WebTV automatically wraps your words to the next line. When you've finished writing a paragraph, press Return twice. This inserts a blank line in your letter between paragraphs. Don't confuse the Return key with the down-arrow ($\downarrow$) key. Otherwise, you will move the yellow box onto Send. If you do this by accident, press the up-arrow ($\uparrow$) to return to your letter.

USING WEBTV CLASSIC

WebTV Classic supports multiple recipient addresses in the same way as WebTV Plus.

③ Type additional addresses, separating each with a comma.

④ After adding all desired addresses, proceed with the letter as normal. That is, move the cursor to the space just below the **Subject:** line and type your letter.

⑤ To send the letter to all the listed addresses, move the yellow box to **Send** and press Go on your remote control.

Replying to Electronic Mail

When someone has sent you e-mail, it's a simple matter to reply to their message. You do not need to remember their address. You do not need to refer to an address book. When you choose to **Reply** to a letter, WebTV automatically understands that the e-mail goes back to the person who sent it to you.

The **Reply** option appears on the list to the left of the text of a letter. To find this option, first select a letter from the Mail list and press Go. The letter is displayed and the **Reply** option is now available. Select **Reply** and activate it.

WebTV places you in a Reply to a message screen and you are ready to type your reply. Do so in the same way that you would type a letter you were sending without using **Reply**. Finish the letter as you otherwise would, by activating **Send**.

Relax and step back

You need not reply to a letter the instant you get it. Feel free to wait a few hours, days, or even weeks, if you like. Many people new to electronic mail feel pressured to reply to letters as soon as they are received. Replies lead to more replies, and the e-mail novice quickly feels overwhelmed by the pressure of replying to everyone. Step back. Remember that electronic mail is a social tool, not a social pressure.

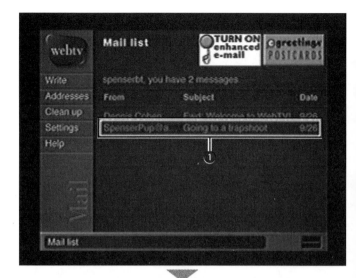

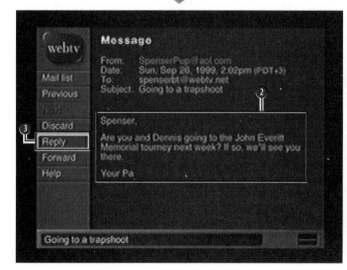

❶ From the Mail list, select the letter you wish to reply to and press Go on your remote control.

❷ WebTV displays the letter for you to read. To the left of the letter is a list of options, including **Reply**. You use this option to reply to the letter.

❸ Move the yellow box to **Reply** and press Go.

CROSS-REFERENCE

You can include a copy of the original letter in your reply. Learn how in Chapter 10.

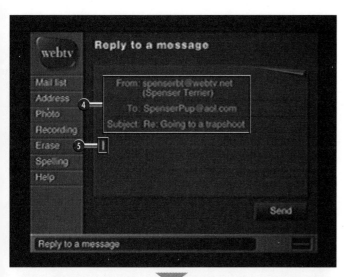

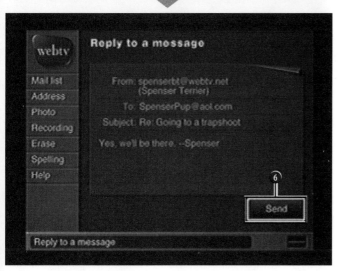

4 WebTV creates a reply-letter for you. Notice that the To: and Subject: lines have been filled out automatically.

5 Write the letter as you normally would when sending e-mail.

6 Move the yellow box to **Send** and press Go.

TAKE NOTE

TIME OUT

If you take a long time to write a letter, your WebTV unit may "time out:" The unit hangs up and prompts you to reconnect to the WebTV service. This happens because the process of typing e-mail does not activate any "page changes," which is what WebTV monitors to reflect user activity. If time outs keep happening to you, consider performing the following little "fix." Every few minutes simply press Home followed by Back. This will take you to your home page and back to your letter. It lets WebTV know that you are still around and active.

DON'T REPLY TO SPAM

Spam refers to unsolicited e-mail, generally advertisements. As a rule of thumb, never reply to spam, even when they say things such as, "If this letter was sent to you in error, just send a reply to the following address." This is a sucker's ploy. When you reply, you confirm your address as valid. Confirmed addresses mean money to spammers — they can sell your e-mail address to others and you will receive even more unwanted e-mail.

USING WEBTV CLASSIC

Reply to electronic mail on WebTV Classic exactly as you would on WebTV Plus.

FIND IT ONLINE

Want to write mail using other language systems? Check out **http://help.webtv.net/mail/compose/language.html.**

135

Forwarding Electronic Mail

Sometimes you receive e-mail that you think will be of interest to another party. Why not send it to them? You can easily forward a copy of any e-mail. This creates a duplicate of the letter you received and sends it off to an electronic mail address (or to several addresses) that you specify.

Like replying, the option to forward is only available at the actual display of a letter and not in the Mail list. To forward a letter, you must first choose it in the Mail list and open it. Once you have done so, the options, such as **Forward** and **Reply**, appear to the left of the e-mail.

After activating **Forward**, it might seem that the original message disappeared. This is not so. Look at the very bottom of the Forward a message screen. Notice the downward-pointing bright green arrow? Press Scroll Down to see the rest of the letter. Press Scroll Up to return to the top.

When forwarding a message, WebTV enables you to add a subject and a short note before the actual forwarded letter. This is a good way to provide context. Let the person to whom you are forwarding the letter know why you are sending it.

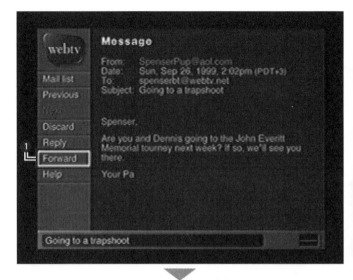

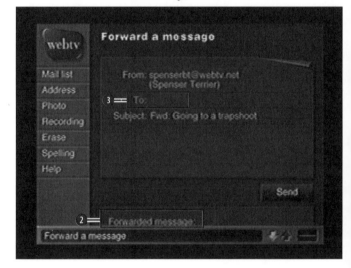

❶ After opening and reading a message, move the yellow box to **Forward** and press Go on your remote control.

❷ In the Forward a message screen, WebTV creates a new letter for you with the forwarded information at the bottom.

❸ Fill in the **To:** line to address this message.

CROSS-REFERENCE

You can forward mail to several people, too. Learn about mailing multiple recipients earlier in this chapter.

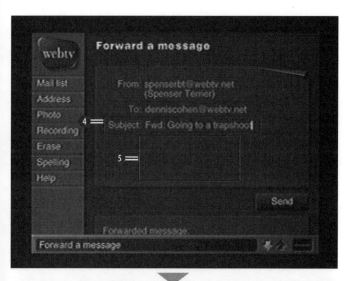

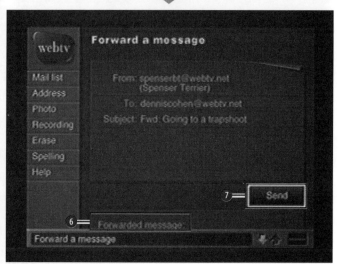

SEND A JOKE

Have you heard a good one? Why not pass it on to a friend. A lot of forwarded electronic mail on the Internet is shared humor. New jokes are created and transmitted around the world in a matter of days or even hours. If you find something particularly humorous, share it with a friend.

JUST SAY NO

Is someone sending you a lot of jokes that you'd rather not see? Send them a letter and tell them so. The Internet culture of "pass-along-a-joke" is based on courtesy and kindness — they may think they are brightening your day. Unless you let people know that you do not want to participate, you're going to get a lot of jokes in your mailbox!

DON'T FORWARD CHAIN LETTERS

When it comes to chain letters, do not forward them to 10, 20, or 50 of your friends. You will not receive 10 years' bad luck.

USING WEBTV CLASSIC

Forward electronic mail on WebTV Classic exactly as you would on WebTV Plus.

④ Move down to the Subject line below the **To:** line and either accept the default subject or edit it more to your liking. WebTV automatically inserts Fwd: and the subject of line of the forwarded message.

⑤ If you wish, you can add a few lines of explanation below the **Subject:** line.

⑥ The forwarded message appears at the bottom of the screen. You can scroll down to see it using either the arrow on the screen or Scroll on the remote.

⑦ Move the yellow box to **Send** and press Go to forward the letter.

FIND IT ONLINE

Want more information about forwarding e-mail? Visit
http://help.webtv.net/mail/sending/forward.html.

Adding a Picture to Electronic Mail

A dding a picture to your electronic mail is one of WebTV Plus's most charming features. Simply by hooking up a video camera to your WebTV unit and following a few steps, pictures of yourself and your family can be sent to other people around the Internet.

The joy of sending pictures doesn't stop there. You can send pictures of your pets, your home, your garden, and your hobby. Are you selling something secondhand? You can send a picture of that old couch or flower vase as well. Antiquing enthusiasts regularly send each other pictures of their prized possessions. Bicyclists send pictures from their latest road trips. The possibilities are endless.

What you need

So what do you need to take advantage of this? First, you need WebTV Plus. The Classic units of WebTV do not support photo capture from video.

Second, to take a picture you need a video camera. To hook up your video camera directly, it must have an audio-visual output cable. This cable usually has two or three jacks: a video-out and one or two audio-outs. Hook these jacks to your WebTV Plus unit's video-in and audio-in. Remember to match the colors: yellow goes to yellow, red to red, white to white.

An alternative to connecting your video camera is to connect your VCR. Some video cameras record directly to a cassette and do not have cables. If so, you can play the cassette in your VCR and freeze a picture from the playback. You will need a cable to connect the video- and audio-out jacks of your VCR to the video- and audio-in jacks of the WebTV Plus unit. Once again, colors

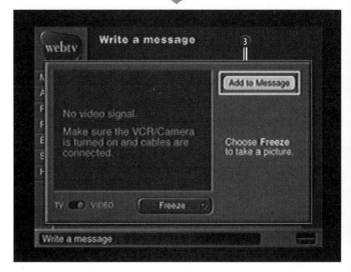

❶ Address and write a message as you usually would.

❷ Move the yellow box to **Photo** and press Go on your remote control.

▶ Attach the video camera cable to the video-in port on the back of your unit. Refer to the instructions that came with your WebTV unit.

❸ If you receive this message, check the connection between your video camera and the WebTV unit.

CROSS-REFERENCE

Want to forward a picture you've received? See the previous topic.

match: yellow to yellow, red to red, white to white. If you use coaxial cable instead of the jacks, be sure to choose **TV** input rather than **VIDEO**, as the signal will be coming in through the television feed.

Another alternative is to use one of the many inexpensive video cameras available on the market that are intended for children. These video cameras typically cost about 50 dollars. They only take black and white pictures, but most run on batteries, have the correct cables to hook to WebTV, and are small and convenient to use.

Digital cameras with video-out work, too. Plug the video cable into the camera and connect the jacks to the WebTV Plus unit. The camera will only produce still images, but this is a big advantage when using the WebTV Freeze feature. You never miss that "perfect shot," like you do when freezing live video.

Continued

④ Take a live picture with your video camera or play back from the camera's tape. The video signal displays on WebTV.

⑤ Make certain that the VIDEO button is lit, not the TV button.

⑥ When you see a picture you like, activate **Freeze**. Its green light will go on.

▶ If you do not like this picture, press **Freeze** again to choose another picture.

FIND IT ONLINE

Want to know which video sources can be used? Visit
http://help.webtv.net/multimail/videotype.html.

Adding a Picture to Electronic Mail

Continued

No matter how you hook up your video signal to the WebTV Plus unit, you will not be able to hear sound. It can be a little disconcerting when you are monitoring the video input and are not hearing any sound associated with it. This is, however, usual.

If you see the No video signal message, even when your camera or VCR is turned on, make sure the cables are connected correctly. If they are, try changing the video input button from VIDEO to TV and back.

You can capture pictures from the same video-in signal that provides WebTV Plus's picture-in-picture capability. This allows you to capture still images from a videotape, if you have a VCR hooked up.

Some tips

Consider turning on a few lights before taking your pictures. Although modern video cameras are very good at adapting to low-light conditions, your pictures will turn out better if there is plenty of ambient light.

Also, consider using a tripod. This steadies the picture. It further enables you to go across the room, join in on the picture (holding your WebTV Plus remote, of course), and snap the picture by pressing Go.

If at any time you change your mind about adding a picture and want to make the freeze-frame display go away, simply press Back on your remote or keyboard.

❼ Move the yellow box to **Add to Message** and press Go.

❽ If you are happy with the image, activate **Send** now.

❾ If you are not happy with the image, scroll down below the picture. Highlight the down arrow (↓) and press Go.

CROSS-REFERENCE

Want to add sound too? See the next topic.

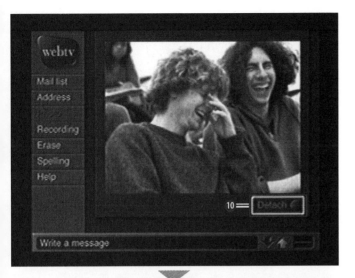

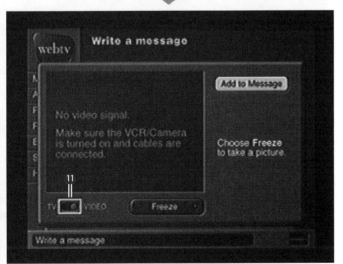

10 To remove the picture, move the yellow box to **Detach** at the very bottom of the letter. Activate **Detach** by pressing Go on your remote control or Return on your keyboard.

11 If you have an antenna or cable hooked into your WebTV unit, you can attach a picture from television by following the same procedure. The TV-VIDEO selector chooses whether to accept the signal from your video camera or from your television.

TAKE NOTE

▶ WHAT YOU SEE IS WHAT YOU SEND

If the picture you freeze is fuzzy or out of focus, it will be sent to others fuzzy and out of focus. You can improve your picture's quality by asking people to stay still as you take it. This avoids blurring caused by motion.

▶ KEEP IN TOUCH WHILE FAR AWAY

As nice as it is to keep in touch with your friends and family with e-mail, it's nicer still to attach a picture so that they can see how everyone is doing. My parents and my mother-in-law love to see new pictures of the baby. It's a great way to feel close when far away.

▶ DON'T SEND PICTURES WITHOUT PERMISSION

Pictures are big — they take up a lot of Internet bandwidth and computer memory. Don't send pictures to people unless they have told you it's okay in advance. Some people have small mailboxes, and some cannot receive electronic mail attachments at all. As a rule, be courteous and ask before you send.

FIND IT ONLINE

Read more about adding video to mail. Visit **http://help.webtv.net/multimail/addimage.html.**

Attaching a Sound Clip

A picture may be worth a thousand words, but a sound clip of a baby's words, a pet's bark, or a group singing "Happy Birthday" is surely of high value too. The sound of a human voice adds immeasurable warmth to an electronic letter. WebTV Plus enables you to record a greeting and attach it to your e-mail.

Attach a microphone

To record a message, you need to attach a microphone to the Mic jack on the back of your WebTV unit. Do not confuse this jack with the red and white RCA Audio jacks. The Mic jack uses a standard "mini"-plug instead. When you are ready to send a letter with an attached recording, use the microphone to capture your words.

If you do not have a microphone available, you can cheat and use a pair of earphones instead. Earphones and microphones work on the same principle: they convert electric signals to vibrations and back. Earphones do not make the best microphones, but you can use one in a pinch. I've sent several WebTV recordings using only a Sony Walkman earphone set that I had lying around the house. If you try this trick, remember to speak loudly and hold the "ears" close to your mouth. Use the **Play** feature to confirm that your recording was successful.

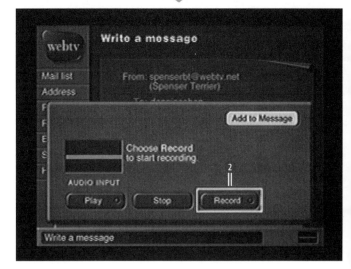

▶ *Write a message as you usually would.*

❶ *Move the yellow box to **Recording** and activate it by pressing Go on your remote or Return on your keyboard.*

❷ *Move the yellow box to **Record** and activate it to start recording.*

CROSS-REFERENCE

Want to add video to your e-mail, too? See the previous topic.

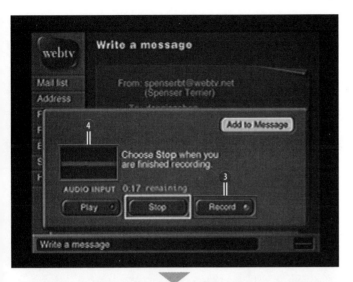

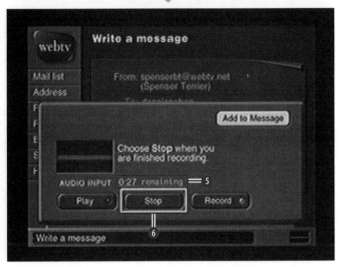

Make sure they can hear it

Before you send an audio greeting, you may want to make sure that the person who is receiving your mail both can receive attachments and has audio capabilities on their system. I remember one person who just couldn't make audio playback work on his computer. It turns out he had never bought speakers! Fortunately, if you are sending to anyone who owns a WebTV unit, this is not a problem. His or her TV acts as the speaker system.

Continued

TAKE NOTE

▶ **SEND A BIRTHDAY GREETING**

Birthdays are great times to send a recording to someone special. Sing them the "Happy Birthday" song and wish them a great year.

▶ **SONY WEBTV UNITS**

Sony WebTV units do not have Mic jacks. To hook in a microphone, you must use a minijack-to-RCA adapter and connect to the red or white "audio-in" jacks on the back of the unit.

---

❸ The red light next to **Record** illuminates when you are recording.

❹ As you speak or sing, this area shows a waveform of your voice.

❺ WebTV allows you 30 seconds of recording time and tells you how much time remains.

❻ When you have finished your recording, activate **Stop**. (If you run out of time, WebTV automatically stops for you.)

FIND IT ONLINE

Read more about supported microphones. Visit **http://help.webtv.net/multimail/microphone.html**.

Attaching a Sound Clip
Continued

Listen to music

You can bring sounds to your electronic mail from a variety of sources. You don't have to limit yourself to speaking into a microphone. If you have a CD-player, radio, or cassette player that you wish to record from, use a mini-to-mini cable to connect the sound output from your device directly into the Mic jack on your WebTV unit.

Fair use copyright law limits you to 30 seconds maximum use of a copyrighted piece of music — which is exactly the amount of time allotted by WebTV for recording. However, do not use recorded copyrighted music for any commercial purpose without prior permission from the copyright holders.

Troubleshooting

The most typical problem with creating a recording is the lack of sound input. If this happens to you, first check your connections. The microphone should be plugged firmly into the Mic minijack on the back of your WebTV unit.

You may also be dealing with a broken microphone. Try another microphone. If you don't have one around, try the earphone trick described on the previous page.

If you still cannot record a sound, check whether you are using a microphone with an on-off switch. If so, make sure the switch is set to "on" or "record."

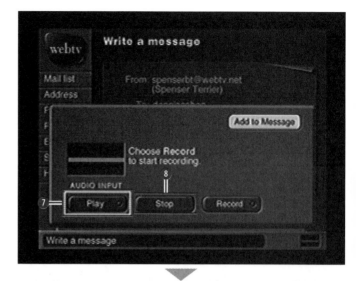

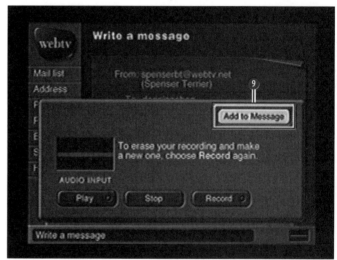

7 Activate **Play** to listen to your recording. The green light indicates playback is in progress.

8 To stop playing back, activate **Stop**.

▶ If you are unhappy with the message, you can activate **Record** and compose a new message.

9 If you are happy with the message, move the yellow box to **Add to Message** and press Go.

CROSS-REFERENCE

Want to forward a good sound bite? Discover how to forward e-mail earlier in this chapter.

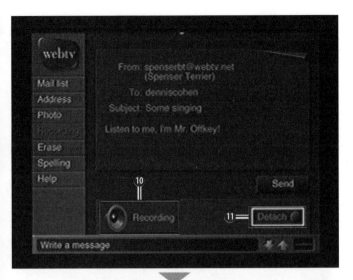

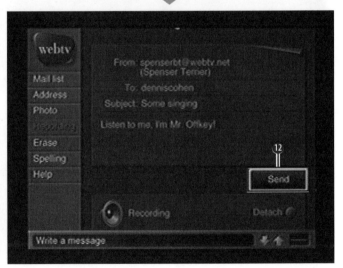

⑩ *You can move the yellow box to **Recording** and activate it to hear the message again.*

⑪ *If you are dissatisfied with the message, you may activate **Detach** to remove the recording from your letter before sending it.*

⑫ *To send the e-mail message with the recording, activate **Send**.*

Getting Help with E-Mail

Do you have questions about e-mail viruses, spam, using audio and video attachments, or managing your mailbox? If so, WebTV's Mail Help function will usually have an answer all ready for you.

WebTV's Mail Help gives you three broad categories: Getting Started, Detailed Instructions, and Frequently Asked Questions (also known as FAQ).

Getting Started tells you how to get set up to use e-mail and Detailed Instructions gives you a step-by-step walkthrough of sending and receiving e-mail. In short, these sections give an abbreviated version of this chapter's early sections.

Unless WebTV modifies their service, adding new capabilities, you probably won't find anything in the first two categories that isn't in this book. The meat of Help is the FAQ. This section answers which microphones work with which WebTV units, how to manage your E-Mail storage space on WebTV, how to access mail you've received on a non-WebTV e-mail account, and many other questions.

If you can't find the answer for which you're searching, there will be links to send your question to WebTV Customer Support on every page of the FAQ.

You should make it a practice to periodically check the FAQ as you will frequently find answers to questions you might not have known you had. There are frequently many ways to do the same thing and the FAQ will often give you alternative methods which will prove more convenient than the way you're currently doing things.

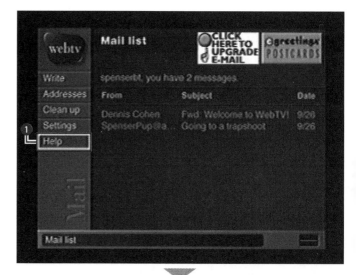

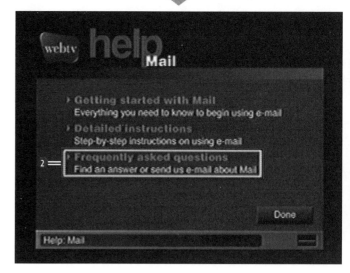

1 Choose **Help** while viewing one of the WebTV Mail screens.

2 Select one of the Help categories with the yellow box and press Go.

CROSS-REFERENCE

Learn about your e-mail address book in the next chapter.

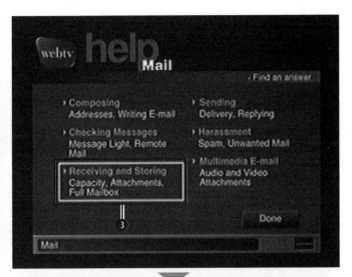

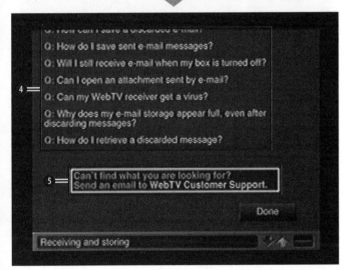

TAKE NOTE

▶ **BEYOND HELP**

Sometimes, you'll receive an e-mail with one or more attachments (like the pictures or recordings you sent earlier in this chapter). Once in a while, these attachments will be something that WebTV is unable to process for you. There are a lot of people out there who compress their attachments to make them smaller and transmit more quickly or send something that takes a specific program on a Windows or Macintosh computer to read, forgetting that not everyone runs the same programs on the same kinds of computers.

▶ **WEBTV CLASSIC**

WebTV Classic supports Mail Help the same as WebTV Plus.

❸ Assuming you chose **Frequently Asked Questions**, select a general topic area with the yellow box and press Go.

❹ Scroll through the list of questions to find one whose answer you wish to learn.

❺ If you can't find the question you want answered, choose that option to send an e-mail to WebTV Customer Support.

FIND IT ONLINE

Learn about IMAP (Internet Message Access Protocol) at **http://www.imap.org.**

Personal Workbook

Q&A

1 What does an e-mail address look like?

_____

_____

_____

2 Why does the red message light on your WebTV unit illuminate?

_____

_____

_____

3 How should you address an e-mail when you are sending it to more than one person?

_____

_____

_____

4 What is *spam?*

_____

_____

_____

5 What should you do about spam?

_____

_____

_____

6 What does it mean when the **Previous** option is displayed in very dim blue rather than yellow?

_____

_____

_____

7 What does it mean when both the **Previous** and **Next** options are displayed in very dim blue rather than yellow?

_____

_____

_____

8 When should you not send a sound recording attached to an e-mail?

_____

_____

_____

ANSWERS: PAGE 337

Building Basic E-Mail Skills

1 Forward e-mail to yourself.

2 Try sending e-mail to several friends at once.

3 Reply to e-mail.

4 Practice sending a picture or a recording with e-mail.

✔ You are in love. On February 13, at 9 p.m., you still cannot find the perfect gift, but you want to send a special Valentine to that special someone. So you record yourself singing "I Love You Truly" and attach it to a letter.

✔ You have a brother-in-law who's a doctor. You attach a picture of your sprained ankle to an e-mail and ask him for a diagnosis. He replies with a recorded attachment directing you to apply ice, wrap your ankle tightly, and send $50 as payment for his services.

Visual Quiz

How could you read the letter from SpenserPup?

_____

_____

_____

_____

_____

_____

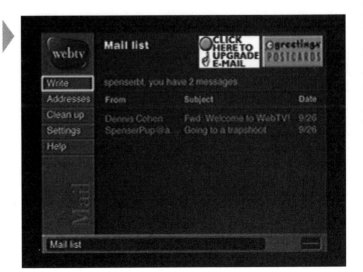

CHAPTER 9

MASTER THESE SKILLS

- ▶ **Adding to the Address Book**
- ▶ **Adding to the Address Book from E-Mail**
- ▶ **Addressing a Letter with the Address Book**
- ▶ **Updating Address Book Entries**
- ▶ **Removing Names from Your Address Book**
- ▶ **Finding E-Mail Addresses**

Creating and Maintaining Your Address Book

Just as physical address books help us keep track of people, their phone numbers, and their addresses, WebTV's address book keeps track of e-mail addresses. Memory is fleeting, and permanent storage of important information is invaluable. E-mail addresses are particularly hard to remember. With an e-mail address book you need never forget a person's electronic mail address. Whenever you are preparing to type a letter, the address is only a few keystrokes away.

You can build an address book slowly. As you learn new e-mail addresses, you can add one or two at a time. Don't feel pressured to fill out the address book all at once. WebTV takes care of alphabetizing the names. You can type them in whatever order is most comfortable for you.

One of WebTV's marvelous features is the capability to add an address to your book directly from an e-mail someone has sent to you. You can store the address and later, if you like, dispose of the original letter. When people move or drop out of sight, it is easy to update or remove those addresses.

With your WebTV address book, you can make sure you never misplace or lose an important e-mail address.

This chapter teaches you to create and maintain the WebTV address book. You learn to add and remove names and to update information. You learn to send a letter using the address book and to find addresses for people over the Internet. When you finish this chapter, you will have a good understanding of how the address book works and how using it can help you create electronic mail.

Adding to the Address Book

When someone gives you his or her electronic mail address, you can easily add it to your WebTV address book. You can use this address book to keep track of e-mail addresses without having to remember them or rely on easily misplaced written lists or notes. The addresses are kept on WebTV and are always there to use whenever you power on your WebTV unit.

Adding a new address is simple. Activate **Addresses** from your Mail list and then **Add**. Type in the person's name and e-mail address and activate the **Add** button at the bottom of the screen. That's all. With these few steps, the address will be available to you whenever you are ready to write an electronic letter.

WebTV stores addresses in alphabetical order according to the first letter of the name. This helps you find the proper address quickly when you are ready to add an e-mail address to a letter. If you store a lot of addresses, you may want to use "Last Name, First Name" listings, which enables WebTV to sort by the first letter of the last name.

When a person has two e-mail addresses, you can choose to list both addresses under one entry or to list the addresses separately. Each choice has its tradeoffs.

To list both addresses for a single name, type them into the Address space on the Add an e-mail address screen. Separate them with a comma followed by a space. This enables you to send e-mail to both e-mail addresses using a single entry in your address book. However, this also means that your recipient will receive two copies of any electronic mail that you send, which may prove undesirable and/or cumbersome. Your correspondent may ask you to refrain from this practice.

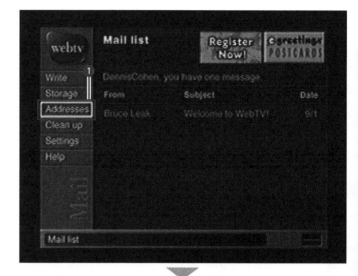

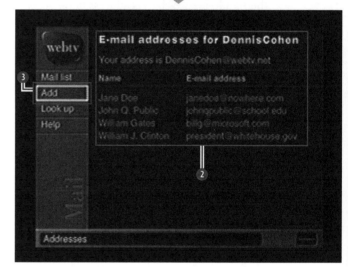

❶ In the Mail list, move the yellow box to **Addresses** and press Go on the remote or Return on the keyboard.

❷ WebTV moves you to the E-mail addresses screen. This screen lets you add or modify address book entries.

❸ Activate **Add**.

CROSS-REFERENCE

Need to find an e-mail address? Find out how later in this chapter.

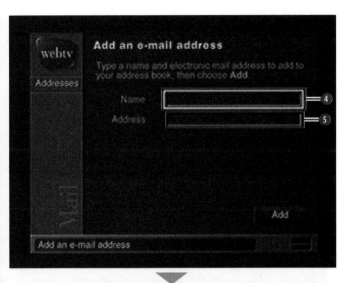

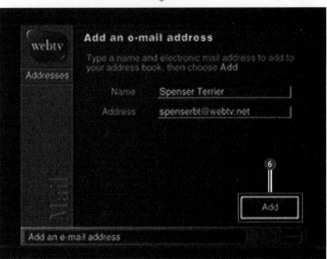

Listing each address separately provides an alternative. You may want to list addresses for both "Bernard (at the office)" and "Bernard (at home)." Unlike the dual-address scheme above, this lets you select the address to use and to send only a single copy of your letter. On the other hand, people with multiple electronic mail accounts may not check each account every day. For example, when people go on trips, they often neglect their home e-mail accounts in favor of their business accounts. For important messages, you may still wish to send a copy to each account. You can do this easily, however, by checking off both addresses when directing an e-mail.

TAKE NOTE

▶ USE DISCRETION

If it is unlikely that you will ever write to someone, it may not be worth cluttering your address book with his or her address.

▶ LIMITS

WebTV permits a maximum of 150 names with addresses in an address book.

▶ USING WEBTV CLASSIC

WebTV Plus and WebTV Classic address books work in the same fashion.

④ Type a **Name** for the new address book entry and press the down arrow (↓) to move to the **Address**.

⑤ Type the e-mail **Address**.

⑥ Move the yellow box to **Add** and press Go on the remote. WebTV will add this entry to your address book.

▶ Repeat steps 2 through 5 to add more addresses.

FIND IT ONLINE

Experiencing e-mail delays? Visit **http://help.webtv. net/mail/sending/longtime.html**.

Adding to the Address Book from E-Mail

WebTV provides a tremendously easy shortcut for adding an entry to your address book. Once someone has sent you an electronic letter, you can grab his or her address and add it to your address book. Just activate the blue-colored address in the **From:** line of your letter and WebTV walks you through the steps.

So, how does WebTV know how to do this? Electronic mail programs attach information to each e-mail message. This information, as a whole, is called a "header." As you might expect, WebTV can find information about the sender's address, the date the letter was sent, and the subject. WebTV lists these three pieces of information when you display an e-mail. When you save the address, WebTV recovers the e-mail address and, if provided by the sender, the real name, and stores the information in your address book.

More data is provided in e-mail headers than the sender, date, and subject. WebTV hides this extraneous information to provide a clearer and more succinct presentation of the e-mail content.

Headers also contain information about how the e-mail was sent to you. This includes the path your letter took, which computers were involved in routing it, and so forth. It also might include specifications about how pictures and text were encoded, which protocols were used and so forth. Fortunately, you can live quite happily without ever seeing this information.

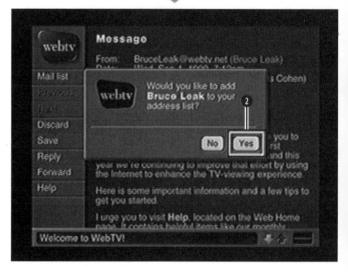

❶ Move the yellow box to the blue address in the **From:** line and press Go on the remote or Return on the keyboard.

❷ Confirm that you would like to add the address to your address list by pressing Go. (The **Yes** option is highlighted by default.)

CROSS-REFERENCE

Want to add an address by hand? Read the previous topic.

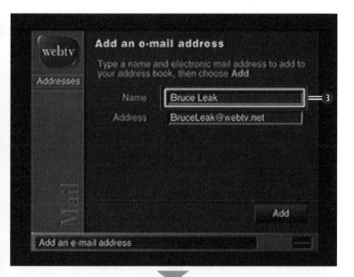

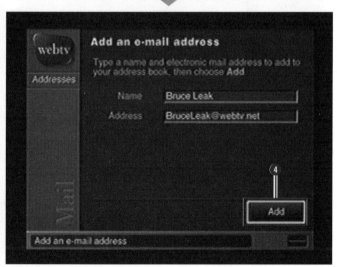

WebTV, however, does save this information for you for a very important reason. If at any time you receive threatening or unwanted e-mail, you may wish to forward a copy of that e-mail to the sender's system administrator or other proper authority. When you forward e-mail, WebTV resends the full header information. This allows the authorities on the other end to investigate how the mail was sent to you and provide you with better protection.

TAKE NOTE

▶ PICK SENSIBLE NAMES

Pick easily understood names for your address book. If you have only one friend named Jane, you might store her address simply as "Jane." For a business acquaintance, the full name is often easier, "Jane Doe." Perhaps you know several Janes on a casual basis. "Jane D." may suit you best.

▶ THE RIGHT NAME

Sometimes you'll find that, unlike the example on the facing page, both the name and address are filled in correctly right away. This is because many computers that send electronic mail attach a person's name to the incoming mail as well as the address. If you are happy with both the Name and the Address that WebTV has read from the letter, simply activate **Add**.

▶ USING WEBTV CLASSIC

WebTV Plus and WebTV Classic address books work in the same fashion.

③ *In the Add an e-mail address screen, edit the **Name** field to a more appropriate name, if necessary. For example, change this entry to "Jane Doe."*

④ *Move the yellow box to **Add** and press Go.*

FIND IT ONLINE

Read more about saving addresses. Visit **http://help.
webtv.net/mail/compose/saveaddress.html**.

Addressing a Letter with the Address Book

WebTV provides two ways to access the address book when sending a letter. First, and most obviously, is to highlight and activate **Addresses** on the left side of the Mail list display or activate **Address** on the Write a message display. Less obvious, but far more convenient is the shortcut provided by To:. Move the yellow box to the blue-colored word and activate it for a simple shortcut to the address book.

You can scroll up and down through your address book using the keys on your remote. When you have found the name you want, use the yellow box to highlight it and select it with Return or Go. A red check mark next to the name indicates it has been selected as a recipient. If you select a name in error, activate it once again with Return or Go, and the check mark will be removed.

You can send an e-mail to several people as easily as to one. Select additional names in the address book and each is added to the list on the **To:** line. WebTV automatically inserts commas and spaces between the names. As with single recipients, if you add a name in error, WebTV lets you remove it and updates the addresses to reflect your change.

When you use the address book in this way, you can start your letter with just a few keystrokes. You spend more time writing the letter than filling out the mail form.

There is another big advantage in using the address book to address your letters. You bypass typographical errors in your addresses completely. Assuming that you entered correct address information in your address book, you completely avoid the problem of misspelling an address or hitting a comma rather than a period. These sorts of mistakes are common when typing from memory, and virtually impossible when using your address book.

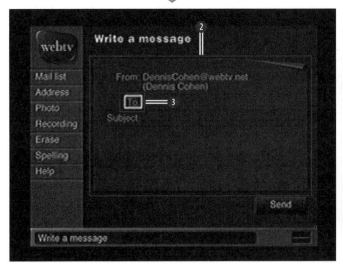

❶ Move the yellow box to **Write** and press Go on the remote or Return on the keyboard.

❷ WebTV creates a new letter for you to edit.

❸ Highlight **To:** and press Go.

CROSS-REFERENCE

Read more about writing a letter in the previous chapter.

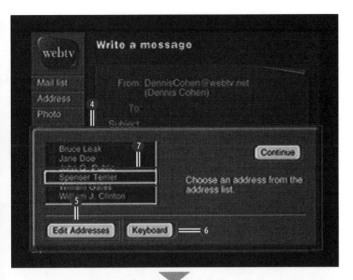

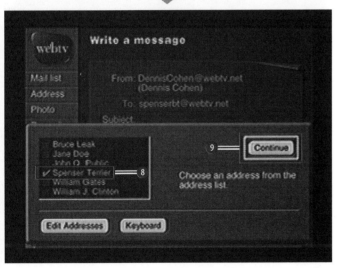

▶ GROUPS

You may often send mail to an unchanging group of people. If so, you can create an address book entry for that group. Rather than mark every name each time, you can select a single address book entry, such as "The Gang," and send to the whole group at once. To create a group list start by adding a new entry to your address book. Name it "The Gang," or "Whole Family," or something similar. Move to the address line to type the addresses. Separate each address with a comma followed by a space. For example: "joesmith@bob.net, fredjones@nowhere.com, janedoe@nowhere.com."

▶ USING WEBTV CLASSIC

You can use WebTV Classic address books to automatically address messages in the same way as WebTV Plus.

④ *The address book pops up from the bottom of your screen.*

⑤ *Use the **Edit Addresses** button if you need to change or update your address book.*

⑥ *Activate **Keyboard** to bring up the onscreen keyboard.*

⑦ *Move the yellow box to each intended mail recipient's name and press Go.*

⑧ *A check mark appears next to the name of each recipient in the address book and their address is added to the To: line of the message.*

▶ *To remove an address from the message, highlight that person's name in the address book and press Go.*

⑨ *Activate **Continue** and proceed with your e-mail.*

Updating Address Book Entries

People move, graduate, change jobs, and marry. For these reasons, and for others, their names and electronic mail addresses may change. When someone sends you notice that his or her address is about to or has just changed, it's a simple matter to update entries in the address book.

To update an address book entry, follow these steps. First, make the address book active. From the Mail list, move to **Addresses** and press Go or Return. This brings you to the E-mail addresses page for your WebTV account.

Use the arrow keys to move to the name and address you wish to update. Once again press Go or Return to move to the Change an e-mail address screen.

This screen lets you directly edit either the name or the address. Use the arrow keys to select either one and press Go or Return to enter the edit mode. Once the yellow cursor appears, the arrow keys move you within the line of text. Recall that Delete erases the character to the left of the yellow blinking cursor. The up ($\uparrow$) or down arrow ($\downarrow$) keys enable you to move between the two fields and down to **Done**.

When you have edited the address to your satisfaction, use the arrow keys to move the yellow box to **Done** and activate it with either Go or Return. If you wish to remove the entry from your address book completely, highlight **Discard** from the list of options at the left of the screen and press Go.

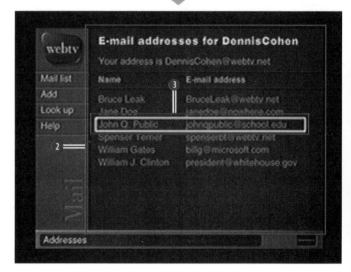

❶ From your Mail list, move the yellow box to **Addresses** and press Go on the remote or Return on the keyboard.

❷ WebTV moves you to the E-mail addresses screen. You can add to or edit your address book from this screen.

❸ Highlight the name you wish to update. Press Go.

CROSS-REFERENCE

Want to erase an e-mail in progress? Read about it in the next chapter.

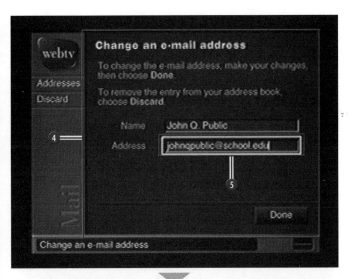

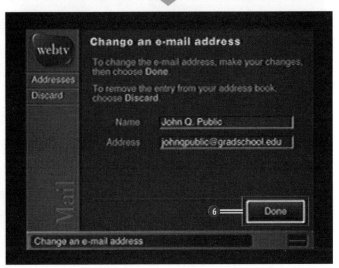

NAME CHANGES

When people's names change — for example, when Laura Ingalls becomes Mrs. Laura Wilder — the order of your address book may change to reflect the new alphabetical order.

OLD AND NEW

Sometimes it is valuable to store both the old and the new addresses. You may have been given a month's advance warning, or more, when a person's e-mail is about to change because of, for example, a change in jobs. However, the new job may not be assured. In such a case, you will want to store both addresses in your address book. WebTV, however, does not allow you to store two addresses under identical names. Instead, you can store the names as "Jane Doe (old)" and "Jane Doe (new)," or come up with a similar strategy to differentiate the addresses.

USING WEBTV CLASSIC

WebTV Plus and WebTV Classic address books work in the same fashion.

④ WebTV displays the Change an e-mail address screen. This screen enables you to update or correct an address book entry.

⑤ Edit the **Name** and **Address** field to update the information.

⑥ Move the yellow box to **Done** and press Go. WebTV updates your address book to reflect the changes you made.

Removing Names from Your Address Book

From time to time, address books require trimming. People drop out of sight. Your address book becomes overly large. Friends and colleagues change their e-mail providers without sending you any notification. For whatever reason, you may wish to remove an address or two from your WebTV address book.

Ideally, your address book mimics the one you keep at home — those names and addresses of people you hold dear and whose information you want to keep at your fingertips. WebTV address books should not necessarily contain the name of every friend or relative who's on the Internet. Instead, your WebTV address book should list those people you want to write to without having to think about e-mail addresses.

You may wish to review and weed your address book once or twice a year. You can store up to 150 names and addresses in your address book. Although excess names and addresses are not a drain on your WebTV resources they do tend to encumber the process of sending e-mail. Scrolling through an unnecessarily long list of names requires time and effort.

On the other hand, avoid thinning your address book to the point where it becomes unusable. Remember that the **Reply** function, which one uses for the most frequent correspondents, bypasses the address book entirely. The address book is a valuable resource for keeping track of those people who are not in daily correspondence but whose importance demands a record of their e-mail address.

Removing a name from the address book cannot be "undone" without reentering a new listing. As a precaution, if you have a printer and the optional printer port, you may want to print a hardcopy of your address book before discarding any addresses.

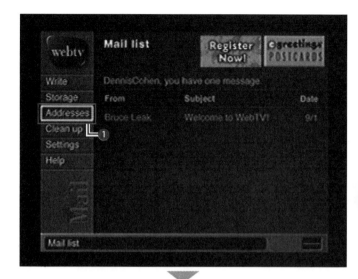

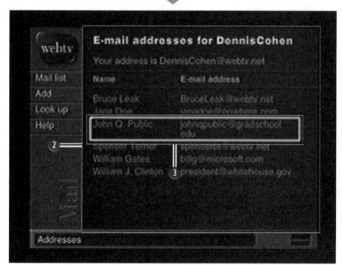

❶ Select **Addresses** from the Mail list and press Go.

❷ WebTV moves you to the E-mail addresses screen. This screen enables you to enter or update address book entries.

❸ Use the arrow keys to highlight the name you wish to remove and press Go.

CROSS-REFERENCE

See "Printing a Letter" in Chapter 8 for tips on using a printer with your WebTV unit.

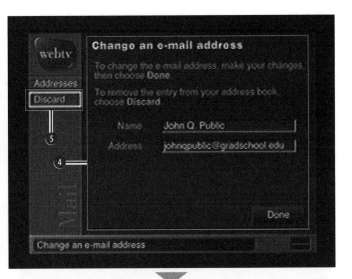

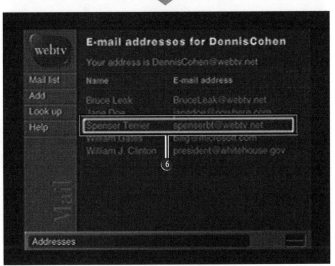

TAKE NOTE

TAKE NOTE

▶ LOSING AN ADDRESS

If you discard an address and later find you really needed it, you may want to use one of the many e-mail search engines available on the World Wide Web. These search engines help you match a person's name to any known e-mail addresses.

▶ KEEP A BACKUP LIST

You may want to keep a printed version of your current address list to guard against any unforeseen problems. These lists are also handy to take along when you travel and are away from your WebTV unit.

▶ REINSTATING AN ADDRESS

If you have a current e-mail, you can always replace an address book entry after it has been deleted. Simply follow the directions in the previous section on adding addresses from e-mail.

▶ WEBTV CLASSIC

WebTV Plus and WebTV Classic address books work in the same fashion.

④ *WebTV moves you to the Change an e-mail address screen. Although you can use this screen to update an address book entry, this example makes use of the options on the blue menu bar found to the left.*

⑤ *Highlight and activate* **Discard.**

⑥ *WebTV returns you to the Address book. The name you selected was discarded, and the next name on the list is automatically highlighted.*

FIND IT ONLINE

Visit **http://people.yahoo.com** for a good e-mail search engine.

Finding E-Mail Addresses

Search engines are the Internet's equivalent of directory assistance. If you want to find a person's e-mail address, you can use a search engine. WebTV provides a direct link from your E-mail addresses page to the WhoWhere search engine.

Of course, only those people connected to the Internet have e-mail addresses, and of those people, a search engine may not locate many. It may be difficult to find a person who is new to the Internet, or who only occasionally uses the Internet. The more a person uses the Internet, however, the more likely it is that the person can be found with a search engine.

When searching for e-mail addresses, don't overspecify. Many people are listed only by their first initial and last name. You will do better searching for "J Public" than for "John Public." The former produces more matches and may overcome errors when, for example, you are not sure if the correct name is Jon, John, or Jonathan. Similarly, search for just a last name when you are unsure about whether a person is listed by a proper or nickname. William Doe might be listed as "W. Doe," "Will Doe," or "Bill Doe," for example.

Before sending e-mail, try to confirm the identity. Some names are so unusual a single match suffices. Other names are much more common. For example, WhoWhere found many matches for "Albert Gore." In this example, the White House service provider indicates a clear match. When the information is ambiguous, however, you can activate **More Details About ... ?**. WhoWhere will show you more details about the person listed and boost your confidence before you send e-mail.

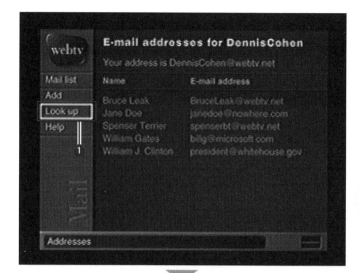

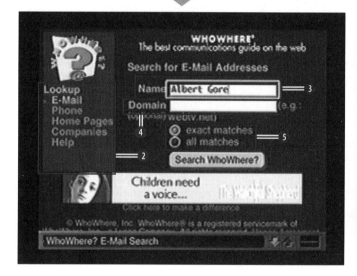

❶ From the E-mail addresses display, move the yellow box to **Look up** and press Go on the remote.

❷ There are several options under Lookup: E-Mail, Phone, Home Pages, Companies, and Help.

❸ In the WhoWhere display, move to the **Name** line and enter the person's name.

❹ If you know the person's domain, enter that as well.

❺ Choose **exact matches**, if you are sure of the name, or **all matches**, if you are not.

CROSS-REFERENCE

Section II discusses searching for information on the World Wide Web.

Creating and Maintaining Your Address Book

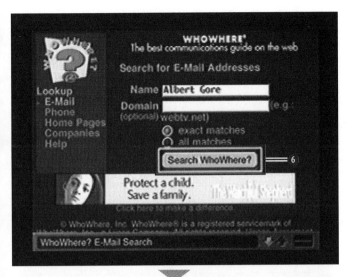

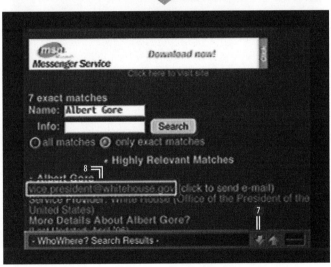

TAKE NOTE

STAYING ANONYMOUS

As with phone numbers, some people have unlisted e-mail addresses. With phone directories, you pay a fee to keep a number out of the white pages. With the Internet, however, search engines constantly scan the net to find new names and addresses to add to their listings. To stay anonymous, a person must avoid certain activities that announce his or her presence to the Internet community.

To keep your address private, follow these rules. First, distribute your address only to those people you trust to keep it private. Second, do not post articles to Usenet newsgroups. Third, do not enter contests or fill out forms that ask for your e-mail address. Finally, if you know a search engine has your address, you can write to the maintainers of that site and ask that your name be removed. In all practicality, though, it is easiest not to worry about whether or not your e-mail address can be found by other people. There may be an old friend out there whom you would love to find you.

USING WEBTV CLASSIC

Search for e-mail addresses on WebTV Classic the same way you do on WebTV Plus.

---

⑥ *Activate **Search WhoWhere?***

⑦ *WebTV displays the search results for you. Scroll down to see what matches WhoWhere made to the name.*

⑧ *To send a letter to any person in the results list, move the yellow box to their blue colored address and press Go.*

FIND IT ONLINE

Looking for a name? Visit **http://help.webtv.net/ search/addresses.html**.

Personal Workbook

Q&A

1 How many addresses can you store in an address book?

_____

_____

_____

2 How can you store an old and a new address for a friend?

_____

_____

_____

3 How can you send an e-mail to more than one person using the address book?

_____

_____

_____

4 How can you change your mind about sending mail to someone when using the address book?

_____

_____

_____

5 Why should you print your address list before removing a name?

_____

_____

_____

6 When should you update names and addresses?

_____

_____

_____

7 When should you remove names?

_____

_____

_____

8 What might be the problem when you are unable to find someone's e-mail address?

_____

_____

_____

ANSWERS: PAGE 337

Creating and Maintaining Your Address Book

1 Add some names to your address book.

2 Remove a name from the address book.

3 Change a name or an address in the address book.

4 Send a letter using the address book.

5 Add a name to the address book from an e-mail you've received.

6 Search for a friend on the Internet.

✔ You attend a family reunion and decide to start an e-mail family newsletter. You ask family members for their e-mail addresses and add them to your address book.

✔ You are too busy (or forgetful) to write out holiday greetings and send them by regular mail. You add an entry to your WebTV address book titled Christmas mail, and you type in the e-mail addresses of everyone you normally send a card to. You write a single letter and use your address book to send it to your entire Christmas mail list at once.

Visual Quiz

How can you add Bruce Leak's name and address to your address book?

CHAPTER **10**

MASTER
THESE
SKILLS

▶ **Using an E-Mail Signature**

▶ **Choosing a Mail List Order**

▶ **Enabling Carbon Copy (cc:)**

▶ **Sending E-Mail Using Carbon Copy**

▶ **Replying to All E-Mail Recipients**

▶ **Enabling E-Mail Inclusion**

▶ **Including the Original Letter**

▶ **Stopping and Continuing E-Mail**

▶ **Erasing an E-Mail in Progress**

▶ **Correcting Misaddressed E-Mail**

Building Intermediate E-Mail Skills

WebTV provides a number of flourishes that make electronic mail easier to read, more convenient to send, and so forth. This chapter discusses techniques that you can use to make the process of sending and receiving electronic mail more efficient. These techniques include customizing the way you send and reply to mail, starting and stopping the letter-writing process, and fixing mail when it has been addressed incorrectly.

There are several ways to customize sending and replying to e-mail. You can attach a custom signature to the bottom of each e-mail message. You can activate the carbon copy feature to send electronic mail to additional recipients. You can also enable e-mail inclusion that enables you to attach a copy of the letter that was sent to you.

In this chapter, you also learn about the process of writing an e-mail. WebTV enables you to take a break in the middle of writing a letter and to return later to finish it. You can change your mind about a letter and erase it entirely. Also, if you sent a letter to an invalid address, WebTV lets you go back, fix your mistakes, and try again.

By the time you finish this chapter, you will have mastered skills that enable you to fully control the process of sending and replying to electronic mail.

Using an E-Mail Signature

In the old days of the Internet — by which you can read "the early eighties" — the last line or so of mail often failed to arrive with the rest of the message. Thus the tradition of e-mail signatures began. A signature was a bit of extra text attached to the bottom of a letter to let the mail be clipped without losing any of the words within the main text of the letter. Over time, signatures took on a culture of their own. Long after e-mail became reliable, and message text was unlikely to be clipped, signatures became the norm in electronic communications.

What is in a signature? Typically a signature contains a person's name and contact information: e-mail address, office phone, fax number, and so forth. This is the sort of information often included on a business card. Sometimes a signature contains a short but amusing quote as well. Signatures "stamp" the bottom of your letters with this information each time you send an e-mail, saving you the bother of typing it in each time.

Internet etiquette (also called "netiquette") suggests that signatures be short, limited to no more than four lines. The four-line rule also dates back to the 1980s. Four lines of message text was about 300 characters long (assuming 80 characters per line). As the last 'block," or 256 characters, were at risk, a 300-character/4-line signature file would easily prevent information loss. More than four lines were not needed, because they would burden the Internet with unnecessary information transfer, called "excess bandwidth."

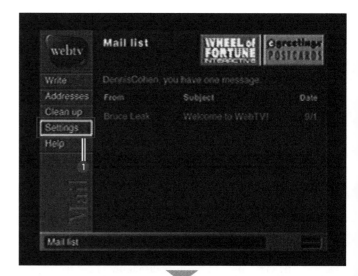

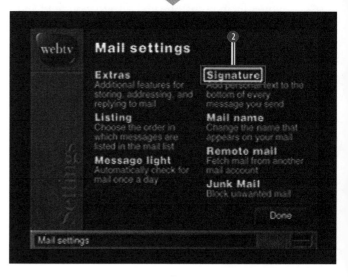

❶ Starting in your Mail list, move the yellow box down the list of options to **Settings** and press Go on the remote or Return on the keyboard.

❷ On the Mail settings page, highlight **Signature** among the list of options and press Go.

CROSS-REFERENCE

Later in this chapter, read about setting other options, such as carbon copy.

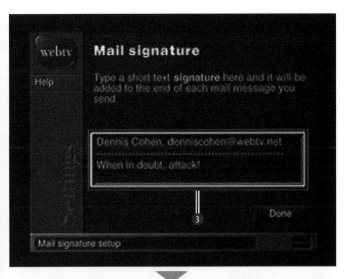

Shortly after signatures were introduced, people started using them to add contact information and amusing quotes to the ends of their letters. If the signatures got clipped, then fine; if not, they provided helpful information and entertainment. Because of this usefulness, signatures remain in use long after the need for extra padding on the mail disappeared.

TAKE NOTE

▶ ASCII (TEXT-BASED) CLIP ART

Signatures are not the place for text-based clip-art, no matter how cute the picture. Keep your signatures short and to the point.

▶ HYPERLINKS

Many people use their signatures to reference their World Wide Web home page. Type the home page's URL into a signature so that everyone who receives your mail will know where to find your home page.

▶ QUOTING

There are marvelous quotes that make good signature fodder. Be sure, if possible, to provide proper attribution when quoting.

▶ USING WEBTV CLASSIC

WebTV Plus and WebTV classic signatures work in the same fashion.

③ *WebTV displays the Mail signature page with a large textbox in the middle for your signature. Type the text for the signature in the box.*

④ *Move the yellow box to **Done** and press Go.*

FIND IT ONLINE

Read more about it. Visit **http://wecare.webtv.net/ mail/sending/signature.html**.

Choosing a Mail List Order

WebTV lets you order your Mail list in two ways. You can have the newest messages appear at the top of the list or at the bottom. There is no "better" choice between these two options. This is strictly a matter of taste.

If at any time you find you dislike the ordering scheme you chose, it is only a matter of a few steps to switch to the other scheme.

Changing the order of the Mail list does not affect the mail itself. You will neither gain nor lose messages by changing the message ordering.

This feature showcases WebTV's commitment to user-centered design. Rather than force you into one listing style or another, WebTV has thoughtfully provided the option that enables you to select between the two. Some people might believe that it matters little whether your mail is listed in oldest-first or newest-first order. Others are adamant about one style or the other. Small touches such as this put you in command of WebTV's presentation and enable you to control your environment.

A detail, such as a mail list order, can make or break a user interface. Some people really are firmly committed to a particular mail order. Whether previous computer experiences or simple prejudice about how mail should be ordered influences them, their opinions and desires count. Their enjoyment of, and ultimately their use of, the WebTV mail system can be greatly influenced by their ability to choose the way the mail is listed. Kudos are due WebTV for including such a minor, but ultimately influential, preference.

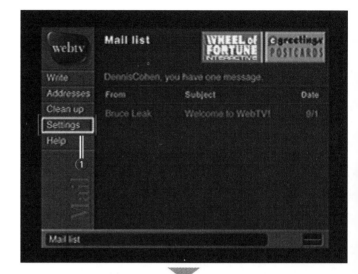

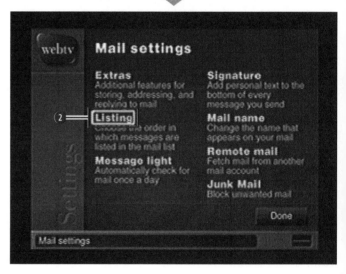

❶ Starting in your Mail list, move the yellow box to **Settings** and press Go on the remote.

❷ In the Mail settings screen, highlight **Listing** from among the options and press Go.

CROSS-REFERENCE

Later in this chapter, find out about replying to electronic mail.

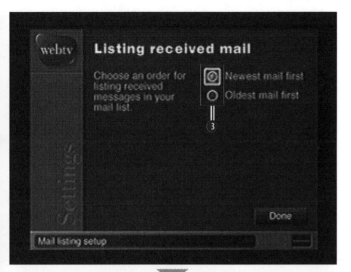

③ In the Listing received mail screen, choose either **Newest mail first** or **Oldest mail first**. Highlight the corresponding radio button and press Go to activate it.

④ Move the yellow box to **Done** and press Go on the remote.

TAKE NOTE

▶ NEWEST FIRST

If you tend to keep a lot of old mail in your mail list, you may prefer newest-first ordering. This way you do not have to scroll down to see any new mail. New mail consistently appears at the top and can be seen immediately upon entering your mail list.

▶ OLDEST FIRST

If you are moving to WebTV from another personal computing system, you may feel more comfortable with oldest-first ordering. This is the ordering used by most commercial electronic mail packages. New letters appear at the bottom of your mail list. If you retain old mail in your mail list, you may need to scroll down to see any new e-mail. Remember, however, that the red message light always lets you know when new mail has arrived. You need not visually scan your mail list to determine this.

▶ USING WEBTV CLASSIC

WebTV Plus and WebTV Classic Mail list ordering work alike.

FIND IT ONLINE

Read about extra mail features. Visit **http://wecare. webtv.net/mail/receive/extras.html**.

Enabling Carbon Copy (cc:)

Using carbon copies is the polite way of including a third party on a letter without addressing the letter directly to that party. This dates back to more traditional methods of correspondence. One could send a letter to one party and, as a courtesy, or simply for the record, send a copy of it to another. The memo would read "To:" one party and "cc:" another or several others. Back in the days when I was a Kelly Girl, people often referred to these as "courtesy copies" as well as "carbon copies," meaning the same thing.

Electronic mail has, in a lovely touch of quaintness, preserved this scheme. You can send e-mail to your main addressee using the **To:** line and send copies with the **cc:** line. People will say "when you drop a line to Mitch, please cc me on it."

By default, WebTV hides the **cc:** line, assuming this feature is not necessary for day-to-day e-mail use. It takes only a few steps, however, to enable it to let you send "carbon copies" with your e-mail.

Enabling carbon copy also adds another feature to your Mail list options: a **Reply All** button, which lets you reply both to the person who sent the e-mail to you, and to all addressees in both the **To:** and **cc:** lines of the e-mail. This makes it easier to carry on a group correspondence. When the Reply all feature is used, all addressees will receive e-mail copies.

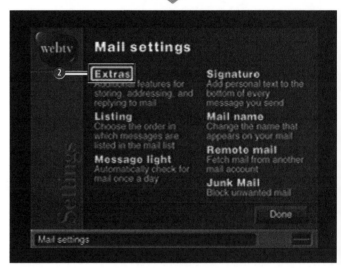

❶ Starting in your Mail list, move the yellow box to **Settings** and press Go.

❷ In the Mail settings screen, highlight **Extras** and press Go.

CROSS-REFERENCE

Learn how to write a letter with carbon copy in the next topic.

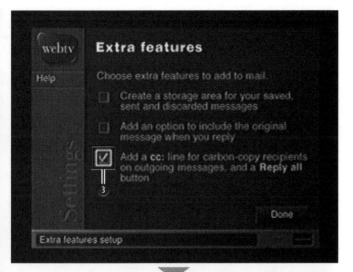

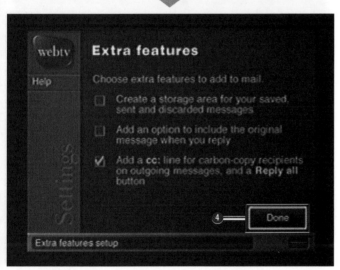

CC: CANNOT WORK ALONE

You cannot send e-mail using only a cc: address. E-mail requires a primary addressee before it can be sent.

DISABLE AT WILL

The same steps that you follow to enable carbon copies let you disable them whenever you want. Simply follow the steps below to turn off the check mark next to the carbon copy option.

USING WEBTV CLASSIC

Enable carbon copies on WebTV Classic just as you do on WebTV Plus.

③ *In the Extra features screen, use the arrow keys to move to the box to the left of "Add a cc: line for carbon copy recipients…" Press Go to place a check mark in the box. This will also add a* **Reply all** *button to your* **Mail list** *options.*

④ *Move the yellow box to* **Done** *and press Go.*

Sending E-Mail Using Carbon Copy

When WebTV's carbon copy feature has been activated, an extra line labeled **Cc:** appears below the **To:** line in the Write a message screen. To use this feature, simply use the arrow keys to move to the **Cc:** line and type the addresses of those to whom you wish to send carbon copies of your message.

You can use the address book to add to the carbon copy line in exactly the same way that you do for the normal address line. Move the yellow box to the blue-colored **Cc:** and press Go on your remote or Return on your keyboard. Proceed as described in Chapter 9.

Other than allowing another path for specifying recipient addresses, carbon-copy e-mail works exactly the same as e-mail with the cc: feature turned off.

When carbon copies are enabled, however, do not think that you must always use this feature. Using the **Cc:** line is always optional. You can turn this feature on and never use it.

There are two reasons why the feature is not normally enabled. First, most people never use carbon copies in casual use of their electronic mail. Second, and more importantly, a carbon copy line takes up screen space. WebTV considers screen space to be valuable. Many features that are not regularly used have been carefully hidden away. Other obscure features that WebTV does not expect its users to ever need, such as "blind carbon copies" and "x-headers," have been taken out entirely. This simplifies and streamlines the WebTV electronic mail interface.

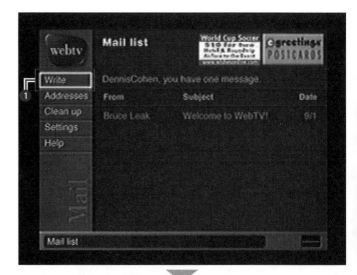

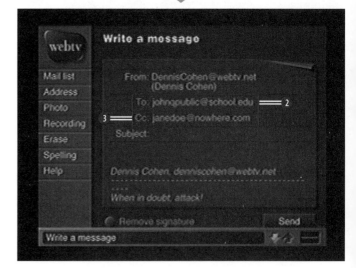

❶ Starting in your Mail list, move the yellow box to **Write** and press Go on the remote or Return on the keyboard.

❷ In the Write a message screen, move to the **To:** line and type the address of the primary recipient.

❸ Move to the **Cc:** line and type the address(es) of the secondary recipient(s).

CROSS-REFERENCE

Need to set up carbon copy? Read the previous topic.

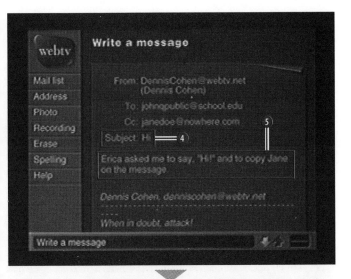

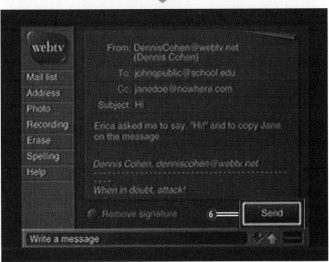

④ *(Optional) Move the yellow cursor to the **Subject:** line and add a subject.*

⑤ *Move to the main text area, just below the **Subject:** line and write your letter.*

⑥ *Move the yellow box to **Send** and press Go. WebTV sends your letter to each addressee listed in either the **To:** or **Cc:** lines.*

TAKE NOTE

▶ EXTRA SPACE

Some people use carbon copy lines as extra space for addresses when sending letters. While this is certainly not an inappropriate way to use the carbon copy feature, it may be misleading. People whose addresses appear in the carbon copy list may assume that the letter is not meant directly for them. Placing an address in the **To:** line makes recipients feel more as if the letter was truly intended for them.

▶ SEND YOURSELF A COPY

Some people use carbon copies to send themselves a copy of their letter. This happens for several reasons. First, unlike WebTV, their e-mail service might not automatically make copies of mail that has been sent. Second, a person may want to send the copy to another account he or she uses. This behavior is used particularly when the e-mail has attachments. Sometimes WebTV users capture a memorable image when attaching a video picture to their mail. They may send themselves a carbon copy of the message at another account so that they can store the picture for later use.

▶ USING WEBTV CLASSIC

WebTV Plus and WebTV Classic carbon copies work alike.

FIND IT ONLINE

Want to keep WebTV from timing out during mail? Visit http://help.webtv.net/mail/compose/disconnect.html.

Replying to All E-Mail Recipients

To reply to a letter's sender as well as to the other recipients of the letter, the Reply all feature must be enabled. The details of how to do this are described in the Enabling Carbon Copy lesson earlier in this chapter.

When a letter has been sent to multiple recipients, **Reply all** is added to the list of options to the left of the letter's display, directly under **Reply**. This option is not displayed when a letter has been sent solely to you. Nor is it displayed when the Reply all feature is inactive.

Reply all enables you to send an electronic message to several people at once without typing names in by hand, and without needing to use your address book. It is a convenient way to carry on a conversation with a group. Everyone within the group gets to read all the replies made to each member of the group.

This sort of conversation typically goes on when people are working together on a project, planning a family vacation together, discussing politics as a group, and so forth. You can easily imagine situations where one might want to converse with a group rather than with a single individual.

The person who originates the letter must, of course, address it to all the parties with whom he or she wishes to communicate. Once one has received the letter, it is a simple matter to reply to all parties.

Do not confuse this sort of communication with "mailing lists," which are discussed in Chapter 13. Mailing lists use a special mail server to coordinate communications between a large group of people. When you receive a message from a mailing list, you need only reply to that list to have a copy sent automatically to all members of the list. For day-to-day communications, using the Reply all feature is much more convenient.

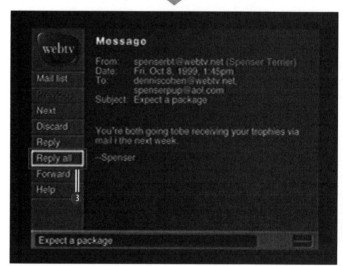

▶ Open a message from your Mail list.

❶ The Message screen indicates that the letter has been sent to multiple recipients.

❷ **Reply all** appears among the Mail list options in the left column.

❸ Move the yellow box to **Reply all** and press Go.

CROSS-REFERENCE

Need to enable **Reply all**? Read about it in the Enabling Carbon Copy topic earlier in this chapter.

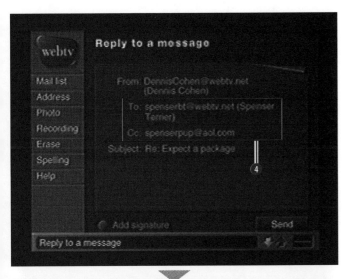

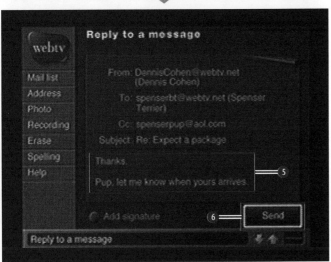

TAKE NOTE

▶ COPIES TO YOURSELF

On many systems (not including WebTV), when you reply to all, a copy of your letter is sent to you. WebTV does not because copies of your e-mail are automatically kept for seven days. These copies are kept even when you have turned off the Create a storage area option in the Extras section of Mail settings.

▶ WHEN NOT TO REPLY TO ALL

Avoid replying to all when your message is personal in nature and not of interest to the other parties listed in the To: or Cc: lines. Remember this, especially, when replying to point out an error or take a person to task. Many "flame wars," that is, heated group debates, can be avoided by sending messages directly to one person and avoiding involving the rest of the group.

▶ USING WEBTV CLASSIC

Reply all works the same on WebTV Classic and WebTV Plus.

④ *WebTV creates a new letter for your reply. WebTV automatically sets the addresses in the* **To:** *and the* **Cc:** *lines. Everyone will receive a copy.*

⑤ *Move to the main text area and write your letter.*

⑥ *To finish and send your letter, move the yellow box to* **Send** *and press Go on the remote or Return on the keyboard.*

FIND IT ONLINE

Learn how to spell check your e-mail messages. Visit
http://help.webtv.net/mail/compose/checkspell.html.

Enabling E-Mail Inclusion

Context is vital in e-mail, especially because electronic mail tends to be terse. Seeing a single electronic letter is similar to hearing one phrase of a conversation. Often, little information is added in each letter — it is the back and forth, give and take, that builds meaning. To add to the confusion, people tend to carry on several e-mail correspondences at once.

Imagine receiving this letter: "Sounds good to me. Go for it." What sounds good? Go for what? If you had written to the sender just a few minutes ago, you would probably know what he or she is talking about. The chain of conversation would still be fresh in your mind. Consider, however, the effect if you had written him or her a few weeks or even months ago.

There is a simple and obvious way to include context in electronic mail. Include a copy of the letter to which you are replying. "Sounds good to me. Go for it," makes a lot more sense when it's attached to a letter that says, "I'd like to hold the party on the 15th of July."

WebTV enables you to attach original letters to replies. Before you can do so, you must activate an option in the Extras area of the Mail settings. This option reads "Add an option to include the original message when you reply" and must be turned on manually. Follow the steps on the facing page.

Unlike other mail systems, WebTV does not let you edit the included mail. It simply attaches it to the bottom of your letter. If the letter you are replying to is long or cumbersome, you might want to consider "gisting" it, instead of, or in addition to, including it in its entirety.

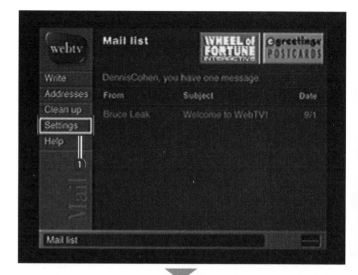

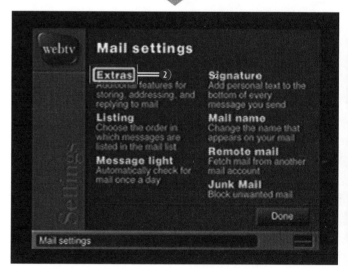

❶ Starting in your Mail list, move the yellow box to **Settings** and press Go.

❷ In the Mail settings screen, highlight **Extras** at the top of the list of options and press Go.

CROSS-REFERENCE

Want to include an original letter in new e-mail? Read the next topic.

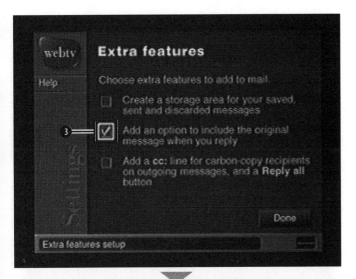

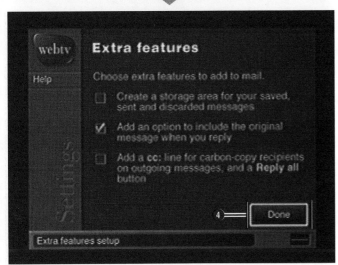

3 Use the arrow keys to highlight the box to the left of "Add an option to include the original message when you reply." Press Go to place a check mark in the box.

4 Move the yellow box to **Done** and press Go.

To "gist," put main ideas in short summaries and mix them into your text. For example, consider the letter about the July picnic. You might type "[You asked about holding the picnic on July 15th]" at the top of the letter before writing your reply. Typing text in brackets or parentheses is common shorthand. You can place these context bites throughout your letter and make your e-mail more understandable.

TAKE NOTE

▶ KEEP IT ON

Even if you only occasionally include an original letter in your mail, consider keeping the **Attach original message** feature active all the time. It's always easier to have an option available when you need it, than to go through the steps to turn it on. The option sits just to the left of the word **Send** on your screen and takes up relatively little space.

▶ USING WEBTV CLASSIC

E-mail inclusion works the same on WebTV Classic and WebTV Plus.

FIND IT ONLINE

Read more about it. Visit **http://help.webtv.net/mail/ sending/originalmail.html.**

Including the Original Letter

To include a copy of the letter to which you are replying you must enable "Add an option to include the original message when you reply," found in WebTV's Mail list Settings, under Extras. You can find instructions for setting this option in the previous topic.

Once this WebTV feature is enabled, you will find a new element on your Reply to a message screen. Next to **Send** will be the words **Attach original message**. Like **Send,** these words appear in yellow, surrounded by a lightly colored three-dimensional box. When **Attach original message** is activated, the included message appears below the **Send** button.

Notice the **Attach original message** option disappears after use. This highlights one example of WebTV's excellent design strategy. After attaching the original letter, it no longer makes sense to include the option — the original has already been attached. Therefore WebTV hides it, letting it reappear if you later **Detach** the message. Because the WebTV screen is fairly small, use your scroll keys, Scroll Up and Scroll Down, to see the included letter. The entire letter is attached and WebTV does not provide any way to edit the included message.

You can remove a letter that has been attached. Below the **Send** button is the blue word **Detach**. Move the yellow box to this word and press Go or Return. WebTV removes the original letter from your reply. The **Attach original message** option reappears. If you change your mind, you can always reattach the letter.

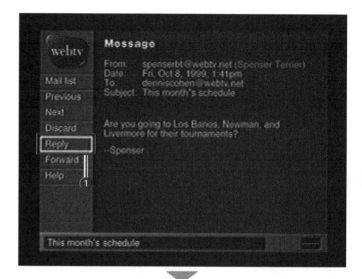

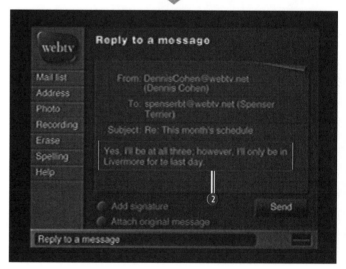

❶ When reading an e-mail message, move the yellow box to **Reply** and press Go on the remote or Return on the keyboard.

❷ Type the reply in the space below the **Subject:** line.

CROSS-REFERENCE

Need to turn on e-mail inclusion? Read the previous topic.

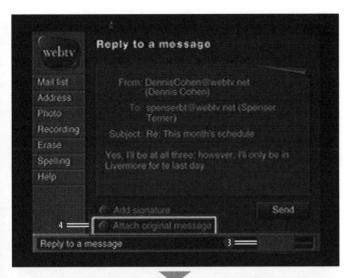

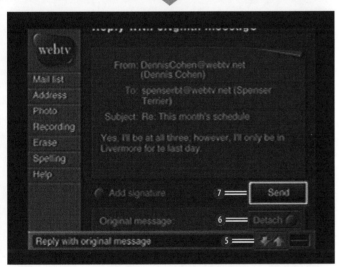

TAKE NOTE

INCLUDED PICTURES AND SOUNDS

You may receive electronic mail that includes pictures or sounds. When you reply and attach the original letter, those pictures and sounds are still included. This can be problematic. Pictures and sound resources take up a lot of memory and are slow to transfer. One picture can strain some people's electronic mailboxes. Several pictures might break them. Always ask in advance whether your recipient can accept pictures and sound.

SEND A "FILM STRIP"

The above note provides important caveats. That being said, there is a marvelously cute trick that you can use to send a series of pictures to people. What you do is this: Send a picture to yourself. Reply to yourself, include the original mail and add another picture to the reply. Do this two or three times and you will make a "film strip" of three or four images. Then, you can forward the letter and pass on the entire collection of pictures in one electronic message. Just remember those caveats!

USING WEBTV CLASSIC

You can include the original letter on both WebTV Classic and WebTV Plus units in the same way.

③ The darkened downward-pointing arrow shows you are at the bottom of the letter.

④ Highlight **Attach original message** and press Go.

⑤ The glowing downward arrow now indicates that there is more mail (the newly attached letter) to see below. Use the scroll keys to view the full letter.

⑥ If you change your mind, move the yellow box to **Detach** and press Go.

⑦ To send the letter with the original attached, highlight **Send** and press Go.

FIND IT ONLINE

Concerned about viruses? Read more about it at
http://help.webtv.net/mail/receive/virus.html.

Stopping and Continuing E-Mail

Sometimes the phone rings. Sometimes you have to run out to an appointment. Sometimes you want to check out a fact on a Web page. Sometimes you simply lose your train of thought. In these circumstances, and in others, you may want to stop in the midst of writing a letter and pick up writing it after some time has passed.

WebTV enables you to pause in the middle of letter composition. You can go on to other tasks and come back to your letter as needed. You can even turn your WebTV unit off and continue your letter days or weeks later. WebTV remembers what you were doing, what you had written, and where you were in the letter.

When you come back, you can finish the letter and send it off. Or, you can write a bit more and go away again. WebTV will continue to remember your letter until you send it or you instruct WebTV to begin a fresh letter.

You may need to check out information on the World Wide Web while in the middle of writing a letter. Go to the Web site as usual, using Favorites, Search, and so on. When you are done, use the Back key on your remote or keyboard to return to and finish your message. Similarly, you can check out the news on MyWebTV and return to your mail.

Sometimes WebTV remembers a letter that you do not. When you activate **Write**, you may find that you were in the middle of a letter that you had forgotten about. You may want to finish the letter and send it. If so, fine. If not, you to erase the letter and start from scratch.

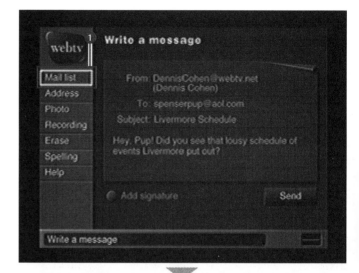

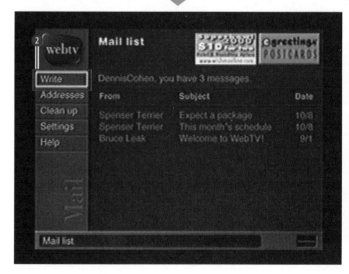

❶ *To pause while in the middle of a letter, simply press another button such as Favorites, Home or (in this example) activate Mail list.*

❷ *From the Mail list, activate* **Write**.

CROSS-REFERENCE

Want to start an e-mail from scratch? Read the next topic.

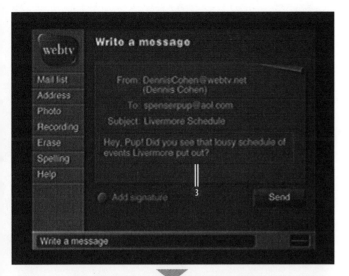

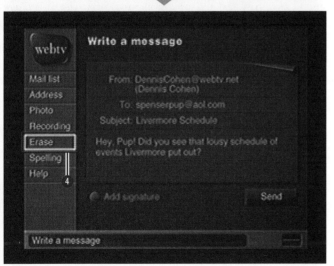

❸ *When the Write a message screen reappears, continue writing the letter from where you left off. WebTV remembers your letter.*

❹ *To start a new letter and discard the one in progress, activate **Erase**.*

FIND IT ONLINE

Read more about it. Visit **http://help.webtv.net/mail/ compose/leavepage.html.**

Erasing an E-Mail in Progress

At times, you may change your mind about an e-mail that you are writing. You may decide that an issue is not important enough to write about. You may have calmed down from an argument. A letter may arrive in your Mailbox that obviates the need for your message. You may simply want to start from scratch.

To erase a letter in progress, move the yellow box to highlight **Erase**. This feature erases all the work you have done on the letter to date. It will return you to a fresh slate. Consider carefully before erasing a letter, however, because this action cannot be undone.

You cannot "unerase" a letter. Once you have erased it, it is gone. Be extra cautious before making this decision. Whether you invested minutes or hours in a message, all your work is lost if you erase it.

WebTV asks you to confirm your decision: "Are you sure you want to erase the changes to this message?" If you are sure, select **Erase** to begin fresh; if you are unsure, select **Don't Erase** to leave your message as it is.

If you choose to continue and erase the letter, WebTV starts you with a new Write a message screen. You can go ahead and write a new message here or you can go on to other WebTV activities. There is no need to write another letter at this point. Leaving you with a fresh letter is merely a courtesy on the part of WebTV, which assumes that you intended to write a letter.

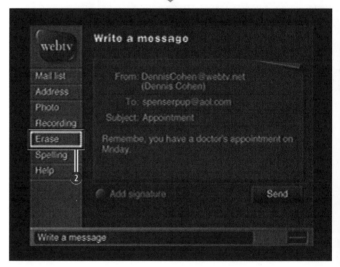

❶ *Begin by writing a letter as usual.*

❷ *Highlight **Erase** and press Go on the remote or Return on the keyboard.*

CROSS-REFERENCE

Want to start and stop writing an e-mail without erasing it? See the previous topic.

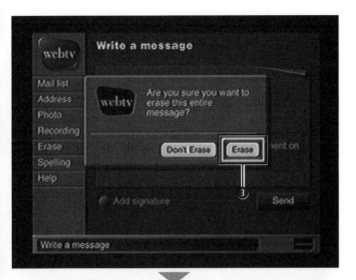

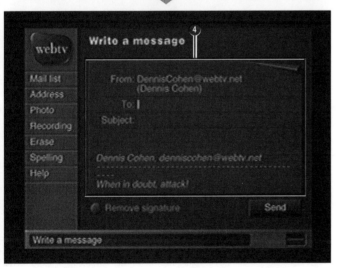

③ In the confirmation box, select **Erase**, if it is not already highlighted, and press Go.

④ The message is erased and you are placed in a fresh Write a message screen.

TAKE NOTE

▶ REUSING TEXT

Before you erase a letter, you can copy parts of it into memory to use again. Use the arrow keys and Shift to mark the area you want to copy. Then press the cmd+C combination on your keyboard to copy it. When you start a new letter later, you can paste this stored text with cmd+V.

▶ USING WEBTV CLASSIC

The technique for erasing in-progress e-mail does not vary between WebTV Classic and WebTV Plus units.

FIND IT ONLINE

Read about returned e-mail. Visit **http://help.webtv. net/mail/sending/returned.html.**

Correcting Misaddressed E-Mail

The red light has gone on. You have received a message from a mysterious "Post Office." It contains a lot of confusing information and makes very little sense.

To the new WebTV user, there is perhaps nothing more puzzling about electronic mail than these letters from the Post Office. As disconcerting as they are, they are little more than a notice that your mail was misaddressed or otherwise undeliverable.

Spelling mistakes account for the majority of Post Office letters. The remainder is due to unavailable computers or changing information. These latter happen rarely, so when you receive a Post Office notification, you can more or less assume you made a mistake in typing an address.

Of all the systems I've ever used, WebTV provides the simplest way to correct an address and resend the letter. Start by reading the message from the Post Office.

Look for two options in the message display: **Edit Message** and **Show Details**. The former enables you to correct your address, the latter shows the complete delivery rejection notice in all its detail. Ignore the latter and activate **Edit Message**.

Incorrect addresses usually occur for one of two reasons. First, the person you are writing to may have changed his or her address. If so, there is little you can do other than try to get a new address.

Second, you may have misspelled the address in some fashion. Typical mistakes include substituting a comma for a period, dropping a letter, or adding one. These

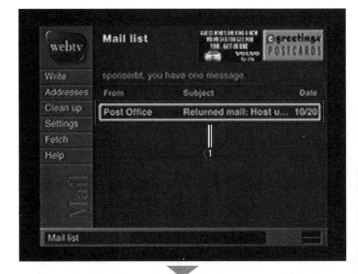

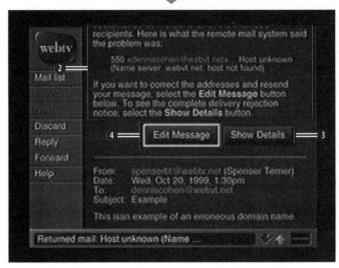

❶ *A letter from the Post Office means a letter did not go through. Highlight the listing, then press Go or Return to view this notice.*

❷ *WebTV describes the problem, although it may not make sense to you.*

❸ *You can activate **Show Details** to see more information about the attempt to deliver your mail.*

❹ *Activate **Edit Message** to correct your mistake and resend your message.*

CROSS-REFERENCE

Want to start from scratch? Learn about discarding a letter in the next chapter.

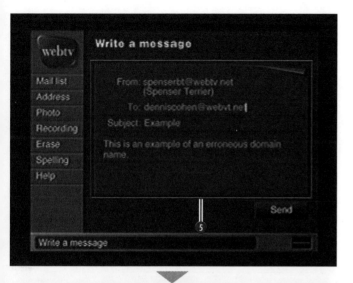

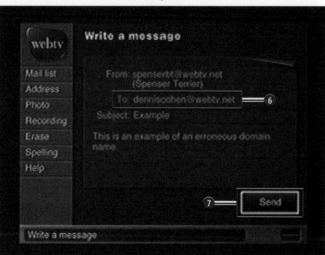

sorts of mistakes can be found through careful inspection of the address. In the example on the facing page, webtv was accidentally mispelled "webvt."

Sometimes the letter from the Post Office helps you find the error; most often it will not. Consider the error message included in the example: "Name server webvt.net host not found."

When you do find a misspelling, it is a simple matter to amend it and resend the message. Use the arrow keys to move around the message and fix the erroneous address. WebTV includes the message as originally written in a Write a message screen. Activate **Send** and your message is sent to the now correct address.

TAKE NOTE

▶ BEDTIME FOR MAIL SERVERS

Some mail servers "go to sleep" during the evenings to save energy, or for maintenance or security purposes. During this time they cannot receive mail. WebTV will try to send your mail for five days to bypass any mail server downtime.

▶ USING WEBTV CLASSIC

Correct misaddressed letters in the same manner on both WebTV Classic and WebTV Plus.

⑤ *A new Write a message screen appears containing the original message. The domain name in the e-mail address was misspelled. Webtv is misspelled webvt.*

⑥ *Move the yellow box to highlight the mistaken address. Retype the address to correct the misspelling.*

⑦ *Activate **Send** to mail the letter again.*

FIND IT ONLINE

Learn more about it. Visit **http://help.webtv.net/mail/ sending/bounced.html.**

Personal Workbook

Q&A

1 Why do people use e-mail signatures?

_____

_____

_____

2 Why do people use different e-mail ordering?

_____

_____

_____

3 What difference is there between sending a letter to person X with a cc: to person Y and just sending the letter to both X and Y?

_____

_____

_____

4 When should you "Reply to all"?

_____

_____

_____

5 Why do people include e-mail in a reply?

_____

_____

_____

6 Why do some people erase a letter that they are writing?

_____

_____

_____

7 What does it mean when you get a letter from the "Post Office?"

_____

_____

_____

8 Why are most letters returned to you by the "Post Office?"

_____

_____

_____

ANSWERS: PAGE 338

Building Intermediate E-Mail Skills

EXTRA PRACTICE

1. Create an e-mail signature.

2. Send a letter to a friend and "Cc:" yourself on it.

3. Reply to everyone on a group e-mail message.

4. Reply to a letter and include the original.

5. Send a letter using the address book.

6. Power your WebTV unit off and on when in the middle of a letter.

REAL-WORLD APPLICATIONS

✔ All of your friends like to include jokes or clever quotes in their e-mail signatures. You find a particularly clever phrase and add it to your signature.

✔ You are already using a signature, but you consider changing it every now and then. Friends tell you this makes your e-mail more interesting and keeps jokes from going stale.

✔ You start a discussion group! You send a letter to a group of friends and use the reply-to-all feature to keep in touch. Discussions about religion and politics ensure lively responses.

Visual Quiz

You are in the middle of writing the following letter. How can you take a break?

_____

_____

_____

_____

_____

_____

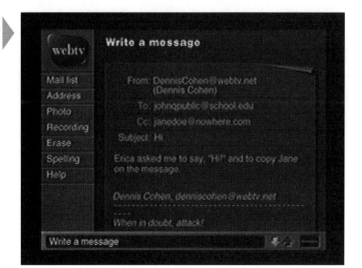

CHAPTER **11**

MASTER
THESE
SKILLS

▶ **Enabling Storage**

▶ **Storing a Letter**

▶ **Discarding a Letter**

▶ **Cleaning Up Storage**

▶ **Discarding a Letter Permanently**

▶ **Retrieving a Discarded Letter**

▶ **Resending a Sent Letter**

Taking Charge of E-Mail Storage

WebTV provides four areas that store electronic messages. These include the Mail list, and the Saved, Sent, and Discarded message folders. Each area is responsible for storing a different type of message. Each provides a different storage function for your e-mail.

The first storage area, the Mail list, is available whenever you press the Mail key. The other three are accessed from the **Storage** option on the Mail list screen. A special Storage option must be enabled before these secondary areas become available to you. The first topic in this chapter discusses how to enable this feature.

The Mail list acts as your "in box." It stores incoming mail. When your WebTV unit receives new mail, its red Message light illuminates. The new mail appears on your Mail list in brighter, bigger letters. These visual cues remain until all new mail is read. Mail will remain in your Mail list until you save or discard it. There are no time limits associated with your Mail list. However, you are allocated only 2 megabytes (MB) of memory for your mail list.

As with physical mail, you can sort through your WebTV mail, choosing which mail to file and which to discard. The Saved folder provides message archives, allowing you to store e-mail in a "file folder" for later review. When you save an e-mail message, WebTV moves the message from your Mail list to the Saved folder. As with the Mail list, the message will remain until you choose to discard it.

The Sent folder saves copies of outgoing messages for a period of seven days. After seven days have passed, messages are automatically and permanently removed. Use the Sent folder to review, save, or resend letters that you have written.

The Discarded folder saves copies of discarded messages. As with the Sent folder, these messages are kept for seven days before they are automatically and permanently removed. Use the Discarded folder to recover mail that you've accidentally disposed of.

WebTV allocates 2MB of Storage per user. You cannot store more than this allocation between the Saved, Sent, and Discarded storage areas. If your Storage space exceeds the space allotted, you will be prompted to permanently discard messages until you fall below the 2MB quota.

When you have finished this chapter, you will have mastered the skills that allow you to fully understand and control your e-mail storage.

Enabling Storage

Enabling **Storage** forms the first step towards allowing you to save important mail, review outgoing messages and recover deleted letters. Unfortunately, these options are not available until you take the first step. Before you can save, review, and recover, your storage option must be chosen and enabled.

Start by activating **Settings** from your mail list. Next, activate **Extras**. On the Extra features screen, check the box before "Create a storage area for your saved, sent and discarded messages" and activate **Done** to continue.

Guard against disaster

By enabling storage, you guard against disaster. Discarded letters may be recovered. Messages already sent can be reviewed and saved or forwarded to other parties. WebTV storage provides an important safeguard for your use. When WebTV saves copies of e-mails, you're saved the worry of taking irreversible steps. By neglecting or disabling this option, you are refusing an important safety net.

I strongly recommend that you set, and always leave on, the option that enables storage. For those of you worried about security issues, remember that you can still permanently discard letters. It just takes a few extra steps to do so. The long-term gain in e-mail safety surely offsets the extra work to ensure privacy.

The techniques for recovering and reviewing messages are covered later in this chapter.

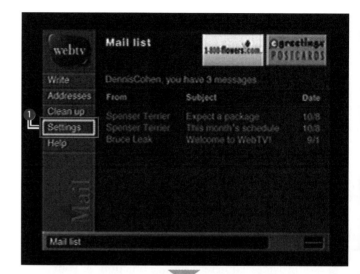

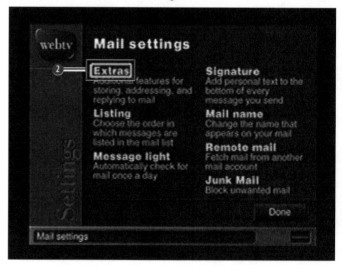

❶ *Starting in your Mail list, move the yellow box to **Settings** in the list of options along the left-hand side of the screen and press Go on the remote.*

❷ *In the Mail settings screen, activate **Extras**.*

CROSS-REFERENCE

The rest of this chapter covers all the features available once you activate storage.

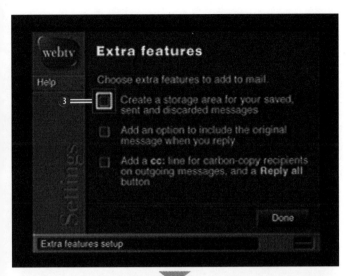

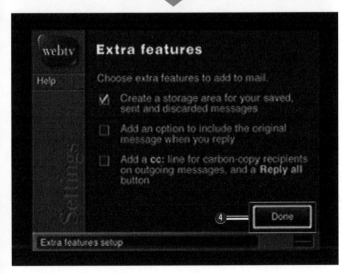

3 In the Extra features setup screen, highlight the box next to **Create a storage area for your saved, sent and discarded messages**. Place a check mark in the box by pressing Go or Return.

4 Activate **Done** to finish.

▶ OTHER OPTIONS

The Extra features screen offers a couple of other options. These options include adding an option to include the original message and enabling carbon copy recipients. You can set these options at the same time that you enable storage. You need not set them one at a time. Select and check off those options that you wish to enable and activate **Done** to confirm your choices.

▶ DISABLING OPTIONS

Disable options in the same manner in which you enable them. Return to the Extra features screen and remove the check marks to disable these features. Move the yellow box to the checked box you wish to disable and press Go or Return. This turns the option off. To reenable an option, press Go or Return again. WebTV toggles the check mark between off and on.

▶ FORWARD IT

In addition to saving accidentally discarded e-mail, WebTV enables you to forward it. This lets you send copies to other parties without moving the e-mail out of the "garbage can." You can also reply to discarded e-mail.

▶ USING WEBTV CLASSIC

Storage activation works the same on WebTV Classic and WebTV Plus.

FIND IT ONLINE

What is storage? Visit **http://help.webtv.net/ glossary/gloss_s/storage.html**.

Storing a Letter

To save a letter for future reference, store it. This moves the letter out of your mail list and into the WebTV Saved folder within the Storage option. Letters in the Saved folder are kept until you decide to discard them. The storage folder enables you to keep important letters without cluttering your inbox.

What sort of things might you want to store? There are many to choose from. Consider storing memorable personal messages, letters with important phone numbers, e-mails that reference interesting Web sites, and so forth. Use WebTV's Saved folder as you would a physical one: to store those e-mails that you do not wish to lose. To store a letter, activate **Save**. WebTV does the rest.

Once a letter has been saved, you can reread it at any time. Choose **Storage** from your Mail list and your letters appear in the **Saved** message folder.

WebTV stores saved messages on the main WebTV server, not on your WebTV unit. It saves your messages until you remove them or cancel your account. Saved messages count as part of your 2MB Storage quota, so use care when choosing which messages to save.

If your messages are precious and space is limited, there are three other options. First, you can attach a printer to your WebTV unit and print out e-mail for permanent physical storage.

Second, you can create additional users for your WebTV account. Forward copies of your e-mail to these secondary accounts. Each secondary user is allocated an additional 2MB of e-mail storage. WebTV lets you add up to five secondary user accounts to each primary WebTV account. For further information about adding secondary accounts, call 1-800-Go-WebTV.

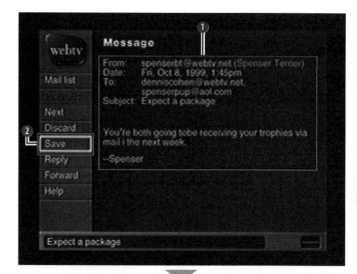

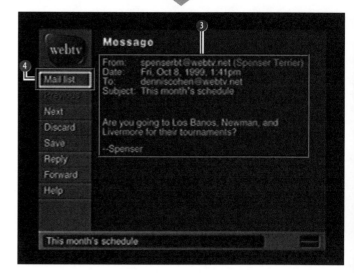

❶ Display the message you wish to save.

❷ Highlight **Save** and press Go on the remote.

❸ WebTV saves the message and displays the next e-mail in your Mail list.

❹ To review the saved message, you must return to the Mail list. Highlight **Mail list** with the yellow box and press Go.

CROSS-REFERENCE

Do you want to remove a letter from your Mail list, but not save it? Read the Discarding a Letter topic in this chapter.

194

Third, if you have a non-WebTV account, you can forward a copy of your e-mail there. Most other Internet Service Providers furnish greater storage limits, although without WebTV's excellent design and ease-of-use.

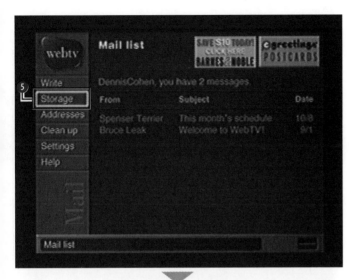

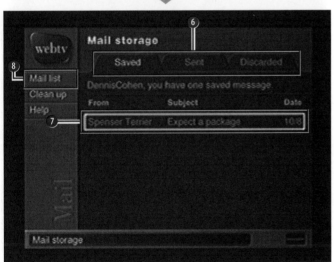

TAKE NOTE

▶ **PERIODICALLY REVIEW SAVED MAIL**

Make sure to review your saved messages regularly. Messages that seemed irreplaceable when you first saved them may appear less valuable when you re-view them a few months later. Plan on sorting through and cleaning up your saved messages every few months.

▶ **NO WAY BACK TO THE MAIL LIST**

Unfortunately, once you have saved a letter, you cannot move it back to the Mail list from the saved mail storage.

▶ **USING WEBTV CLASSIC**

Save your letters on WebTV classic as you would on WebTV Plus.

⑤ In the Mail list screen, highlight the **Storage** option and press Go.

⑥ WebTV provides three Mail storage folders: **Saved**, **Sent**, and **Discarded**.

⑦ The message saved in step 2 appears in the **Saved** folder. (Optional) Move the yellow box to the saved message and press Go to review the saved message.

⑧ Activate **Mail list** to return to your mailbox.

FIND IT ONLINE

You can save sent e-mail. Visit **http://help.webtv.net/mail/receive/save.html**.

Discarding a Letter

After you have read or replied to a letter, you may wish to discard it. Keeping old, unimportant, or finished correspondence clutters your Mail list and may, if your mailbox is full, prevent you from receiving new letters. It also confuses the wheat of important mail with the chaff of extra letters. With WebTV it's a matter of a few simple steps to dispose of a letter: To remove a letter from your Mail list, display it and activate **Discard**. That's all. WebTV removes the letter from the mailbox.

Remember that WebTV lets you store a maximum of 2MB of e-mail in your Mail list and 2MB more in your storage areas. According to WebTV's help center, this is equal to approximately 150 "standard-length" text messages. Long messages and messages with pictures and sound attached can quickly fill up your mailbox. The more mail you discard, the more space you will have for incoming mail.

You can get an idea of how much memory each message occupies by activating **Clean up** from any of the four storage areas: Mail list, saved mail, sent mail, and discarded mail. The right-hand column shows the size of your messages as a percentage of 2MB. The clean up feature is discussed in further detail in the next topic.

Of course, there's a sneaky way around this. The 2MB storage limit applies to each user. You can create as many as five secondary user accounts in addition to your main account. You can forward your mail to these accounts and use the extra storage provided there.

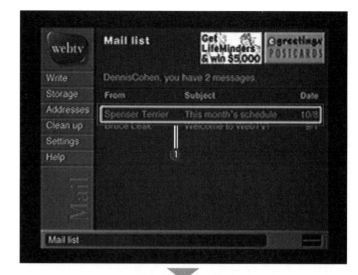

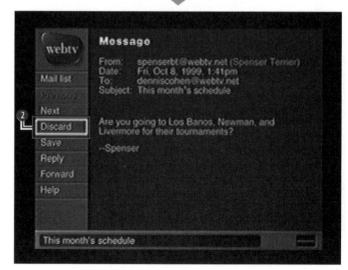

❶ Starting in your Mail list, select a message to read and press Go on the remote.

▶ In the Message display, Discard appears among the Mail list options.

❷ Highlight **Discard** with the yellow box and press Go.

CROSS-REFERENCE

If security is an issue, you can permanently dispose of e-mail. Read "Discarding Letters Permanently" later in this chapter.

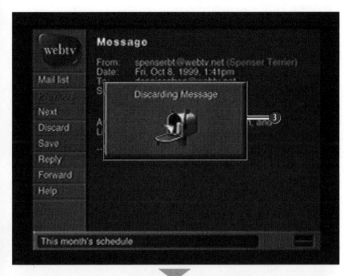

③ *WebTV displays a Discarding Message box as it discards the message. Once begun, there is no option to cancel the process.*

④ *When finished, WebTV displays the next message in your Mail list. The **Discard** option remains highlighted, enabling you to continue cleaning out your mail.*

FIND IT ONLINE

How many letters can you store on WebTV? Visit
http://help.webtv.net/mail/receive/howmany.html.

197

Cleaning Up Storage

The **Clean up** option appears in all four of your e-mail storage areas: the Mail list, the Sent mail, the Discarded mail, and the Saved mail. The option works the same in each area. The examples on the facing page demonstrate cleaning up the Mail list, but the same technique can be used for the three areas of the Storage option.

Cleaning up a storage list involves two choices. First, you may discard items. This removes the items from your list. WebTV keeps any item you discard for a week, which enables you to correct mistakes or change your mind about discarding it. During this time, these disposed items are kept in the Discarded storage folder.

Second, you may store items. These items are stored indefinitely in the Saved storage folder. By saving an item, you remove it from your list and move it to a permanent folder. You can, of course, later discard it from that folder.

The Clean up screen

To enter the Clean up mail list screen, highlight and activate **Clean up** from the list of options. The Clean up screen is arranged as a list of messages, with each message preceded by a gray square, and followed by a date and size. Take careful note of the size. This number refers to the size of a message as a percentage of the 2MB space WebTV allows each user.

When activated, the options **Discard** and **Save** apply to each message that has been checked. To check a message, move the yellow box to the gray square before the message and activate it with Go or Return. You can also activate **Mark all** to put a check before all messages.

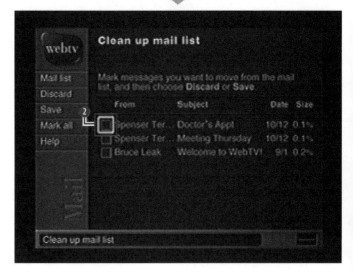

❶ From the Mail list, highlight the **Clean up** option and press Go on the remote or Return on the keyboard.

❷ When the Clean up mail list screen appears, use the arrow keys to highlight the box next to the message you wish to discard. Place a check in the box by pressing Go.

CROSS-REFERENCE

To discard a single letter without using the Clean up screen, consult the previous topic.

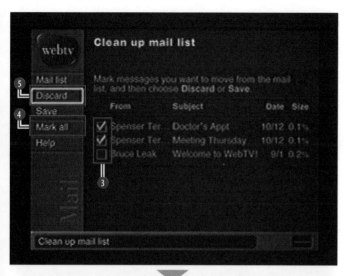

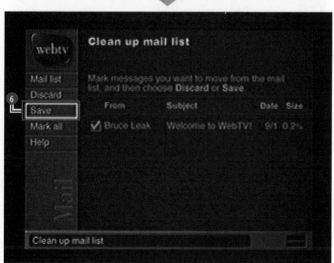

Mark and Unmark

The **Mark all** option selects every message. Once it is activated, WebTV replaces the **Mark all** option with **Unmark**. This feature, unsurprisingly, unmarks all the messages in the list. After using either of these options, you can still use the arrow keys to move to individual letters and toggle the check marks on and off.

Once an item has been discarded or saved, you cannot move it back to the Mail list. However, you can always "save" a discarded item. This recovers items that were accidentally disposed and moves them to the Saved mail folder.

There is, of course, a tricky way around this. You can forward letters from the Discarded mail. Simply forward the letter to yourself and it will "move" back to the incoming Mail list.

TAKE NOTE

▶ **DISCARDING FROM DISCARDED MAIL**

If you discard a letter when cleaning up the discarded mail list, it is removed permanently and irrevocably.

▶ **USING WEBTV CLASSIC**

You can clean up mail on WebTV Classic as you would on WebTV Plus.

---

③ Place check marks next to each message that you wish to discard. Remove the check mark to preserve the message in the mail list.

④ (Optional) Activate **Mark all** to discard all messages.

⑤ To remove messages, highlight **Discard** and press Go on the remote.

⑥ To store messages, follow steps 1 through 4, check marking all messages you wish to store in your Saved storage folder. Highlight **Save** and press Go.

FIND IT ONLINE

Read more about it. Visit **http://help.webtv.net/mail/receive/storage.html.**

Discarding a Letter Permanently

There are times when you will want to discard a letter permanently. You may wish to do this for one of two reasons. First, you may not want or need to save the letter any longer. Second, you may need to free up space in your mailbox. For whichever reason, WebTV enables you to remove letters completely from your mailbox.

To remove a letter from your discarded folder, follow the steps illustrated on the facing page. Following these steps will fully erase discarded letters. You cannot "undo" this action. Once you have permanently discarded a letter, it is gone forever.

Security

Security can be an issue for people who are using their WebTV accounts to write sensitive or personal electronic mail. WebTV keeps a copy of both outgoing and discarded messages for one week. This policy enables you to review messages that you've sent and recover messages that you've deleted. This also means that anyone with access to your WebTV account and the proper know-how can read these messages. To avoid this, you can permanently remove messages from both your Sent and Discarded storage folders.

To remove a letter from your Sent folder, you must first discard the letter (which is described in the previous topic). Next, you must remove the letter from the Discarded folder. Permanent disposal can only be performed in the Discarded folder.

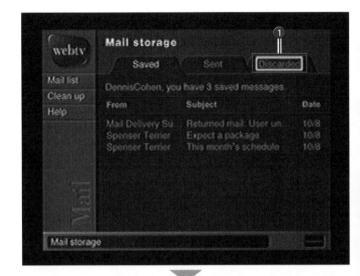

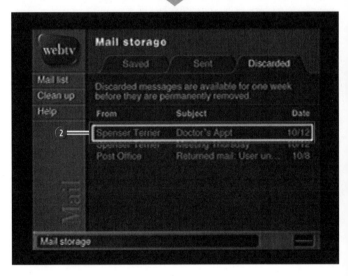

❶ On the Mail storage screen move the yellow box to the tab on the **Discarded** folder and press Go on the remote or Return on the keyboard.

❷ Select the message you wish to discard permanently and press Go. This displays the discarded message for you to review.

CROSS-REFERENCE

If neither security nor space is an issue, remove letters as discussed in Discarding Letters earlier in this chapter.

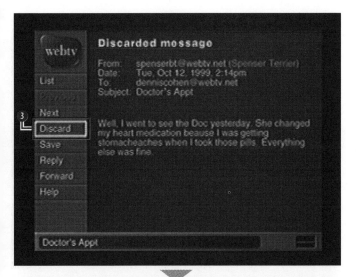

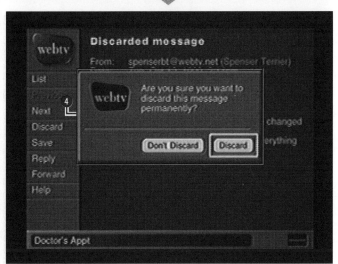

Space Limitations

Space becomes an issue quickly for those people who send and receive lots of attachments, such as pictures and audio clips. Space is also a factor for those who engage in frequent correspondence and who save all the back-and-forth e-mail. Because WebTV keeps your discarded and sent mail for a week before disposing of them permanently, this extra storage may eat into your 2MB storage allotment. The Clean up screen (as described in the previous topic) always shows, as a percentage, how much space each message occupies of your allotment.

When space is limited and you are worried about having enough storage available for incoming messages, you can use permanent mail removal. This forcibly clears out some of your storage allotment and prevents the messages about full e-mail storage.

TAKE NOTE

▶ **DID YOU REALLY MEAN TO DO THAT?**

Think long and hard before removing a message permanently from your WebTV mailbox. Once a message has been removed in this way, it is gone forever.

▶ **USING WEBTV CLASSIC**

You can discard letters on WebTV Classic as you would on WebTV Plus.

---

③ On the Discarded message screen move the yellow box to **Discard** in the List of options and press Go.

④ When prompted, confirm that you wish to **Discard** the message permanently by pressing Go.

▶ If you decide not to permanently discard the message, move the yellow box to **Don't Discard** and press Go.

FIND IT ONLINE

Read more about it. Visit **http://help.webtv.net/mail/ receive/storagefull.html**.

Retrieving a Discarded Letter

The time will come, unfortunately, when you activate **Discard** rather than **Next**. WebTV will display a picture of a mailbox and inform you it is busy Discarding Message. Fortunately, disposing of a letter is reversible if you have enabled storage, as discussed earlier in this chapter.

WebTV keeps all discarded letters for a week after they have been removed, which gives you time to realize that a letter may have been discarded in error and to recover that letter if necessary.

Discarded letters are kept in a special folder in WebTV's storage area. To enter the storage area, activate **Storage** from the Mail list. WebTV's Mail storage provides three folders: Saved, Sent, and Discarded.

The Saved folder stores those letters that you have saved from your Mail list. This provides a permanent mail storage solution without crowding your Mail list in-box. The saved messages form an archive that can be used for reference at any time.

The Sent folder stores a copy of all outgoing messages. This feature enables you to review messages that you have sent, send copies of already sent messages to additional people, and save copies of your outgoing e-mail. WebTV stores a copy of all sent mail for one week.

The Discarded folder stores copies of all discarded mail. This folder acts as your garbage pail. It enables you to review those messages that you have chosen to dispose of and to recover any messages discarded in error. As with the Sent mail, these letters are stored for one week.

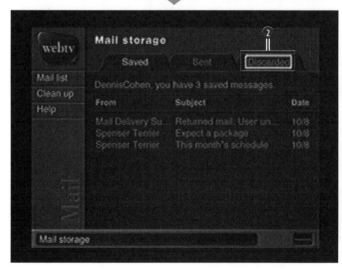

❶ On your Mail list screen, activate the **Storage** option.

❷ From Mail storage move the yellow box to the tab on the **Discarded** folder and press Go on the remote.

CROSS-REFERENCE

If security or space is an issue for you, you can permanently dispose of e-mail. Read "Discarding a Letter Permanently" earlier in this chapter.

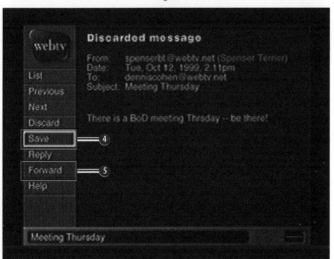

To recover a discarded letter, you need only follow a few steps. First, display it from the Discarded folder. Second, activate Save. WebTV moves the message to the permanent Saved message folder. WebTV does not provide a direct way to move it back to your Mail list, although you may forward a copy to yourself and achieve the same result, more or less.

TAKE NOTE

▶ **TIME OUT**

The one-week time limit on storing discarded messages starts when you activate Discard.

▶ **PRINT IT**

You can print a discarded letter exactly as you would a letter in your Mail list. You do not need to "save" it first. Press the Options button on your remote and then activate **Print**.

▶ **DISCARDING DISCARDED LETTERS**

When you discard a letter that is already in the Discarded folder, you are asked, "Are you sure you want to discard this message permanently?" from your WebTV account.

▶ **USING WEBTV CLASSIC**

You can recover discarded letters on WebTV classic as you would on WebTV Plus.

③ Select the message you wish to recover with the yellow box and press Go.

④ When the Discarded message is displayed, activate **Save** from the list of options along the left-hand side of the screen.

⑤ (Optional) You can also highlight and activate the **Forward** option to send a copy of the discarded letter to yourself or another recipient.

FIND IT ONLINE

Read more about it. Visit **http://wecare.webtv.net/ mail/receive/discarded.html**.

Resending a Sent Letter

On occasion, you might forget to include an address as a recipient on an e-mail. You need not retype the entire letter to send it to that additional recipient. Instead, you can forward a copy of the message from the Sent mail storage folder.

It takes a few steps to find your sent mail folder. Start from the Mail list. Activate **Storage** to move to WebTV's Mail storage folders. Move the yellow box to the **Sent** tab, which will appear in blue letters. Press Go. You can tell you are now in the correct folder because the word Sent appears in yellow rather than blue, and the letters that you recently sent are listed below.

All sent messages are kept by WebTV for one week before they are automatically and permanently removed.

To display a message, move the yellow box to the letter you wish to see and press Go. Once a message has been displayed, you can Save it, Discard it, or, as shown on the facing page, Forward it.

Copy the text

Another way to recover a sent letter is to copy the text within the letter and paste it into a new message. Start by moving the yellow box to your name in the **From:** line. This ensures that you will be copying the text in the letter rather than the options on the left side of your screen.

For the next few steps you will need to press and hold the cmd key on your keyboard while typing other keys. Start by selecting the entire message with cmd+A. Next, copy the message with cmd+C. Remove the selection with cmd+A again. This copies the entire letter to WebTV's memory. You are now ready to start a new letter and recover the message from memory.

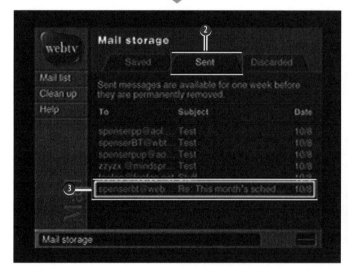

❶ On the Mail list screen, activate **Storage**.

❷ On the Mail storage screen, activate the **Sent** tab.

❸ Display the message you wish to forward by highlighting it with the yellow box and pressing Go.

CROSS-REFERENCE

Learn more about using cut, copy and paste in Section I.

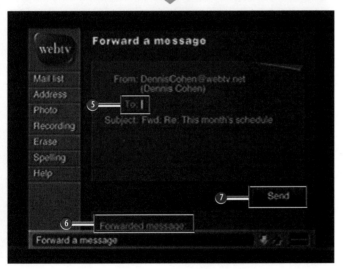

Start by writing a new e-mail message. Paste the old message text with cmd+V. You may find that unwanted header information appears at the start of the copied letter. You can remove the header by moving to the start of the text that you wish to keep and repeatedly pressing Delete to remove the unwanted material before that text.

TAKE NOTE

▶ **DOUBLE HEADERS**

When you forward a saved letter, the message will arrive with two sets of headers (the information that appears at the beginning of an e-mail message). One belongs to the original message. The second belongs to the forwarding e-mail. You cannot edit out the original header when forwarding a saved e-mail.

▶ **FORWARDING USING WEBTV CLASSIC**

Forward saved letters on WebTV Classic as you would on WebTV Plus.

▶ **EDIT USING WEBTV CLASSIC**

The command (cmd) key combinations that copy and paste mail work identically on WebTV Classic and WebTV Plus.

---

④ When the Sent message displays, activate **Forward** from the list of options to the left.

⑤ In the Forward a message screen, type the new recipient's address in the **To:** line.

⑥ The forwarded message appears below. Scroll down to review it, if necessary.

⑦ Move the yellow box to **Send** and press Go.

FIND IT ONLINE

Read more about it. Visit **http://help.webtv.net/mail/sending/forward.html**.

Personal Workbook

Q&A

1 What does WebTV's Storage option enable you to do?

_____

_____

_____

2 How many storage areas does WebTV provide?

_____

_____

_____

3 Is discarding a letter from the Mail list a permanent action?

_____

_____

_____

4 How long is saved mail kept?

_____

_____

_____

5 How long is discarded mail kept?

_____

_____

_____

6 How long is sent mail kept?

_____

_____

_____

7 How much storage is allocated to each WebTV user?

_____

_____

_____

8 How can you determine how much space a letter takes up?

_____

_____

_____

ANSWERS: PAGE 338

EXTRA PRACTICE

1. Use Clean up to discard letters.

2. Save a letter.

3. Discard a letter and then recover it.

4. Discard a letter and then remove it permanently.

5. Save a letter you have sent.

6. Forward a sent letter to another party.

7. Discard a sent letter and then save it back to your "saved" folder.

8. Forward a copy of a sent letter to yourself.

REAL-WORLD APPLICATIONS

✔ You want to save a photo sent to you in e-mail but you are unsure how much Storage space is left in your mailbox. You use the Clean up screen to determine how much space is available in your Storage folders. You clean up your discarded mail to free up extra space in your mailbox.

✔ You want to understand how storage space can be filled up — before it becomes a problem in real life. You send yourself a series of pictures until you exhaust storage space. You then see what happens when you try to send yourself a letter when you have run out of memory. Later you make sure to discard the extra messages and permanently remove the discarded messages from your Discarded folder to free your mailbox back up.

Visual Quiz

How much space do these sent messages take up?

_____

_____

_____

_____

_____

_____

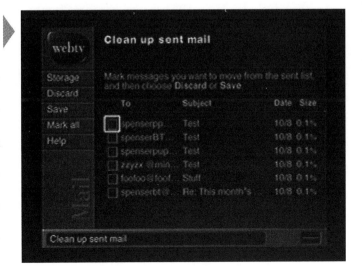

CHAPTER **12**

MASTER ▶ **Checking for E-Mail Automatically**
THESE ▶ **Sending and Retrieving E-mail Hyperlinks**
SKILLS ▶ **Accepting E-Mail Attachments**
      ▶ **Retrieving Mail from Other Accounts**

Mastering Advanced E-Mail Techniques

There's much more to electronic mail than sending, reading, and receiving. With WebTV you can move beyond simple electronic messaging to explore advanced WebTV and Internet techniques. This chapter introduces you to a number of skills that enable you to be a more powerful e-mail user.

These techniques vary from instructing WebTV to automatically check for e-mail to sending and receiving World Wide Web hyperlinks. Whether you want to take advantage of the Hypertext Markup Language (HTML) or retrieve electronic mail from third-party Internet service providers (ISPs), this chapter instructs you in the how-to and why of each.

No single chapter can cover all the intricacies of advanced e-mail skills. The skills you learn in this chapter were selected to give you the greatest gains for the least investment in time and effort.

Remember, too, that the purpose of e-mail is communication. If the person to whom you write is overwhelmed by attachments, embedded fonts, or hyperlinks, you have failed in your mission. Use these features sparingly and meaningfully. While a picture may be worth a thousand words, it may also take up 10 percent of your available mailbox space.

Checking for E-mail Automatically

WebTV's Message Watch feature enables you to automatically check for new e-mail once a day. When this feature is active, your unit will call to the WebTV unit at the same time each day and determine whether you have received any new mail. If you received new mail, the red message light will illuminate. This feature is especially convenient when you connect to WebTV only occasionally.

This feature only works when the phone is not already in use. WebTV will not interrupt ongoing phone calls and will automatically hang up if an extension is picked up to make an outgoing phone call. Try to pick a time for e-mail checks when it is unlikely that anyone will be using the phone line for other purposes.

The time at which WebTV checks your incoming messages is approximate. WebTV does not want several hundred WebTV units calling in, attempting to look for mail at the exact stroke of the hour. Instead, your unit will check for mail at roughly the time you specify.

Choose a time to check mail about an hour before you normally power on your WebTV unit. Many people select a time that they think will be more convenient, such as midnight. They reason that no one is likely to be on the phone line in the middle of the night. This reasoning is faulty. If you use your WebTV unit at eight in the evening, the Mail list will only reflect mail received until midnight the night before. The automatic e-mail check will miss any mail that arrives during the other 20 hours.

WebTV's Message Watch still works when your television and set-top unit are off. As long as there is power available and a phone line attached to your unit, it can call up WebTV and check for mail. The yellow "connected" light need not be on for this feature to work.

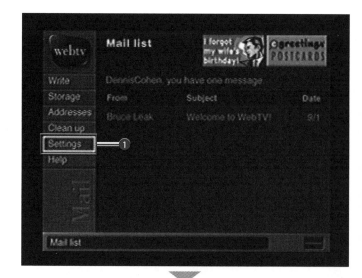

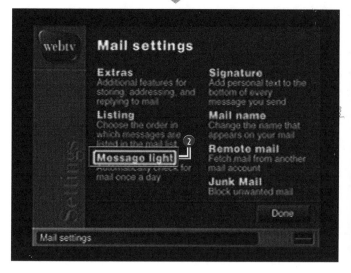

❶ Starting in your Mail list, move the yellow box to **Settings** and press Go on the remote or Return on the keyboard.

❷ On the Mail settings screen, move the yellow box down the list of options to **Message light** and activate it.

CROSS-REFERENCE

Learn more about reading e-mail in Chapter 8.

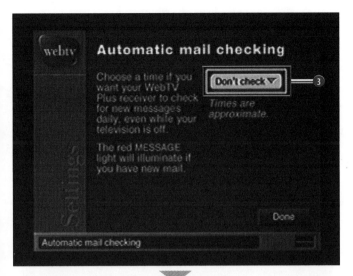

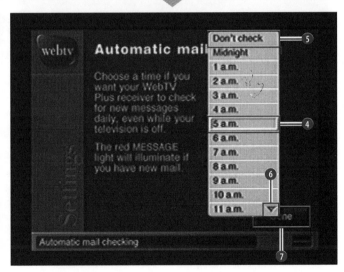

TAKE NOTE

RELAX

Many people feel pressured to turn on their WebTV units when the red message light illuminates. Choosing a mail-check time near to when you usually use your unit relieves some of this pressure. Remember that you do not have to read your mail until it is convenient. WebTV will not lose your mail, nor will your mail expire, even if you unplug your unit. You can delay reading mail for hours, days, weeks, or months. Mail is stored at the main WebTV facility. Although the red message light may not re-light until your unit checks again for mail, the mail itself is still waiting for you in your account.

CHECK TWICE

By setting different times for Message Watch and TV listing updates, you can actually check for mail twice each day.

USING WEBTV CLASSIC

Both WebTV Classic and WebTV Plus offer Message Watch.

❸ On the Automatic mail checking screen, the drop-down list of times is highlighted. The default setting is **Don't check**. Open the list of times by pressing Go on the remote or Return on the keyboard.

❹ Select a time with the arrow keys and press Go to confirm your selection. The gray-rounded rectangle will reflect the new time you selected.

❺ (Optional) Choose **Don't Check** to disallow this option.

❻ Press Scroll Down to view more times.

❼ Activate **Done** to finish.

FIND IT ONLINE

Read more about it. Visit **http://help.webtv.net/ mail/messages/auto.html**.

Sending and Retrieving E-mail Hyperlinks

When other people include hyperlinks in e-mail, you can activate the links directly from the message. Hyperlinks appear in blue. You can move the yellow box to the hyperlink and activate it by pressing Go or Return. WebTV moves you to the address specified in the hyperlink. This address can point to Web pages, pictures, sounds, and so forth. Any place that you can visit on the World Wide Web can be represented as a hyperlink in e-mail.

Hyperlinks can appear as URLs, the address of the hyperlink, or as a blue-colored description of the page. The examples on the facing page show both a straight URL (the first picture) and a descriptive hyperlink (the last). Both hyperlinks work the same way. In this example, both hyperlinks send you to the same Web page.

You may include hyperlinks in mail that you send. Simply type the URL into your message. There is no special formatting other than the standard World Wide Web address conventions for the hyperlink. For example, you can type "Visit the White House! Look at http://www.whitehouse.gov" directly into your letter.

WebTV provides another, extremely convenient, way to send hyperlinks. When you find an interesting Web page, press Send, which is located in the upper-right corner of your remote keyboard. A special window appears and prompts you to enter an e-mail address or to select an e-mail recipient from your address book by activating **Choose Address**. The location of the page will be sent to this address as an included hyperlink.

You can customize the e-mail by adding a personal message. Activate **Edit Message** and WebTV enables you to type a message to accompany the hyperlink. While sending a hyperlink to yourself is generally self-explanatory, other people may find a descriptive message helpful in understanding your intent.

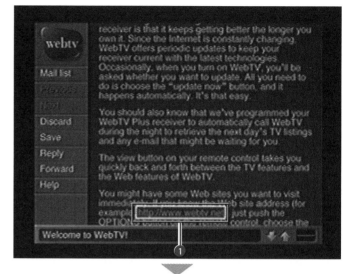

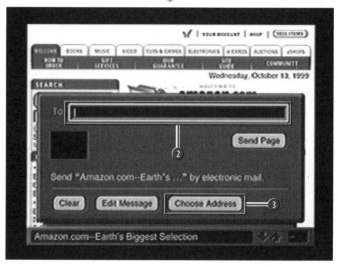

❶ Hyperlinks appear in blue. Move the yellow box to the hyperlink and activate by pressing Go on the remote or Return on the keyboard.

▶ Press Send on the keyboard to mail a hyperlink.

❷ In the Send Page dialog box, fill in the address of the person to whom you wish to mail the hyperlink.

❸ (Optional) Activate **Choose Address** to select an address or addresses from your WebTV address book.

CROSS-REFERENCE

Learn more about hyperlinks in Chapter 4.

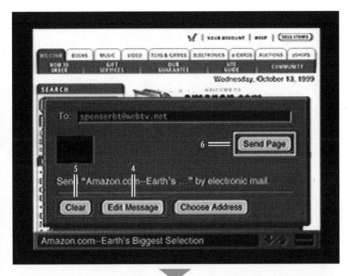

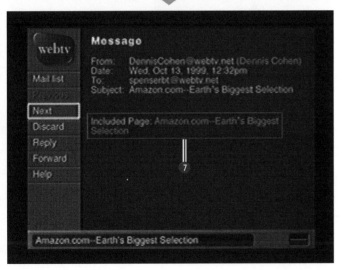

④ (Optional) activate **Edit Message** to add a message with the hyperlink.

⑤ (Optional) activate **Clear** to revert to no recipient and a blank message.

⑥ Activate **Send Page** to mail the hyperlink to the address you specified.

⑦ Hyperlinks may appear as a series of words rather than as a URL. This hyperlink, which was just sent, is equivalent to the one shown in step 1.

FIND IT ONLINE

Amazon.com is a great place to buy books. Visit
http://www.amazon.com.

Accepting E-mail Attachments

When another WebTV user sends you a picture, it appears directly in the message you receive. When you receive pictures, recordings, and so forth from people outside the WebTV network, these arrive as attachments, that is, you cannot see the picture or hear the sound directly. Instead, you need to activate part of the e-mail message to view the picture or hear the sound.

Attachments are secondary items that people send attached to an e-mail message. In addition to pictures and sound, attachments can be documents, data files, image movies, or compressed archives, among others. Anything that exists in a digitized — hence computer-readable — format, in theory can be attached to a message and sent via electronic mail.

Attachments appear in messages as a small picture followed by a name and a description. An example can be seen on the facing page. This example shows a GIF format picture attached to an e-mail message. To view or listen to an attachment, activate it. That is, move the yellow box around the attachment notice and press Go or Return.

Sometimes people will send you attachments that you cannot read on your WebTV account. WebTV supports certain file types, but not others, because set-top units cannot store and process the attachments as regular computers do. Unreadable attachments will not damage your WebTV unit or mailbox.

To open an attachment, WebTV must support it. Because there are hundreds, if not thousands, of computer "file types" associated with attachments, WebTV cannot support every attachment type. WebTV enables you to view GIF and JPEG images and listen to WAV sound recordings. These are, however, just three of the

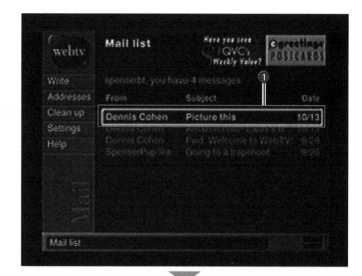

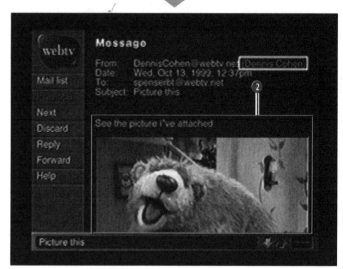

1 E-mail messages with attachments are indistinguishable from other e-mail in your Mail list.

2 However, the image appears below the message when the e-mail is opened.

CROSS-REFERENCE

Learn about sending photo attachments with WebTV e-mail in Chapter 8.

214

many types of attachments that WebTV can handle. WebTV plans to expand its attachment support in future software upgrades.

You cannot, however, use your WebTV account to view an Excel spreadsheet that someone has attached to a letter. Other attachments that WebTV does not support include Microsoft Word documents and Adobe Acrobat PDF files, among others. WebTV focuses on allowing you to see and hear images and sounds. This means that WebTV is unlikely to support these types of computer application files in future upgrades.

TAKE NOTE

▶ SOUNDS

As of spring 1999, WebTV supports these sound formats: RealAudio 1.0, 2.0, 3.0, .WAV, General MIDI, MIDI Karaoke, QuickTime Audio, .AU, .SND, MPEG-2 Audio, MPEG-3 Audio, Shockwave Audio, and .AIFF (Mace 3:1 and Mace 6:1 compression of AIFF files are unsupported).

▶ PICTURES

As of spring 1999, WebTV supports these image formats: MPEG movies, GIF, GIF89a Animation, JPEG, and Macromedia Flash 1.0.

▶ CLEAN UP

Attachments can occupy a lot of memory. Pictures and sound are tremendously memory intensive. Take care when sending and receiving attachments so as not to fill up your mailbox. Remember that you must permanently discard a message (from the Discarded storage folder) to force it out of your account without waiting for a seven-day period to elapse.

FIND IT ONLINE

Discover which technologies WebTV supports. Visit http://help.webtv.net/mail/receive/attachment.html.

Retrieving Mail from Other Accounts

o you have another e-mail account? Would you like to read and reply to that e-mail account from WebTV? If your other account supports the POP3 standard, be glad. You can use WebTV to retrieve mail from your other account.

POP3 stands for the Post Office Protocol version 3. A protocol provides a way for networked computers to talk to each other. You may have already encountered other protocols such as the Hypertext Transfer Protocol (HTTP) for the World Wide Web, and the File Transfer Protocol (FTP), which allows computers to transfer files. The POP3 protocol permits remote access to electronic mailboxes.

Most Internet service providers support POP3 e-mail. However, you may want to check with your ISP before trying to use this feature. Many free e-mail accounts and older computer systems do not support POP3. Still, POP3 has become an almost universal standard for electronic mail retrieval.

You will need some account information in order to fetch electronic mail with WebTV. First, you need your account name. Your account name is usually the first portion of your e-mail address, although see below for a caveat. This name is the part that precedes the @ sign. Second, you need your service provider's domain name. This domain name is the second portion of your e-mail address, that which follows the @ sign. Third, you need a password. E-mail accounts are secure. Your service provider will not allow you to access your e-mail account without a proper password.

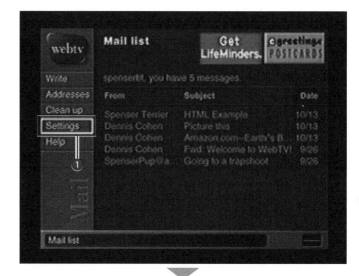

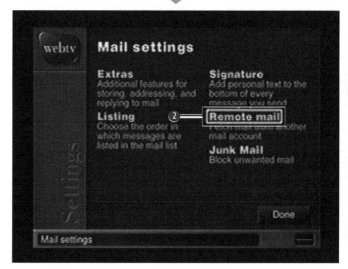

❶ Starting in your Mail list, select **Settings** and activate it by pressing Go on the remote or Return on the keyboard.

❷ On the Mail settings screen, activate **Remote mail** from the list of options.

CROSS-REFERENCE

Learn about reading WebTV e-mail in Chapter 8.

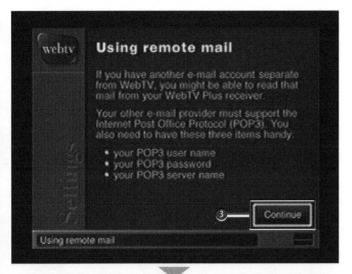

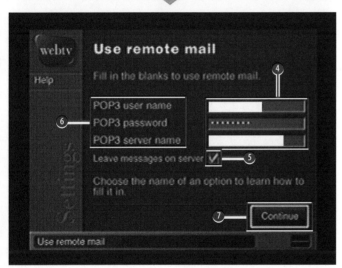

Once you have gathered this information, you can set up WebTV to fetch remote mail. Your password will not be shown on the screen. Instead, you will see a series of dots. Each dot represents one character that you have typed. WebTV hides your password to provide greater security and to prevent password theft by anyone looking over your shoulder.

Continued

TAKE NOTE

▶ ATTACHMENTS

When you receive attachments, you may or may not be able to read, view, or listen to them. Regardless, they still take up space on your WebTV account. WebTV does not provide a filter-before-download option as many other e-mail programs, such as Eudora, provide. This option enables you to see the type of attachment before choosing to retrieve it.

▶ AUTOMATIC FORWARDING

As of spring 1999, you cannot set your WebTV account to automatically forward e-mail to another account. You can, however, automatically forward e-mail from another account to your WebTV address.

③ *The first Using remote mail screen reminds you that your other ISP must support POP3. It also tells you the three pieces of information that you need to continue. If this information is handy, activate* **Continue***.*

④ *Type in your POP3 user name, server name, and password. For security, your password appears as a series of dots.*

⑤ *Check the Leave messages on server box to retain mail on your other server.*

⑥ *Activate any of the blue words for further guidance.*

⑦ *Activate* **Continue***.*

FIND IT ONLINE

Read more about it. Visit **http://help.webtv.net/ mail/messages/pop3.html**.

Retrieving Mail from Other Accounts

Continued

On the Use remote mail screen, a small box below the account information entry spaces gives you the option to "Leave messages on server." When this box is checked, your mail is read and copies of any new letters are sent to your WebTV e-mail account. When it is not checked, your mail is retrieved, sent to WebTV, and removed permanently from your server. Be sure to check this box if you intend to retrieve your letters later from your other account.

Most people choose to leave messages on the server. When you read your letters later, on your other non-WebTV account, already-fetched letters will appear as "old" read mail rather than "new" unread mail. Your server knows that they have already been retrieved and read once by WebTV. For the same reason, once fetched, WebTV will not retrieve a letter again. Only new mail is and should be fetched by WebTV. This prevents retrieving multiple copies of the same message.

When you set up WebTV to retrieve POP3 e-mail, a new option, which is called **Fetch**, is added to your Mail list screen. When you activate Fetch, WebTV retrieves mail from your other e-mail account and places those messages in your WebTV mailbox. The messages are displayed in your Mail list.

WebTV remembers your password. Once remote mail is enabled, WebTV stores your password between sessions. Conveniently, this means that you do not need to reenter your password each time you fetch mail.

Some Internet service providers do not allow accounts outside their system to access electronic mail via the POP3 server. If this is true for your secondary e-mail account, you will not be able to retrieve messages using WebTV.

Be aware that some e-mail addresses are "aliases," convenient and easily remembered names (such as "JohnQPublic"). Mail sent to the alias still arrives at

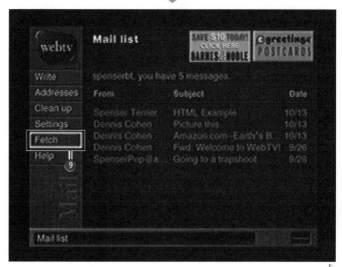

▶ The *Remote mail is on screen tells you what options you enabled. To disable, repeat steps 1 through 7 leaving the user, password, and server name blank.*

❽ Activate **Mail list** or **Done**.

❾ The **Fetch** *option now appears on the Mail list. Activate it to retrieve mail from your POP3 Server.*

CROSS-REFERENCE

Learn about replying to multiple e-mail recipients in Chapter 10.

your mailbox. However, some service providers insist that you use a special account address (usually a hard-to-remember sequence such as ms9992gt03b) to access your e-mail. If your account name does not work as expected, check with your ISP.

Your e-mail password may differ from your account password. This allows another layer of security when using your Internet account. Again, check with your ISP if your password does not work as expected. Your account may support two passwords — one primary and one for mail.

⓿ *Retrieved POP3 mail appears in your Mail list and is indistinguishable from WebTV mail.*

TAKE NOTE

▶ WEBTV AND POP3

WebTV does not provide POP3 access for its own e-mail. You cannot read your WebTV e-mail on any system or computer other than your WebTV set-top unit.

▶ ON THE ROAD

To read your WebTV mail on the road, simply bring your WebTV unit, cables, keyboard, and so forth with you as you travel. WebTV does not permit e-mail to be read by anyone other than the physical owner of the WebTV set-top unit. Whenever your unit has been unplugged, it will ask on powering on if the unit was moved. If you are on the road with your WebTV, agree. WebTV will attempt to find a local toll-free number for your unit to call.

▶ USING WEBTV CLASSIC

Both WebTV Classic and WebTV Plus enable you to retrieve e-mail via POP3.

FIND IT ONLINE

What is POP3 e-mail? Visit **http://help.webtv.net/ mail/messages/whatispop3.html.**

Personal Workbook

Q&A

1 If you set WebTV to automatically check e-mail at 11 a.m., at what time will WebTV automatically check your e-mail?

_____

_____

_____

2 How can you set two times to check e-mail?

_____

_____

_____

3 The red message light went on, but no e-mail was received. Why?

_____

_____

_____

4 What kinds of picture attachments can WebTV display?

_____

_____

_____

5 How do you send a message with very large characters?

_____

_____

_____

_____

6 You have another e-mail account and it supports POP3. Can you use WebTV to read that e-mail?

_____

_____

_____

7 What happens if you "send" a Web page to yourself?

_____

_____

_____

8 What do blue-colored words in an e-mail message mean?

_____

_____

_____

ANSWERS: PAGE 339

1 Set up WebTV to automatically check for e-mail.

2 Practice opening attachments.

3 Send yourself e-mail with embedded HTML.

4 Set up WebTV to Fetch e-mail from another Internet service account.

5 Send a Web page to yourself.

✔ You're not sure what is the best time of day to set your WebTV unit for automatic retrieval of your e-mail. You try several times-of-day, but discover that one hour before you usually use your WebTV is better than any other time for you.

✔ Your friend asks you to send a letter with a photo attachment so that he can experiment and find out whether he can open it.

Visual Quiz

What happens when you activate **To:**?

_____

_____

_____

_____

_____

_____

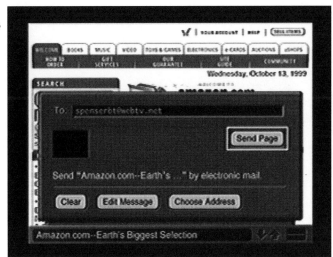

CHAPTER 13

MASTER THESE SKILLS

▶ Finding an E-Mail List with ListServ

▶ Joining an E-Mail List with ListServ

▶ Finding an E-Mail List with Liszt

▶ Leaving an E-Mail List

Joining E-Mail Lists

E-Mail lists enable you to share your interests and experiences. With an e-mail list, you can find and interact with people with similar backgrounds, with an interest in similar issues, or with similar skills and resources. Are you a gardener? Wine enthusiast? Antiquer? Mother-to-be? New grandparent? Do you have arthritis? Allergies? Chronic fatigue? Are you recovering from cancer? Do you want to know more about your heritage? Your genealogy? Folk tales and music of your culture? There are as many e-mail lists as there are interests and interested people to discuss them.

The Internet is a social gathering place. Instead of communicating face-to-face, people communicate using computers and phone lines. E-mail lists enable people to join together based on shared interests to interact, learn, and grow.

Joining an e-mail list is like joining a conversation. People discuss issues back and forth, ask questions, provide answers, and so forth. All messages sent to the main list address are distributed to all members of the list. Lists are usually unmoderated and without much in the way of rules. Once you join the list, you can jump into the conversation any time you are ready to.

E-mail lists may be high- or low-volume. My June 1997 Mommies list often received 100 messages per day. There is no way to "sort" through the messages as you can with Usenet newsgroups. Instead, every message arrives in your mailbox indistinguishable from others until you read them. People sometimes find they must unsubscribe from high-volume mail lists because of the time demands required to read each message.

Joining an e-mail list, however, can be a wonderful and uplifting experience. There are friends to be made, information to be found, and experiences to be shared.

This chapter shows you how to find an e-mail list that matches your interests. Although it focuses on ListServ and Liszt, you learn to find, subscribe, and unsubscribe to e-mail lists that interest you.

Finding an E-Mail List with ListServ

There are many e-mail lists on the Internet. ListServ, in addition to hosting many excellent mail lists, provides one of the most comprehensive collections of mail lists that you can search through. Or you can send a letter to the main ListServ server to discover which lists match your interests.

The ListServ server is found at listserv@listserv.net. To search for a topic, you can send an e-mail to this address. The message (not the Subject line) must read "list global *topic*." In the example on the facing pages, the search is performed on the word *garden*. Send this letter off and you will soon receive a list of related e-mail lists.

When searching, less specific is better than more specific. Searching for *garden* is far superior to searching for *gardens*. This enables the list server to detect more lists that contain the word. For example, searching for *garden* will produce lists with the phrases *gardening, gardens, garden tips,* and so forth. The first and third of these would be ignored if you chose *gardens* as your topic. You can use word fragments, such as *gard*, as well as entire words.

Once the list server has searched through its database of e-mail lists, it sends a reply. This reply will include a list of matching discussion groups and directions for subscribing.

ListServ also provides an excellent World Wide Web interface. Visit **http://www.listserv.net/lists/list_q.html** to search through their catalog online. Enter a search phrase to the right of **Look for:** and activate **Start the Search!** ListServ will create a Web screen that lists each mail list that matches your search phrase.

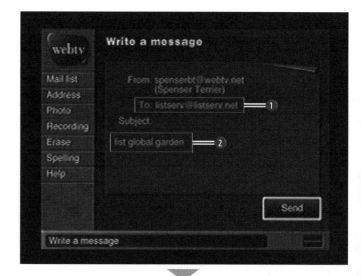

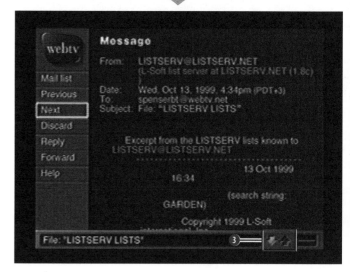

❶ *Send a message to listserv@listserv.net.*

❷ *The message should read "list global topic." This example will search for all e-mail lists whose names or descriptions include "garden."*

❸ *The reply from the list server may initially appear cryptic. Use Scroll Down to see more.*

CROSS-REFERENCE

Learn how to find a list using the Liszt server in the next topic.

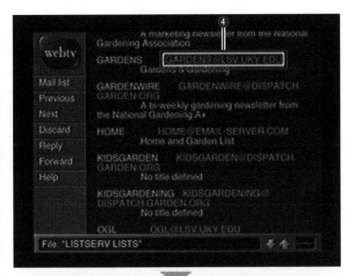

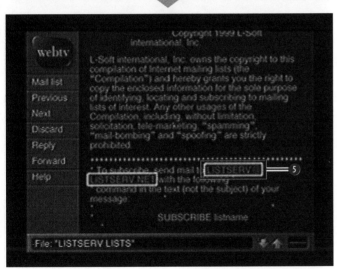

4 Read through the entire message to see if there is a list that interests you. For example, the "Gardens and Gardening" list seems a good match to our "Garden" query.

5 The list server message includes instructions on subscribing to the list you choose. In this case, it directs you to send e-mail to listserv@listserv.net containing the message Subscribe listname. (Replace listname with the name of the list that you'd like to join.)

TAKE NOTE

▶ IF AT FIRST . . .

Although one of the largest e-mail list providers, ListServ is certainly not unique. The next topic discusses using the Liszt Web site to find other mail lists. Many other mail list opportunities exist. A friend may send you a message and mention a new list. Some lists are created and maintained by members of Usenet newsgroups.

▶ COSTS

Membership in e-mail lists is almost universally free. Some professional organizations will not let you join an e-mail list unless you are a member. Still, you are unlikely to even know about such lists unless you are already a member.

▶ CREATING YOUR OWN LIST

You can create your own e-mail list, if you wish. Contact a list server (such as ListServ) for further information. Be aware that there are usually nominal fees associated with creating and maintaining an e-mail list.

FIND IT ONLINE

Read more about it. Visit **http://www.topchoice.com/ ~psyche/lists/index.html**.

Joining an E-Mail List with ListServ

To subscribe to a listserv e-mail list, send your subscription request to the worldwide list server at listserv@listserv.net. This server will get in contact with the local server that hosts the list you are interested in. You will be sent a preliminary acceptance letter and be prompted to confirm your subscription. To do so, you need only reply with a simple "ok" message.

Once you have confirmed your subscription, sit back and wait. You will receive a series of letters that reconfirm and welcome you to your new list. These letters provide hints on how best to use and enjoy your new e-mail list membership. Read these messages carefully and save them to your WebTV storage. You will need to refer to these letters if you ever decide to unsubscribe from the list.

After joining an e-mail list, take time to sit back and "lurk." Lurking means reading an e-mail list without actively participating. Taking time to lurk enables you to sense the social temperature of the e-mail list before jumping in. You avoid making gaffes if you spend a little time observing before making your first post.

When you are ready to write your first post to the e-mail list, consider writing an introductory piece. Tell people who you are, that you are new to the list, and what you hope list membership will do for you. Almost always, you will receive a flood of warm welcomes and wishes for a productive stay in the list.

Remember that joining an e-mail list is like joining a club of people. What you get out of it is a combination of what you put into it and your willingness to be tolerant of personal quirks.

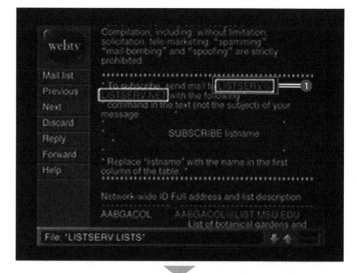

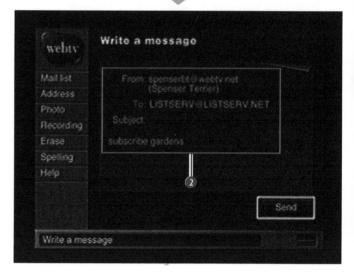

❶ When you search for a list of interest, as discussed in the first topic of this chapter, ListServ includes subscription instructions.

❷ Send a message to listserv@listserv.net, saying "subscribe list-name." For this example, write **subscribe gardens.**

CROSS-REFERENCE

Learn how to find a list using the ListServ server earlier in this chapter.

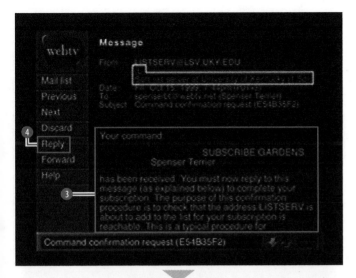

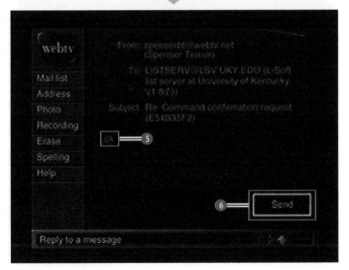

TAKE NOTE

SEND A LETTER

To send a letter to the list, address your message to the list address (in this case, gardens@lsv.uky.edu). Your letter will be distributed to all members of the gardening list. Do not send on-topic letters to list-serv@listserv.net. Similarly, do not send subscrip-tion/information requests to the gardening list.

PLAY BY THE RULES

Usually, you will receive a welcome letter on sub-scribing to a list. These welcome letters often con-tain tips and pointers for list participation. Pay attention to these rules and follow them. You may be told what are acceptable topics for conversation, how to deal with offensive posts, how to be toler-ant of others, how to limit your signatures, and so forth. Following these rules makes e-mail list partic-ipation more pleasant for everyone.

WANT MORE HELP?

Send the message "LISTSERV REFCARD" to listserv@listserv.net to receive more help about us-ing a listserv mailing list.

③ The list server sends a "please confirm" letter. This includes complete instructions on how to confirm your subscription.

④ Activate **Reply**.

⑤ Your message to confirm is the single word "ok."

⑥ Activate **Send**.

FIND IT ONLINE

Read more about subscribing to a ListServ list at **http://www.topchoice.com/~psyche/lists/subscribe. html**.

Finding an E-Mail List with Liszt

Like the ListServ Web site, the Liszt Web site is simple to use and easy to understand. Liszt will find numerous e-mail lists to match your interests and provide exhaustive and simple-to-follow instructions for subscribing, unsubscribing, and so forth. Because these instructions vary by the list, I do not detail the intricacies of list how-to. Instead, you should refer to the Liszt Web site to find the details that apply to the list in which you are interested.

Liszt provides tens of thousands of lists for you to search through and join. Start by typing a search phrase and activating **go**. Liszt will find any list whose name or description matches your search phrase. Always be general. *Antique* is a better search phrase than *Antiques* and *Antiqu* is better than the previous two. *Antiqu* will find e-mail lists about *antiquing* (that is, shopping for antiques) as well as discussion about antiques in general. The missing "e" gives greater search flexibility while retaining enough specifics to limit the search to relevant topics.

Once you find an interesting list, activate it. Liszt will provide the precise information on joining, managing, and leaving the list of your interest.

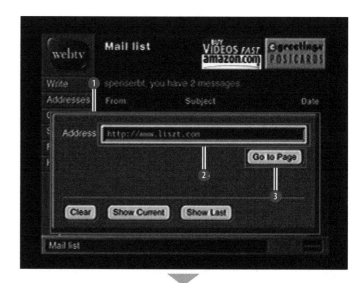

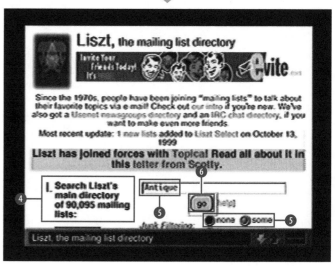

❶ Press Go on the remote control or Return on the keyboard to bring up the special World Wide Web address window.

❷ Type **www.liszt.com**.

❸ Move the yellow box to the Go to Page button and activate it.

❹ The Liszt Web site gives you access to almost 100,000 mail lists.

❺ Enter a search topic. Choose a setting for Junk Filtering and Find groups matching.

❻ Activate **go**.

CROSS-REFERENCE

Learn about ListServ e-mail lists in preceding topics in this chapter.

TAKE NOTE

▶ BE RELEVANT

When taking part in mail list discussions, be relevant. Replying to a message with **I agree** or **Me too** can send unnecessary mail to hundreds of people. If you wish to send a message of support, send it directly to the person who posted the original message. They will appreciate it and you will not burden the list with unnecessary traffic.

▶ USE CONTEXT

When replying to e-mail list letters, include context in your reply. Receiving a message that says, "Right, except you mean arms instead of limbs," makes no sense on its own. Consider, instead, "Jeremy wrote about finding multilimbed chandeliers. I think he meant to say multiarmed instead."

▶ BE TOLERANT

Misspellings and grammatical mistakes are part and parcel of e-mail communication. Do not distract from on-topic discussions by pointing out others' errors. Shaming others in public — and an e-mail list is a public forum — is never a good idea.

▶ LURK BEFORE YOU TALK

Always lurk before making your first posting to an e-mail list. Lurking, or reading the group without participating, enables you time to sense the e-mail list's social temperament before jumping in.

⑦ *Liszt found a large number of lists, including nine Select, or recommended, lists about antiques. Use the scroll buttons to see them all.*

⑧ *Activate a list, in this case "antique-collect" to find out more about it.*

⑨ *Liszt provides information about the list you chose and easy-to-follow instructions for subscribing.*

FIND IT ONLINE

Try it yourself. Visit **http://www.liszt.com**.

Leaving an E-mail List

People leave e-mail lists for all sorts of reasons. Katherine Nagel (katnagel@eznet.net) has written the scathingly funny "Natural Life Cycle of Mailing Lists," which I quote below. This essay not only explains typical list social dynamics, but also offers tremendous insight into exactly why people leave e-mail lists. She describes the steps through which a list evolves.

A thread is a flow of e-mail conversation on a single subject. For example, one might find threads on "quilting techniques," "sewing supplies," and "recycling fabric" when reading a handcrafts-themed mail list. A "newbie," unsurprisingly, refers to a person new to the mail list.

"1 — Initial enthusiasm (people introduce themselves, and gush a lot about how wonderful it is to find kindred souls).

"2 — Evangelism (people moan about how few folks are posting to the list and brainstorm recruitment strategies).

"3 — Growth (more and more people join, more and more lengthy threads develop, occasional off-topic threads pop up).

"4 — Community (lots of threads, some more relevant than others; lots of information and advice is exchanged; experts help other experts as well as less experienced colleagues; friendships develop; people tease each other; newcomers are welcomed with generosity and patience; everyone — newbie and expert alike — feels comfortable asking questions, suggesting answers, and sharing opinions).

"5 — Discomfort with diversity (the number of messages increases dramatically; not every thread is fascinating to every reader; people start complaining about the signal-to-noise ratio; person 1 threatens to quit if *other* people don't limit discussion to person 1's pet

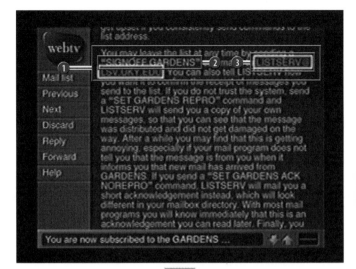

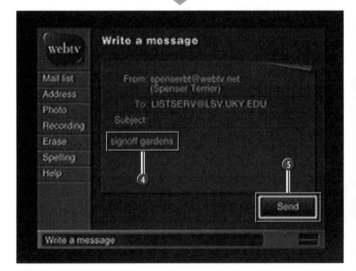

① Most list servers include signoff instructions in their "Welcome" message. Be sure to keep this message around for reference.

② Note the unsubscribe command. You need this for the next step.

③ Highlight the list server address and activate it with Go to send a message.

④ Move the cursor to the message area below the "Subject:" line and type the unsubscribe command.

⑤ Move the yellow box to **Send** and press Go on the remote or Return on the keyboard.

CROSS-REFERENCE

Learn about joining an e-mail list earlier in this chapter.

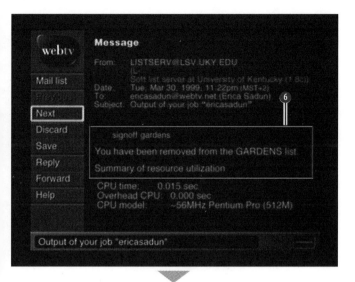

topic; person 2 agrees with person 1; person 3 tells 1 and 2 to lighten up; more bandwidth is wasted complaining about off-topic threads than is used for the threads themselves; everyone gets annoyed).

"6 — Smug complacency and stagnation (the purists flame everyone who asks an 'old' question or responds with humor to a serious post; newbies are rebuffed; traffic drops to a doze-producing level of a few minor issues; all interesting discussions happen by private e-mail and are limited to a few participants; the purists spend lots of time self-righteously congratulating each other on keeping off-topic threads off the list). OR

"7 — Maturity (a few people quit in a huff; the rest of the participants stay near stage 4, with stage 5 popping up briefly every few weeks; many people wear out their second or third 'delete' key, but the list lives contentedly ever after)."

⑥ The list server will send you a signoff confirmation.

TAKE NOTE

▶ **NOMAIL**

If you are happy with your e-mail list, but need to go on vacation, or just need a break, consider setting your subscription to "NoMail." Send a message to the list server along the lines of "Set Gardening NoMail." This command varies by list server, so be sure to check for proper syntax! When you are ready to return to the list, send another e-mail message to your list server, resetting your subscription to "Mail."

FIND IT ONLINE

Read more about it. Visit **http://www.topchoice.com/~psyche/lists/unsub.html**.

Personal Workbook

Q&A

1 What is the difference between an administrative address and a list address?

_____

_____

_____

2 Which search term will find more lists: _Bicyc_ or _Bicycling_?

_____

_____

_____

3 What is _lurking?_

_____

_____

_____

4 What is a _mail list digest?_

_____

_____

_____

5 Why might some people prefer digests?

_____

_____

_____

6 Which is better: Liszt or ListServ?

_____

_____

_____

7 How can you temporarily stop mail from your mail list if you have to go away from your WebTV unit for a period of days or weeks?

_____

_____

_____

8 If you unsubscribe from a list, can you resubscribe to it at another time?

_____

_____

_____

ANSWERS: PAGE 340

EXTRA PRACTICE

① Search for lists that contain the search string "cycl."

② Search for a list that you'd be interested in.

③ Subscribe to an e-mail list.

④ Set an e-mail list subscription to digest and then back.

⑤ Set your list subscription to NoMail and then back to Mail.

⑥ Unsubscribe to an e-mail list.

REAL-WORLD APPLICATIONS

✔ You make a list of your hobbies and special interests. Curious about mail lists, you search Liszt and ListServ to see how many e-mail lists match your interests.

✔ To keep abreast of changes in your professional field, you would like to receive current information and opinions about your line of work. You check with your professional organizations to see if they sponsor e-mail lists. You subscribe to one that discusses standards and practices.

Visual Quiz

This is part of Liszt search for "Opera." How would you narrow the search to find lists likely to interest a soap opera enthusiast?

_____

_____

_____

_____

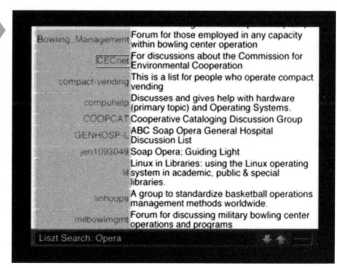

PART

IV

CHAPTER **14** **Introducing WebTV Centers**

15 **Watching TV with WebTV**

16 **Building Community**

17 **Administrating Your WebTV Account**

Making the Most of WebTV

The WebTV experience goes beyond e-mail and the World Wide Web. WebTV provides many varied features that give you instant access to breaking news and weather, enhance your television watching experience, and link you to the "real-time" Internet. If you are using your WebTV account primarily to read and send electronic mail or to surf the Web, you may want to learn more about these exciting features that expand and enhance your WebTV experience.

The first chapter in this section introduces you to WebTV Centers. This innovation provides you with a personal news-clipping service. WebTV Centers enable you to stay on top of the news, weather, finances, sports, and entertainment that you want to track. WebTV Centers enable you to pick stocks and sports teams, and to follow their latest market values and scores.

The second chapter shows you how to expand your television-watching experience with WebTV. WebTV's TV Home gives you immediate access to listings and program information. You can use your WebTV Plus unit to enjoy picture-in-picture programming, even if your television is not set up for picture-in-picture. With TV Home you can set program reminders and even schedule your VCR to automatically record television shows for you! WebTV's TV Home really puts the TV back into WebTV.

The third chapter teaches you to connect to the lively and active Internet community. Whether you are interested in meeting people real-time or joining ongoing Usenet newsgroup discussions, this chapter shows you the ropes of reaching out Internet-style.

The fourth, and final, chapter gives you a tour of skills needed to run your WebTV account. You learn to add or remove secondary users, change system settings, or just get help. Sometimes you have to get to the heart of the WebTV system to accomplish things, and this chapter provides a gentle introduction to WebTV's administrative features.

This section covers a variety of features and how-to topics. You go beyond e-mail and beyond the World Wide Web. When you have mastered the skills in this section, you can truly say that you have made the most of WebTV.

CHAPTER **14**

MASTER
THESE
SKILLS

▶ **Using WebTV Centers**

▶ **Using WebTV Entertainment**

▶ **Reading a News Story**

▶ **Customizing WebTV News**

▶ **Customizing Money**

▶ **Customizing Weather**

▶ **Customizing Sports**

▶ **Shopping Online**

Introducing WebTV Centers

The WebTV Centers feature furnishes you with your own personalized news-clipping service. You can monitor world news headlines, keep on top of your stocks, check the weather for your part of the world, read the latest movie reviews, or catch late-breaking sports scores. Just tell WebTV Centers which topics you want (and do not want) to track.

In this chapter, you learn to use WebTV Centers to discover late-breaking information. You learn to find the story behind a news, entertainment, or sports headline. WebTV Centers connect to some of the most powerful news servers on the World Wide Web. By taking advantage of its links to these servers, you discover the full details of the topics that interest you.

Also in this chapter, you learn to customize WebTV Centers. You can select business headlines and/or world news. You learn to choose hockey and/or baseball scores. You see how WebTV Centers can track the episodes of your favorite television show and tell you what shows are coming up in the week ahead. You learn to add stocks to your "stock watch" portfolio and to receive weather updates for your city.

WebTV Centers are extremely flexible. The main options screen enables you to choose which sections to see and what order to see them in. Furthermore, each section — sports, weathers, news, money, and entertainment — permits individual customization. For example, the financial topic permits you to track up to 75 individual stocks.

Do your secondary users have interests different than yours? Like mail, each user's profile is kept separately and privately. The way each user on your account customizes his or her WebTV Centers home page is preserved uniquely for that person.

Despite its apparent simplicity, WebTV Centers provide surprisingly flexible and powerful tools. Best of all, the WebTV Centers service is included free in your subscription charge.

Using WebTV Centers

WebTV provides up-to-date news, weather, sports, and entertainment reports with its WebTV Centers feature. WebTV Today enables you to access your WebTV Centers from one convenient location. With WebTV News you have a personal clipping service that looks out for the news and features you want monitored.

WebTV Centers operates in two ways. First, you can look at the WebTV Centers hotline feature, which appears in the middle of your home page. Second, you can visit the WebTV Today home page.

The hotline appears in the center of your home page. This area extends from the left margin to about a third of the way from the right. This area acts like the streaming news feed at Times Square, showing rotating news bites from each of the Centers.

Whenever you visit your home page, the hotline automatically updates. News bites might include headline news, current weather forecasts, and so forth. These updates change every few seconds whenever your home page is displayed. This part of WebTV Centers works on its own without any intervention on your part. If you wish to see all the news in the Center currently being displayed, move the yellow box to the hotline area and activate it with the Go button or the Return key.

You could also move the yellow box to the WebTV Today or a particular Center's item in the WebTV Centers list below the WebTV hotline part of the screen when you wish to get a cumulative overview or visit a specific Center.

The WebTV Today home page consists of links to some selected feature articles and a summary of the main news in each of the other five Centers.

▶ At your Web Home page, the WebTV Today Center is the first item in the list of Centers at the bottom.

❶ Move the yellow box to highlight the WebTV Today box and press Go on your remote control to go to your WebTV Today page.

❷ WebTV Today shows the news that you want to see. Scroll down the page to see what's happening in the various Centers. Or click one of the Centers to go there and read more of the headline story.

CROSS-REFERENCE

Need to customize WebTV Today? Instructions follow in the next few topics.

In the next few topics, you learn to customize each Center (except Entertainment) to fit your interests. For example, there's no need to read baseball scores if what you're after is hockey or basketball.

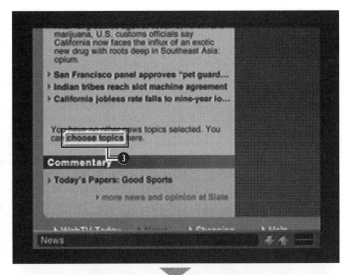

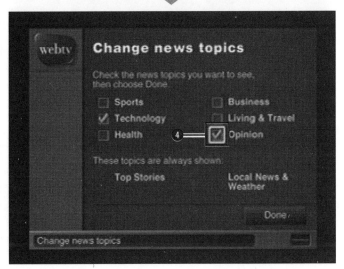

TAKE NOTE

▶ RELOAD FOR THE LATEST INFORMATION

Want to check for the latest information, stock quotes, etc? Press and hold the ⌘ key while typing R to reload your WebTV Today home page with the latest information or press the Option button and select the Reload item. Fifteen-minute delayed stock quotes are updated every 20 minutes. Use this re-load feature to keep on top of the market.

▶ DON'T FORGET TIME ZONES

Is the Dow Jones average "stuck"? Don't forget about time zones, weekends, and holidays. Stock market information is updated only during active Wall Street trading times.

▶ WEBTV CLASSIC

Both WebTV Classic and WebTV Plus support WebTV Today.

③ *Top Stories and Local News & Weather are always displayed. If you would like to display headlines of other news topics, activate the* **choose topics** *link.*

④ *Choose from the list of news topics you would like displayed. Place a check mark next to the ones you want by moving the yellow box and pressing Go.*

FIND IT ONLINE

Visit ABC News at **http://www.abcnews.com.**

Using WebTV Entertainment

The least customizable of the WebTV Centers is the Entertainment. As with each of the other Centers, you have a Feature and Top Stories at the top of the Entertainment page. Entertainment's Top Stories come from E! Online, the Internet side of cable's E! channel.

Although customization is not available, you are tied into E! Online's search engine. If you want to find out about a specific celebrity, type their name into the FIND A CELEBRITY box, select the Find button to its right, and click Go. Do you want to know about a movie, where it's playing, or what the top box office attractions are? Scroll down to New Movies In Theaters and use the Find box and buttons there. Similarly, if you want to find out about what is available on video, scroll down to New Movies on Video and follow the same procedure. Are music CDs your thing? The drill is the same. Finally, the top three fiction bestsellers are listed or you can go to Shopping to find out about more books.

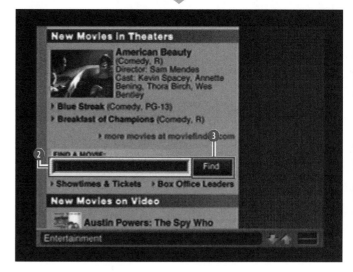

▶ On your home page, select Entertainment with the yellow box and activate it by pressing Go on your remote control. This will take you to the WebTV Entertainment Center.

❶ Select a headline of interest to you or select more news at E! Online with the yellow box and press Go or Return.

❷ Type in the name of a movie you wish to find under New Movies in Theaters.

❸ Select Find with the yellow box and press Go or Return.

CROSS-REFERENCE

Want to select WebTV Today for a collected overview of the Centers? See the previous topic.

TAKE NOTE

▶ **FINDING A MOVIE**

Movies in theaters are linked to the Internet site, moviefinder.com

▶ **WEBTV CLASSIC**

Both WebTV Classic and WebTV Plus support WebTV Entertainment.

❹ Scroll down to New Music CDs and select one of the featured titles.

❺ Alternatively, select **more music in Shopping** with the yellow box and press Go or Return.

❻ If you want to know what the top titles on Billboard's charts are, select Chart Toppers and press Go or Return.

FIND IT ONLINE

Are classic movies more your speed, look at **http:// spotlight.about.com/classicmovies**.

Reading a News Story

Not only does WebTV News show you the headlines, it allows you to read more about them. When a story catches your eye, you can pull up the article behind it. Move the yellow box to a headline and activate it by pressing Go or Return.

WebTV News headlines and news stories are supplied by MSNBC. When you activate a headline, you automatically move to the MSNBC news site on the World Wide Web. At this site, you can read the full article, discover related pieces, search for further information, rate stories, and so forth.

At the MSNBC site, news features typically begin with a large-font summary and a picture. At the bottom of the summary, is the option to view the COMPLETE STORY. Activate this to view the rest of the article. Use the Scroll up and Scroll down buttons to fully view the summary and article.

When WebTV moves you to a different part of a page, you may encounter a "ragged edge" effect. This looks like part of the screen has been "torn." If you see this, it means that you have moved to another part of the article. WebTV uses this effect to differentiate moving between parts of a page and moving between separate pages.

At the bottom of an article is found a collection of related items. These may include older versions of a breaking story, or support materials, or extra discussions. If interested, you can activate these with the yellow box and Go or Return.

To read the article behind another headline, use the Back button to return to WebTV News.

❶ On your home page, select **News** with the yellow box and activate it by pressing Go on your remote control. This will take you to the WebTV News page.

❷ Select a headline of interest to you with the yellow box and press Go or Return.

CROSS-REFERENCE

Read more about the World Wide Web in Section II.

TAKE NOTE

RATE THE STORIES

MSNBC enables you to rate stories on a scale from 1 (not useful) to 7 (extremely useful). When you rate a story, you are shown a list of features to which other people have given top ratings. This enables you to choose and read those stories that other people have rated highly.

TIME PASSES

Sometimes (especially on a heavy news day), it may take a while to connect to the MSNBC news page. If it takes too long, WebTV gives you the option of trying again or picking another activity.

CHANGE YOUR MIND

WebTV calls the host of a Web page a "publisher." You can press Back at any time while waiting for the publisher to be contacted. You may be bored, or you may have changed your mind, or you may have chosen a headline in error. You need never wait for the Web page to actually load before choosing to stop and go back.

WEBTV CLASSIC

Both WebTV Classic and WebTV Plus support WebTV News.

③ MSNBC articles begin with a summary and a picture. Scroll down to see the rest of the summary.

▶ At the bottom of the summary, activate **COMPLETE STORY** to see the full article.

④ As the complete article displays, use the scroll keys to move up and down through the story.

FIND IT ONLINE

You can visit MSNBC directly. Stop by
http://www.msnbc.com.

Customizing WebTV News

Customize WebTV News to show only those topics you want to read. As of summer 1999, optional topics supplied by the MSNBC news feed include Business, Technology, Sports, Opinion, Health, and Living & Travel. You can choose to monitor any, or all, of these in addition to Top Stories and Local News & Weather, which are always presented.

Only the two standard topics plus the optional topics you choose appear under the WebTV news banner. If you have interests in Business and Technology but don't care for Sports news, then turn the Sports news feature off. The example on the facing page shows how to do this.

Although the Sports, Business, and Living & Travel sections do provide some overlap with other WebTV centers, the MSNBC coverage may still prove helpful. Consider the differences in coverage before disabling these topics. For example, the MSNBC Business section provides coverage of global financial happenings. Contrast this with the stock quotes shown in the WebTV Financial section. Do you want to know if Dennis Rodman has signed a new contract? You will not find out by looking at basketball scores in WebTV Sports. Remember that each section provides a different spin on the news and that each news provider provides a different content.

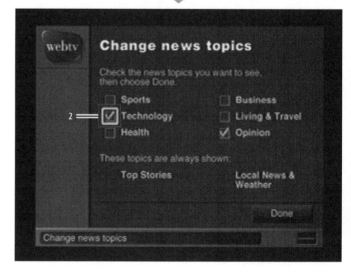

▶ This example shows how to remove the Technology headlines.

❶ Starting at your WebTV News page, activate **choose topics**.

❷ Move the yellow box to the check mark to the left of Technology and remove the check by pressing Go or Return.

CROSS-REFERENCE

Want to select WebTV Today features? See the first topic of this chapter.

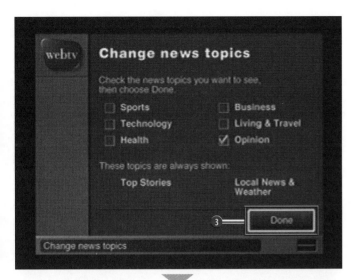

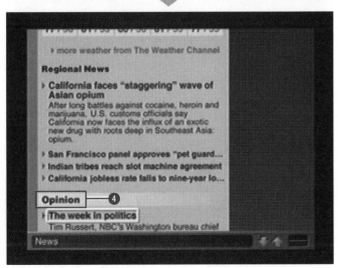

TAKE NOTE

▶ **OVERLAP**

Do not confuse the Sports, Business, and Weather topics with the WebTV centers of similar names. News topics are all furnished directly by MSNBC. The other WebTV centers have different information providers.

▶ **REVERSIBILITY**

Any choice you make is reversible. Did you turn the sports headlines off? You can always turn them back on when you change your mind.

▶ **UPDATES**

News headlines are updated about every two hours.

▶ **WEBTV CLASSIC**

You can customize WebTV news topics from MSNBC with both WebTV Classic and WebTV Plus.

3 When you have checked (or unchecked) all of the news topics you are interested in (or not interested in), activate **Done**.

4 The Technology headlines have been removed. Your WebTV News page now begins with Opinion headlines after the omnipresent topics.

FIND IT ONLINE

To find out how often news is updated on WebTV, visit **http://help.webtv.net/mywebtv/updates.html**.

Customizing Money

Customize WebTV Money to track your current stock portfolio. WebTV updates stock quotes every 20 minutes or so. You can keep on top of your net worth and plan your buy and sell orders.

Adding to and removing stocks from WebTV Money is a simple matter of a few steps. Start by activating **choose stocks**. Enter the name or stock market symbol of a company and activate **Add**. The new company is added to your list of active stocks to track. If you have more stocks to track, type the name of each company and **add** each, one at a time.

If you add a stock by accident, or wish to remove a stock of longer standing, remove the check mark that appears to the left of the company name. Move the yellow box to the check and press either Go or Return. You can uncheck several boxes on the list at the same time.

Once you have added all your new stocks and unchecked all the old stocks you wish removed, activate **Done**. This updates your current list of stocks and finishes your customization.

My WebTV periodically displays stock information on your WebTV home page. This presentation shows three pieces of information about stocks: their symbol, their current value, and the change in their value since the beginning of the trading day.

WebTV stock quotes come from MSNInvestor. WebTV provides this service for free with your account. Stock quotes are, however, delayed by 20 minutes. Remember this when you prepare your buy orders!

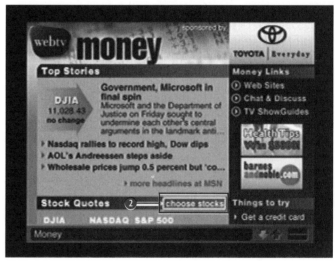

❶ From your WebTV home page, choose Money.

❷ Activate choose stocks on the Stock Quotes banner.

CROSS-REFERENCE

Want to select My WebTV news, entertainment, and sports features? See other topics in this chapter.

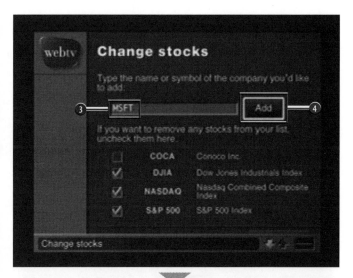

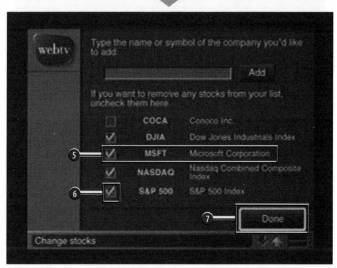

▶ RELOAD

WebTV updates stock quotes every 20 minutes. However, your screen will not automatically update and refresh when new stock quotes are available. You can force a refresh by pressing and holding the cmd button while typing R. This cmd+R combination can be used at any time anywhere on WebTV to refresh a screen and retrieve the latest content.

▶ REVERSIBILITY

Any stock choices you make are reversible. Did you add a stock you didn't intend to? You can always get rid of a stock you don't want or add a stock you do want.

▶ HOW MANY QUOTES

You can select up to 75 stocks to track with WebTV Money. Three stock quotes will appear at a time on the rotating WebTV Centers bar on your WebTV home page.

▶ WEBTV CLASSIC

Both WebTV Classic and WebTV Plus present stock quotes through WebTV Money.

❸ On the Change stocks screen, type in either the name or stock market symbol of a company that you want to add to your display.

❹ Move the yellow box to **Add** and press Go or Return.

❺ The new company appears in your list of stocks.

❻ (Optional) to remove a stock from your list, move the yellow box to the box before the stock's name and press Go to remove the check mark.

❼ When you have added and/or removed all the stocks you wish to, activate **Done**.

FIND IT ONLINE

Do the Dow! Visit **http://www.dowjones.com**.

Customizing Weather

Are you curious about the weather in a far-off city? Going on a trip? Have you moved? WebTV News enables you to display weather forecasts for your own city or any other.

Start by activating **choose city** on the Local News & Weather banner of your WebTV News page. When presented with the Change City page, type in the city's name or ZIP code. Activate **Done** and WebTV updates the forecast for you. That's all you need to do to check the weather in any city.

WebTV provides a five-day forecast for whichever city you pick. The information is provided directly from the Weather Channel. You see predicted highs and lows, and a general forecast. This forecast takes the form of a picture. These pictures are fairly straightforward. A sun means sunny weather. A rain cloud predicts rain. A thunderbolt indicates a thunderstorm. A snowflake means snow. These pictures were designed to provide quick and easy identification of weather patterns.

Further details about the weather are provided in the rotating WebTV Centers panel in the middle of your WebTV home page. There, you can find the current temperature, humidity, and so forth, as well as near-term forecasts for your area.

You can refresh your WebTV News screen to see the latest weather updates. You can force a refresh by pressing and holding ⌘ while typing R. This ⌘+R combination can be used at any time anywhere on WebTV to refresh a screen and retrieve the latest content.

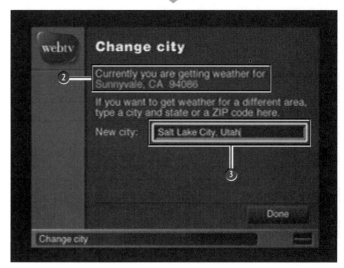

❶ From the WebTV News page, scroll down to the Weather display. Activate **choose city** at the top right of the Local News and Weather display title.

❷ On the Change city screen, WebTV tells you the city for which you are currently getting weather.

❸ Below, in the **New city:** line, type in either the name of a U.S. city and state or its ZIP code.

CROSS-REFERENCE

Learn about WebTV's Around Town feature later in Section IV.

WebTV weather is powered by the Weather Channel. The Weather Channel, which operates out of Atlanta, Georgia, provides up-to-the-minute forecasts for all U.S. cities serviced by WebTV. Unfortunately, you cannot, at this time, select Rome, Italy or Toronto, Canada as your home city.

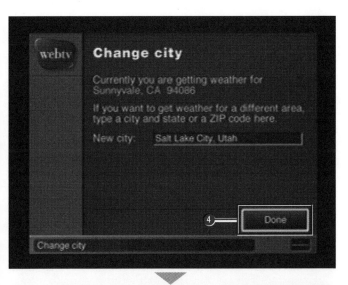

4 Activate **Done**.

5 You now see the five-day weather forecast for your newly chosen city.

TAKE NOTE

▶ **UPDATES**

WebTV updates the weather forecast every few hours.

▶ **VISIT THE WEATHER CHANNEL**

You can visit the Weather Channel by moving the yellow box to the more weather from The Weather Channel (below your five-day forecast) and pressing Go or Return.

▶ **WEBTV CLASSIC**

Both WebTV Classic and WebTV Plus provide weather forecasts and updates through WebTV News.

FIND IT ONLINE

Want to know more about your hometown? Visit
http://help.webtv.net/surfing/specificinfo.html.

Customizing Sports

WebTV gives you the latest in sports scores. CBS Sports Line provides the latest scores for hockey, football, basketball, and baseball. Customizing Sports involves few steps. Activate **Change sports**. Select the topics that you wish to track and activate **Done**. That's all.

The whole sports story

"Seattle 113, LA Lakers 109." Is that all? Isn't there more to the story? If getting the final scores is not enough for you, you can pull up the whole sports summary, blow by blow. Move the yellow box to the score that interests you and activate the story by pressing Go or Return. You automatically move to CBS Sports Line to get the full article. Learn how Gary Payton scored 33 points with 9 assists as the Sonics held off the Lakers.

More than Scores

What? You want to know who's the leading rusher on the Saints, who's playing the Broncos in two weeks, or where the Orioles are in the American League pennant race? Scroll down to the banner for the sport in which you're interested, move the yellow box to either Standings, Schedules, or Stats and press Go or Return. You'll find out what you wish to know.

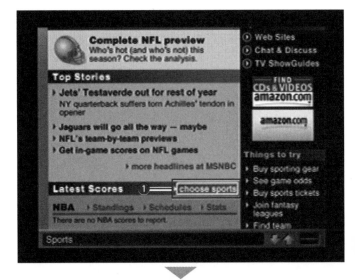

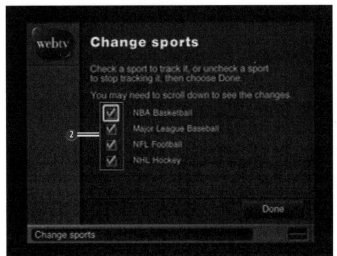

❶ To customize the Sports listings in your WebTV Sports page, activate **choose sports** at the right of the Latest Scores title.

❷ Select the sports that you wish to track. Your choices include NBA Basketball, Major League Baseball, NFL Football, and NHL Hockey.

CROSS-REFERENCE

Found an interesting article and want to send it to someone? Read about mailing a Web page in Section II.

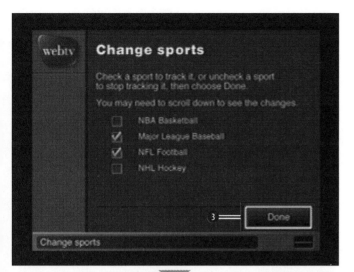

TAKE NOTE

▶ UPDATES

WebTV gets its scores from CBS Sportsline and they are updated frequently. The features and Top Stories are updated daily.

▶ WEBTV CLASSIC

Both WebTV Classic and WebTV Plus provide sports information through WebTV Centers.

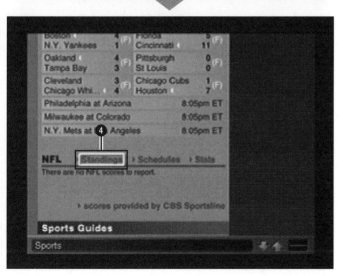

③ *Activate **Done**.*

④ *If you're interested in more than just the scores, move the yellow box to a Sports Guide of interest and click Go or Return.*

FIND IT ONLINE

Want to get up-to-date sports news from CNN and *Sports Illustrated* online? Visit **http://www.cnnsi.com**.

Shopping Online

Online shopping, eCommerce, is the latest rage. Congress and the states are struggling with how and whether to regulate it and most everyone concedes it is one of the fastest growing phenomena on the Internet. WebTV has established an online mall in its Centers, called Shopping.

In shopping you'll find links to hundreds of on-line stores selling all kinds of merchandise, including books, jewelry, food, clothing, toys, and more.

WebTV offers a shopping guarantee to make your online shopping a virtually worry-free experience.

A slightly different center

All of the other WebTV Centers start out with a Feature and Top Stories. Shopping gives you a variation on the theme with featured Specials at the top.

WebTV has certain partner merchants and you're presented with links to their sites along the right side of the screen.

You want something different?

Are you looking for a pet, garden supplies, a florist, or to buy a car? These categories and over a dozen more are available in Shopping. Just move the yellow box to the general category and press Go. You'll be brought to a screen where you can further refine your search within that category.

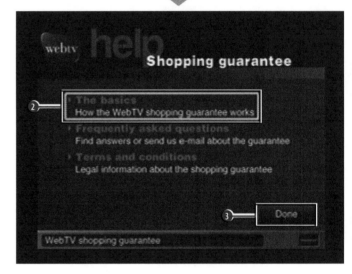

▶ Choose Shopping on your WebTV Home page and press Go to get here.

❶ Select the **WebTV Shopping Guarantee** and press Go or Return.

❷ Select one of the topics and press Go for more information.

❸ When you're done exploring the Guarantee, activate **Done**.

CROSS-REFERENCE

If you want to just know the top movies on video, check out the Entertainment section of this chapter.

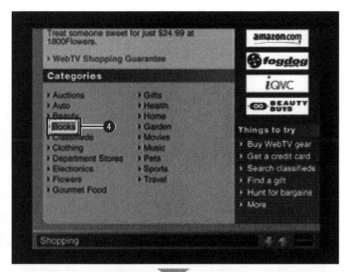

TAKE NOTE

▶ **THE GUARANTEE**

WebTV gives you protection against unauthorized charges when using their featured merchants. Read about it by selecting WebTV Shopping Guarantee just above the Categories heading and pressing Go.

▶ **WEBTV CLASSIC**

Both WebTV Classic and WebTV Plus support Shopping.

④ Back on the Shopping page, select a category of interest, such as Books, with the yellow box and press Go.

⑤ You'll be presented with a screen where you can search for a specific item in that category. In this case, it's the Barnes & Noble Web site.

FIND IT ONLINE

Want to get an online directory to online merchants, just go to **http://www.justshopping.com/**.

Personal Workbook

Q&A

1 How do you get to the WebTV Centers?

_____

_____

_____

2 What topics are covered in WebTV Centers?

_____

_____

_____

3 How do you choose which topics to track?

_____

_____

_____

4 What happens if you choose no topics to track?

_____

_____

_____

5 What are the two ways that you can use to specify a city for weather forecasts?

_____

_____

_____

6 Can you get weather forecasts for Canadian cities?

_____

_____

_____

7 How many stocks can you track at a time?

_____

_____

_____

8 How do you find the details behind a final sports score?

_____

_____

_____

ANSWERS: PAGE 340

Introducing WebTV Centers

EXTRA PRACTICE

1. Set the Weather for your home city.

2. Track the scores for Major League Baseball.

3. Check the latest stock prices for Microsoft.

4. Find out which videos are being released.

5. Read the latest news headlines.

REAL-WORLD APPLICATIONS\

✔ You are travelling to another city and want to pack the right sort of clothes. Use My WebTV to check the five-day forecast for that city and for other cities that you will be visiting.

✔ Your sports-nut brother-in-law is visiting. You sneak into the other room and use WebTV Centers to read the details of last night's Redskins win over the Cowboys. These details help convince him that you're a real sports fan after all.

✔ You want all the news that you can use but don't like reading newspapers. Read all the breaking headlines using WebTV Center's news coverage.

Visual Quiz

You are about to visit Salt Lake City on vacation. What should you pack?

_____

_____

_____

_____

_____

_____

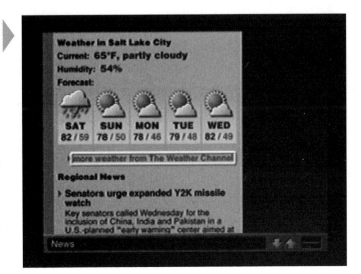

CHAPTER **15**

MASTER THESE SKILLS

▶ Exploring TV Home

▶ Retrieving TV Listings

▶ Retrieving TV Listings Automatically

▶ Selecting a Television Show

▶ Viewing TV Listings by Date and Time

▶ Searching TV Listings for a Show

▶ Searching TV Listings for a Type of Show

▶ Setting Up TV Favorites

▶ Using TV Favorites

▶ Selecting from Recently Viewed TV Shows

▶ Exploring Crossover Links

▶ Planning Television Viewing

▶ Controlling Your VCR with WebTV

Watching TV with WebTV

Most WebTV Classic users have asked the question: "So where's the TV in WebTV?" Happily, WebTV Plus has answered this question with many fully integrated television features. With WebTV Plus you can browse television program listings, schedule program reminders, set up a favorite-channels list, and link to Web sites about television shows.

This chapter covers a number of skills related to using your WebTV Plus unit with your television. You learn to take advantage of those features that enhance watching your favorite television programs.

This chapter starts by introducing WebTV's TV Home. In contrast to your Web Home, TV Home provides a starting place for watching and experiencing television.

Next, you learn to retrieve television program listings. WebTV provides schedules for antenna, satellite, and cable television systems. No matter how your television is configured, WebTV can probably provide a television schedule with full episode information.

You also learn to search through the television program listings to find the show you are interested in. WebTV enables you to search by name for particular shows. You may also browse listings by date and time. WebTV permits you to search for a type of show, such as a children's instructional program or science fiction movies. This flexibility enables you to set your viewing priorities in the way that best matches your interests.

Next, you learn about TV Favorites. This feature enables you to select a subset of preferred channels and surf through them with the skill of an expert channel flipper.

This chapter finishes with a trio of topics. The first shows how to select a program from a list of recently viewed channels. The second explores "crossover links" and "show guides." These features enable you to access special Web sites for more information about a television show. Finally, you learn to set reminders so that you need never miss the start of your favorite programs.

Exploring TV Home

Your WebTV TV Home, available on WebTV Plus units only, provides powerful features that enhance your television viewing experience. Among other features, TV Home provides access to on-screen program listings, shows Web sites, lets you program a VCR and provides a viewing planner. Just as your Web Home provides a central starting point for exploring the Internet, your TV Home acts as a base for television.

You can use your TV Home any time your WebTV Plus unit is powered on, even when you are not connected to the Internet. To connect to the Internet, simply activate the **Web Home** option at the left of the TV Home page. This offers an easy-to-use portal for hooking up to the World Wide Web. If you do not wish to use the Internet, you are still free to take advantage of TV Home's viewing features.

TV Home shares many features with your Web Home. You can use Back on your remote to return to previous channels and screens. Press Home to move to your home page — in this case TV Home rather than your Web Home. The Recent button displays a short catalog of those channels that you have most recently viewed. The Options button displays a short menu of popular choices. The Info button shows you information about the program in progress.

Augmented television

TV Home augments your television in many ways, providing features either unavailable or available only through a premium fee on a cable/satellite service. For example, access to the television program-listing channel on my local cable provider costs an extra dollar per month. In contrast, TV Home, and, thus, television program listings, is included in the standard WebTV Plus service.

▶ *To get to TV Home, simply turn on your WebTV Plus unit. When online, using the View button on your keyboard or remote toggles you from Web Home to TV Home.*

❶ *To view television in full-screen, move the yellow box to the center of your TV Home, where the show is displayed and press Go on your remote.*

❷ *When the television show is displayed full screen, press Home to return to your TV Home.*

CROSS-REFERENCE

Need to customize your favorite channels or set a reminder for a favorite show? Read the next few topics.

Is it hard for you to remember when favorite shows come on? Consider using TV Home's reminder feature. Whether you are surfing the World Wide Web or watching another television show, TV Home can remind you of an upcoming show a few minutes before it begins.

Many Television shows now provide what is called "interactive content" or "crossover links." That is, they set up a Web site associated with their show that offers supplemental information. With just a touch of a button, you can activate this feature through TV home.

TAKE NOTE

▶ KNOW YOUR CABLE

If you have a cable TV converter, be certain that you have identified it properly to WebTV and have attached the control pieces correctly. Other than retrieving and viewing the TV listings, almost everything in this chapter requires a complete installation.

▶ WEBTV CLASSIC

WebTV Classic does not support any TV Home features.

③ To connect to the Internet, activate **Web Home** on the TV Home page.

④ You can display a television window while connected to the Web by pressing cmd and typing W or by pressing Options and then activating **TV Window**.

⑤ Activate TV Home on the screen or press View on your remote. This button moves you back and forth between your TV Home and your Web Home.

FIND IT ONLINE

Visit TV Guide at **http://www.tvguide.com**.

Retrieving TV Listings

You can manually retrieve TV listings. You may wish to do this for a number of reasons. This might be the first time you are using TV Home and you want to see listings right away. You might have chosen not to automatically retrieve daily listings. You might have taken your WebTV unit on a trip and want to acquire television program listings for the city that you are currently visiting. For any of these reasons, you can ask WebTV to access and download current listings for your television viewing area.

Retrieving television program listings takes time. Allow a quarter of an hour or even a bit more. Make time allowances for WebTV redialing—it may take several tries to connect to WebTV, just as it does when you normally connect. Of course, if you are already connected to WebTV, the time to retrieve the television schedule is reduced to just a few minutes. One of the advantages of automatically retrieving television program listings is that you can avoid the wait that is associated with retrieving the information.

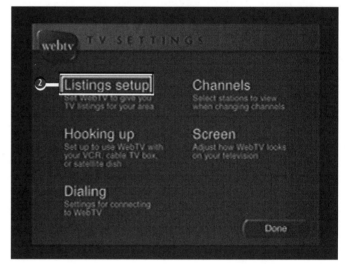

❶ To retrieve television program listings, begin by activating **Settings** from the list of options on your TV Home page.

❷ Activate **Listings setup** from the list of options on your TV Settings page.

CROSS-REFERENCE

Want to set up WebTV to retrieve TV Listings automatically? See the next topic.

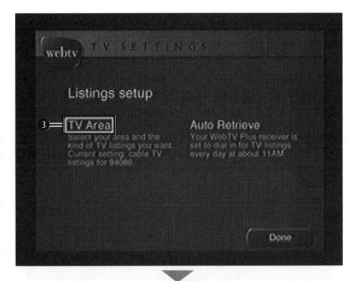

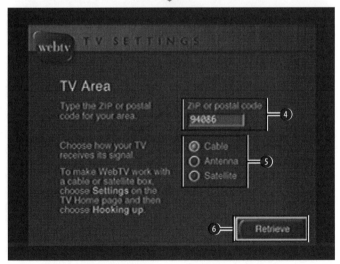

ANTENNA LISTINGS

Be aware that retrieving listings for "antenna" (non-cable, nonsatellite — in other words normal) television can be fairly unreliable. Listings from cable and satellite companies seem to be provided with greater regularity and accuracy.

CHANGING YOUR MIND

Sometimes the process of retrieving listings simply takes too long. Sometimes someone needs to use the telephone. For these and for any other reason you can cancel a listings retrieval at any time.

CHANGING CITIES

Have you changed cities? Follow the directions on the facing page to change your television viewing city and fetch local listings, even if your WebTV unit is set up to automatically retrieve listings. You need do this only once. After a new city has been specified, the automatic listings retrieval will continue to fetch information for the new city.

WEBTV CLASSIC

WebTV Classic does not support any TV Home features. You can, however, visit the TV Guide Web site to preview television program listings for your area.

③ On the Listings setup screen activate **TV Area** to choose the area and kind of settings you want. WebTV tells you the area and type of signal you are currently set for.

④ Move to the ZIP or Postal Code box and type in your ZIP code.

⑤ Select Cable, Antenna, or Satellite reception.

⑥ Activate **Retrieve**. It takes several minutes to retrieve the television program listings.

▶ You may return to the TV Home by pressing Home after the listings are retrieved.

Retrieving TV Listings Automatically

WebTV can automatically retrieve television program listings for you. Using TV Home, you can specify when WebTV is to call in and fetch the latest schedule. This enables you to stay on top of the viewing agenda. Once you have set up this feature, automatic schedule retrieval will continue until you turn the option off. In other words, set it and forget it.

Choose a quiet time of the morning to retrieve your television program listings. You will want a time during which no one is likely to use the telephone. During the wee hours of the morning, the telephone line is generally unoccupied, and the demand on WebTV's services is at its lowest. This helps ensure the greatest reliability for getting your listings.

The time you select to retrieve program listings is approximate. To spread the burden on WebTV's resources, WebTV units do not all phone in exactly on the hour. Instead, times are randomized, to spread the demand for service around the clock. Thus, if you set your retrieval time for 2 a.m., your unit may call in as early as 1:30 a.m., or as late as 2:30 a.m..

Each time your unit accesses WebTV for new listings, it retrieves several days of program information at a time. If your phone line is busy and you have to "skip" a day, you will still have up-to-date television program listings for many days to come.

Automatically retrieving television program listings provides a secret bonus feature. When you retrieve your listings, your WebTV unit also checks for new electronic mail. If new mail has arrived, your red message light illuminates. This means that you can actually check automatically for mail twice a day—once with the e-mail-checking feature and once with the television program-listings feature.

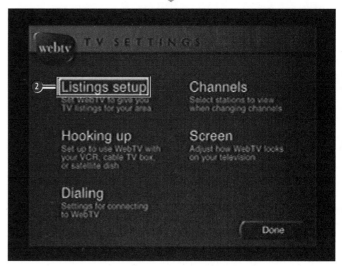

❶ To retrieve television program listings, begin by activating **Settings** from the list of options on your TV Home page.

❷ On the TV Settings screen, activate **Listings setup**.

CROSS-REFERENCE

Want to retrieve television program listings on demand? See the previous topic.

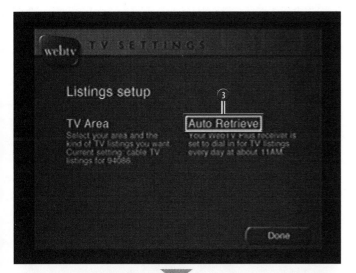

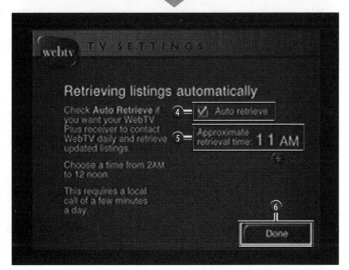

TAKE NOTE

▶ **CHANGING CITIES**

To change cities, please follow the directions in the previous topic. Once you have changed cities, the automatic retrieval time you previously set continues to operate for the new city. No changes need be made.

▶ **TIMES ALLOWED**

WebTV enables you to retrieve television program listings automatically any time between 2 a.m. and 12 noon. These, normally, are WebTV's "slow times." During these hours, WebTV has the fewest customers connected. Your automatic request, therefore, puts the least demand on the system and on other users of the WebTV System.

▶ **WEBTV CLASSIC**

WebTV Classic does not support any TV Home features. You can, however, visit the TV Guide Web site to preview television program listings for your area.

③ On the Listings setup screen, activate **Auto Retrieve**.

④ On the Retrieving listings automatically screen, check the **Auto retrieve** box to have your WebTV unit retrieve listings every day.

⑤ Activate the **+** button to select the retrieval time. This clock scrolls through the hours of 2 a.m. to 12 noon.

⑥ Activate **Done**.

FIND IT ONLINE

Interested in TV Trivia? Visit **http://www.ultimatetv. com/interact/trivia/**.

Selecting a Television Show

WebTV's TV Home allows you to browse the television program listings and select a show directly from those listings. TV Home's show listings provide start and stop times and complete episode information.

To navigate through the listings, use the arrow keys. Up and down arrows move you incrementally through the channels. Channels are listed top to bottom in increasing order. When you reach the last channel available on your system, the first channel follows after it.

Left and right arrows move back and forth between show times. TV Home displays current shows in green and future shows in blue. This way, you can always tell which shows are on and when they end.

A television window in the upper-left corner of the screen enables you to continue viewing your show as you browse through the listings. Make sure to check the **Stay on channel while browsing listings** option on the first TV Listings page. This keeps your show fixed as you browse listings. If you choose not to check this option, the television window shows a preview of each channel you highlight. See the next few tasks to learn how to view TV program listings by day and time and to search TV program listings by program title or category.

Episode summaries appear in the upper right portion of the screen. These summaries give episode information and start and stop times, and indicate (with the diamond-with-an-I symbol) when there is an Internet information site associated with the show.

When you have found a show you wish to view, simply press Go or Return to change channels. You will switch to the full-screen display of that show.

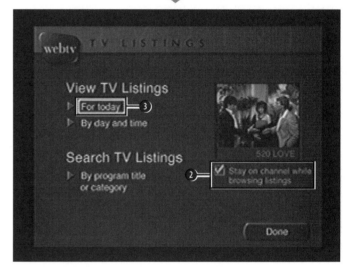

1 *To view television listings, begin by activating TV Listings from the options on your TV Home page.*

2 *(Optional, recommended) Check the Stay on channel option to fix your current show while browsing listings. Leaving this option unchecked may cause visual discontinuity and confusion while browsing listings.*

3 *Activate For today.*

CROSS-REFERENCE

Want to see your show while browsing the Web? See the first topic in this chapter.

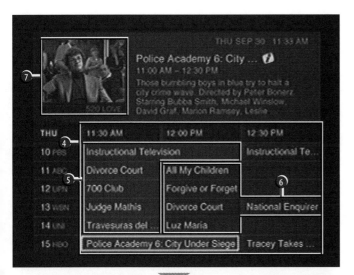

TAKE NOTE

SCROLL UP AND DOWN

If you find the arrow keys tedious when viewing listings, consider using the scroll keys. These keys enable you to move up and down a page of listings at a time. This is particularly useful for those of you with Digital Cable and a plethora of unused channel numbers.

TOP AND BOTTOM

If you want to move to the top and bottom of the television listings, use the cmd key. While pressing cmd press either the up arrow to move to the first channel or the down arrow to move to the last.

DAY BY DAY

You can move forward and backward through the television program listings, a day at a time. Once again, use the cmd key. While pressing cmd, press the right arrow to move ahead or the left arrow to move back 24 hours. Be aware that you cannot retrieve listings for programs in the past, however. You cannot move backward from the present day.

WEBTV CLASSIC

WebTV Classic does not support any TV Home features.

④ *Today's current listings appear. Shows are listed at the bottom of the screen.*

⑤ *Shows in progress appear in green.*

⑥ *Shows yet to air are in blue.*

⑦ *The television window appears in the upper-left corner. If you followed step 2, this window will continue to show your current program as you browse the listings.*

⑧ *The upper-right portion of the screen shows a synopsis of the highlighted show.*

⑨ *Use the arrow keys to select a show. The information at the upper-right of the screen updates to reflect the show currently selected.*

▶ *Press Go or Return to activate the selected show and change channels.*

FIND IT ONLINE

What's the best show on TV today? Visit Ultimate TV at
http://www.ultimatetv.com.

Viewing TV Listings by Date and Time

I f you have a particular date and time in mind, you can instruct TV Home to take you to the TV program listings for that date and time. Your WebTV Plus stores a week of television program listings. You can choose any day and any time within that week. This feature enables you to browse future listings and preview episode information.

You can use the date and time feature to help plan your schedule for the week ahead. Are you trying to decide whether to stay home next Thursday or go to a movie? Pop over to Thursday's listings and find out if you're going to see new episodes or if it will be a whole night of reruns.

When you don't want to miss an upcoming special television event, use the date and time to move quickly to that listing. Activate the name of the show that you want to see and choose **Remind** or **Record** to help make sure that you will not miss that show. The remind feature tells WebTV to warn you when a desired show is about to start. The record feature uses WebTV's IR-Blaster to control your VCR and automatically record a selected show.

When you are not sure of the exact time, select the date and approximate time you think may be correct. WebTV displays 90 minutes of listings at a time. Use the left and right arrow keys to move forward and backward through the time listings until you locate your show.

When you are unsure of the date, you can move through the TV program listings a day at a time. Press and hold cmd while tapping the left or right arrow key. This key combination advances or retraces the listings by 24-hour increments.

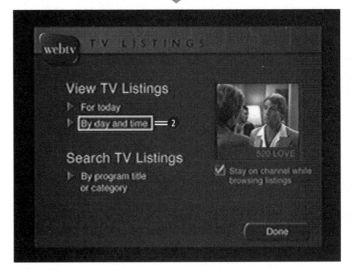

1 To view television listings, begin by activating **TV Listings**.

2 Activate **By day and time**.

CROSS-REFERENCE
Need to retrieve television listings manually? See the second topic in this chapter.

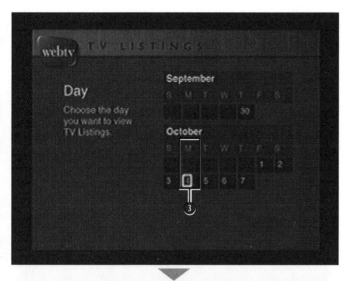

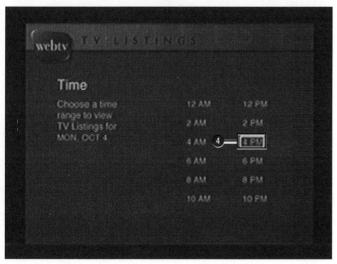

TAKE NOTE

▶ GOING WITH DEFAULTS

If you select **By day and time** from the **View TV Listings** options by accident and do not wish to use Back to change your choice to **For today**, you may press Go or Return on the default date and time provided by WebTV. This automatically selects the current **Day** and **Time**.

▶ TV SITES BUTTON

Activate **TV Sites** from your TV Home page to see which programs have World Wide Web sites associated with them.

▶ WEBTV CLASSIC

WebTV Classic does not support any TV Home features.

❸ *Move the yellow box to a day and press Go or Return. In this screen, I chose Monday October 4.*

❹ *WebTV asks you to choose a two-hour time range for the day you have chosen. Move the yellow box to a time and press Go or Return.*

FIND IT ONLINE

Like soap operas? Visit *Soap Opera Digest* online at **http://www.soapdigest.com.**

Searching TV Program Listings for a Show

With WebTV's TV Home you can search through the television program listings to find a particular show. Use this feature to review all the upcoming episodes of your favorite shows. You tell WebTV what title you are looking for and WebTV does the rest.

Say you are a fan of *Frasier*. As shown on the facing page, you can search through the television listings to find out which episodes are to be shown and when. WebTV displays the show times and the stations, and provides short episode guides for each showing.

To find out more about any program showing, move the yellow box to any presentation and activate with Go or Return. Doing this provides a more full presentation of each episode. If the show has an associated "show guide," you can link to it here.

Do you want WebTV to remind you when a particular show comes on? After activating one of the listings, choose **Remind**. WebTV will alert you a few minutes before the show begins so that you are sure to catch the start of the program. WebTV program alerts work even when you are connected to the Internet.

If you have set up your WebTV unit to control your VCR, you can also choose to **Record** an upcoming show. WebTV remembers the show's date and time. Using the infrared controls shipped with your WebTV Plus unit, WebTV sends signals to your VCR to turn to a particular channel and record the show for its duration.

Of course, to make recordings happen, you must have correctly configured your VCR with the WebTV IR attachments, the VCR must have a fresh tape in it, and both units must be powered on.

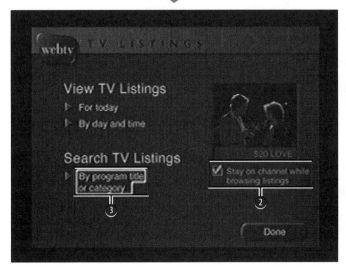

❶ To view television listings, begin by activating **TV Listings** on your TV Home page.

❷ (Optional, recommended) Check the **Stay on Channel** option to fix your current show while browsing the listings.

❸ Activate **By program title or category** under Search TV Listings.

CROSS-REFERENCE

Want to search by category of show? See the next topic.

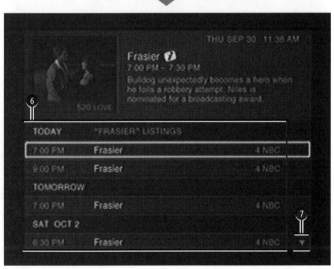

MISSPELLINGS

The most common reason for WebTV failing to find a show is misspelling. If a search produces no results, try checking the spelling.

SHORTER ISN'T BETTER

If you are unsure if the show's title is spelled "Frasier" or "Fraseir," using the shorter search term "Fras" will not help. Unfortunately, TV Home uses entire words when searching. Looking for "Fras" will probably result in no shows being found. Instead, try alternate spellings until you find the show you are interested in.

WEBTV CLASSIC

WebTV Classic does not support any TV Home features.

④ Type in either a word or phrase from the name of a program or the full program title.

⑤ Move the yellow box to **Search** and press Go or Return.

⑥ WebTV searches for your show and displays all the episodes it finds.

⑦ Use the scroll keys to view additional listings.

Searching TV Listings for a Type of Show

With WebTV's TV Home you can search through the television program listings to find a type of show. Do you like Westerns? Children's shows? News features? Sports? Use this searching technique to find specific types of shows.

WebTV has six predefined categories: Movies, Sports, Instructional, Series, News, and Specials. Each category provides options that are more extensive. For example, if you choose Sports, you can search for upcoming golf tournaments, racing events, and soccer matches, and so forth. If you decide to search for News, you can select entertainment, investigative, local, or national. These options help you find the exact type of show that you want to watch without having to know the show's title in advance.

Once you select a category and a topic or topics, WebTV searches for upcoming shows and displays a list of programs that match your criteria. You can scroll through these shows or activate one to see a fuller presentation about the program.

WebTV lists each show it has found in order of date and time. If you have searched for exercise instruction shows, for example, WebTV will display all educational fitness shows for today, tomorrow, and so on for the entire week. Use the scroll keys to move up and down through the listings. As with other TV program listings, earlier shows are listed first, although top to bottom rather than left to right. With this feature, you can see a week's worth of related shows at a glance.

All features associated with normal TV Home television listings are available to you with the category listings. For example, you can move the yellow box to a

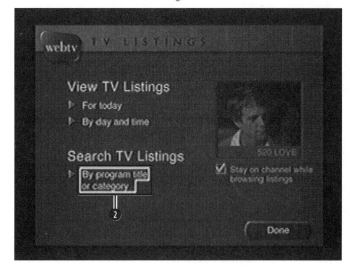

❶ To view television listings, begin by activating **TV Listings**.

❷ Activate **By program title or category**.

CROSS-REFERENCE

Want to search by a show's title? See the previous topic.

270

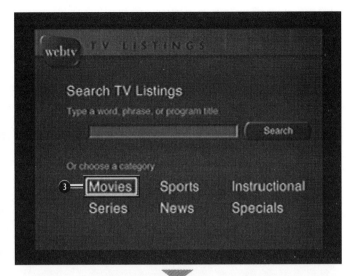

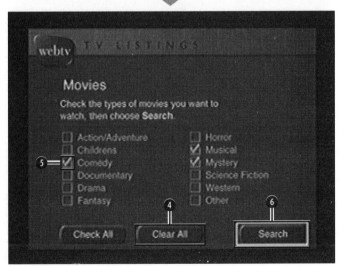

show and see more information about that show at the upper right of your WebTV screen. Similarly, you can activate a show with Go or Return and move to the show's detail screen to get further information. This screen also enables you to set a reminder or request an automated recording.

TAKE NOTE

▶ BE MORE SPECIFIC

The more specific you are when choosing topics, the more focused your search listings will be. I recommend activating **Clear All** when first viewing a category, and only turning on those topics that truly interest you.

▶ SELF-REGULATION

Topics only match when shows tell what they are about. If a show "Great Gunslingers of the West" does not report itself as a "Western" interest show, it will not appear as the result of your search. Fortunately, most television shows provide excellent keyword associations for WebTV searches.

▶ WEBTV CLASSIC

WebTV Classic does not support any TV Home features.

---

③ *Under **choose a category**, select the type of television program listing that you want to see with the yellow box and press Go or Return.*

④ *Activate **Clear All**.*

⑤ *Move the yellow box to the topic to search for and press Go to check it. Check as many boxes as you wish. Or activate the **Check All** option.*

⑥ *Activate **Search**.*

▶ *WebTV searches for all upcoming shows that match your category and topic(s).*

FIND IT ONLINE

See the scripts at **http://www.script-o-rama.com/**.

Setting Up TV Favorites

If you find yourself watching certain channels more than others, you can customize TV Home to provide quick access to these favorite channels. TV Favorites enables you to select channels from a list that you build. This list helps you focus on the channels that you watch the most and skip those — such as the "Home Iguana Shopping Network" — that do not interest you.

Choosing channels is a simple matter of placing check marks next to those channels that you like to watch and removing them from channels that you do not. You may customize directly from the Favorites Channels screen. Activate **TV Favorites** from your TV Home page and then activate **Setup Favorites**; you will move to the complete list of channels. After selecting and unselecting channel choices, activate **Done**. The Favorites page updates to reflect your new channels.

Your favorite channels are listed on the right side of the Favorite Channels screen. Every channel lists the show that is currently playing. This provides an easy way to visually scan the current show listings for your favorite channels and choose a channel to view. Use the scroll keys to move up and down through the listings.

You can select which show to view by moving the yellow box up and down the choices on the right side of the TV Favorites page. Each time the yellow box moves from one listing to another, the TV show updates to that channel. This enables you to quickly surf through your favorite channels using the least number of button presses.

To return to the TV Home page after setting up and selecting favorites, press Home on your remote or keyboard. Alternatively, you can bypass TV Home and select a full-screen display of your current show. To do this, press Go or Return while the yellow box surrounds the channel listing.

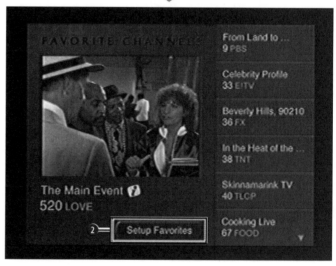

❶ To view television favorites, begin by activating **TV Favorites** at the bottom of your TV Home page.

▶ Your favorite channels, with current program information, are displayed along the right side of the Favorite Channels screen. The television displays to the left.

❷ Activate **Setup Favorites**.

CROSS-REFERENCE

Want to use favorites? See the next chapter.

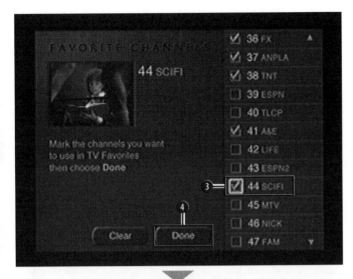

Unfortunately, WebTV does not provide separate favorites for each user. The whole family must share a single Favorites page. However, this is not unlike the existing favorite-channels option found on most televisions, satellites, and cable systems. Perhaps future versions of WebTV will enable you to bypass Junior's list of the "Skateboarding Channel" and the "Super-Loud Hot Rock Favorites Channel."

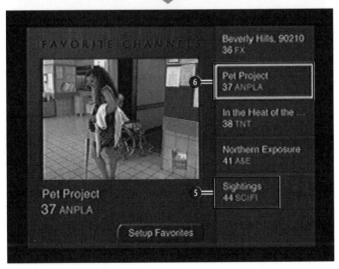

TAKE NOTE

▶ REVIEW PERIODICALLY

You may wish to periodically review your favorite channel choices and customize according to actual use. Space is tight in the Favorite Channels display. The more focused the channels, the easier to select and display them.

▶ WEBTV CLASSIC

WebTV Classic does not support any TV Home features.

---

❸ Move the yellow box to an unchecked channel and press Go to add it to your favorites list. Here, we add channel 44. A preview is displayed to the left.

▶ (Optional) Move the yellow box to a checked channel and press Go to remove it from your favorites list.

❹ Activate **Done**.

❺ Notice that Channel 44 was added to the favorites list.

❻ Channel 37 is highlighted, and the preview is displayed in the television to the left.

FIND IT ONLINE

Visit TVPlex at **http://tvplex.go.com**.

Using TV Favorites

Once you have set up a handful of channels as your "favorites," you can use TV Home to browse through them. TV Favorites provides a quick and convenient way to surf your preferred channels.

Start by activating **TV Favorites**. This brings you to the Favorite Channels page. The list of favorite channels appears on the right side of the screen. If you selected more than six favorites, use the scroll keys to page up and down through the channels.

By moving the yellow box to the list on the right side of the screen, you are ready to scan through your favorite channels. Unlike other WebTV features, you do not need to use the Go button or the Return key to scan through the programs. The yellow box and the arrow keys are all you need to browse through the current shows.

Move the yellow box up and down through the list of programs. As the yellow box moves, the current channel changes. The television screen updates automatically.

When you have found a show that you want to watch, activate it with Go or Return. Alternatively, you can move the yellow box back to the television window and press Go or Return. This enables you to continue watching your new channel using the full-screen display.

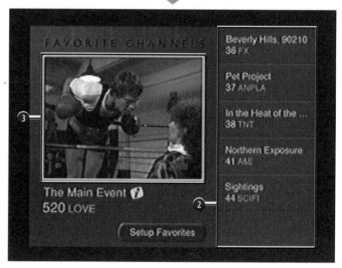

❶ To view television favorites, begin by activating **TV Favorites**.

❷ A list of favorite channels appears on the right-hand side of the display.

❸ The current program appears in the middle of the display.

CROSS-REFERENCE

Want to setup favorites? See the previous topic.

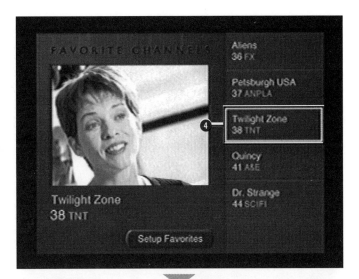

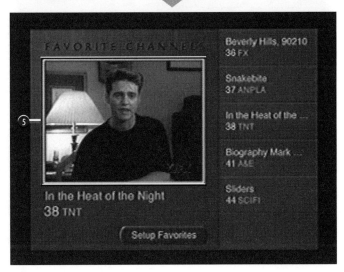

TAKE NOTE

THE HOME KEY

To return to TV Home rather than the full-screen display, press Home after selecting a new channel.

NOTE THE DIFFERENCE

Changing channels by using the yellow box without pressing Go or Return can be a little disconcerting at first. After a little practice, it should become more comfortable. Remember, however, this is not the way that you interact with most of the rest of WebTV's features. This is a classic example of a design tradeoff. WebTV designers had to choose between making channel surfing easier and being consistent with other WebTV features. In this case, they chose to make surfing easier.

WEBTV CLASSIC

WebTV Classic does not support any TV Home features.

④ To select a channel, move the yellow box to it on the right-hand side. You do not need to activate your selection. Simply move the box to any channel and a preview displays in the middle.

⑤ To see the newly chosen channel in full-screen view, either move the yellow box to the television window in the center of the display or surround a show's listing with the yellow box and press Go or Return.

FIND IT ONLINE

Visit the Go Network's Television Center at **http:// infoseek.go.com/Center/Entertainment/Television**.

Selecting from Recently Viewed TV Shows

Television remotes often have a last or back button. These buttons let you flip back and forth between the current channel and the channel that you had most recently viewed. Like a television remote, WebTV also lets you move back and forth between a current and a past channel. Unlike television remotes, WebTV lets you select from the six channels you've most recently visited.

These channels are displayed as two rows of three image spaces. Each image space is accompanied by the name of the show that is playing on that channel, the station, and the channel number. Use this feature to select a show from those channels that you recently visited. Just use the arrow keys to move the yellow box to the channel that you wish to view, and press Go or Return. WebTV takes you to that channel.

Each recent channel displays a screen shot. In a nice touch, as you move the yellow box around the channel selections, each springs to life. You view the show as it is playing. When the yellow box moves away from a channel, the action refreezes to a screen shot.

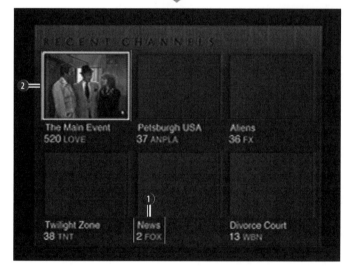

▶ To view recent channels, press the Recent button on your remote. You may press this from any part of TV Home, including the home page (shown here), favorites, full-screen television viewing, and so forth.

▶ Recent channels appear as two rows of three stations, for a total of six recent channels.

❶ Each channel is identified by call letters, channel number, and current program.

❷ The show highlighted by the yellow box appears with full sound and motion. The other five channels show only stills or a blank box.

CROSS-REFERENCE

Want to read more about favorites? See the previous topic.

TAKE NOTE

▶ SOME IMAGES ARE LACKING

Some cable converter boxes do not support retention of the image in the boxes, so you will see blank spaces above the channel number and title as on the facing page.

▶ PASSIVE CHANGE

As with selecting favorites (see the previous topic), channel selections with the yellow box change your active channel. If you press Home after moving the yellow box, the current television show will be that of the highlighted channel. This occurs even though you have not activated any change with Go or Return. Like favorites, this is clearly a design decision on the part of WebTV, but unlike favorites, it does not work well.

▶ WEBTV CLASSIC

WebTV Classic does not support any TV Home features.

3 *Moving the yellow box selects a new channel. The new channel begins to display with full sound and motion. The previous channel reverts to a still shot or a blank.*

▶ *Press Go or Return.*

4 *WebTV displays the channel you selected in full-screen mode. You may return to TV Home by pressing Home or to the Recent Channels page by pressing Recent.*

FIND IT ONLINE

Visit BBC Entertainment at **http://news.bbc.co.uk/hi/ english/entertainment/default.htm.**

Exploring Crossover Links

Many shows provide additional content and associated material through the use of Crossover Links and Show Guides. These two are related in that both provide extra information about the ongoing show. The difference is that Crossover Links appear directly in the show as an icon in a corner of the screen, while the Show Guide is accessed through the program information.

You may, while watching a television show, see a symbol at the upper-right portion of the screen. The Crossover Link symbol is a lowercase letter *i* encased in a slanted diamond. When you see this icon, you can jump to a special Web site that is associated with the show. Simply press Go or Return.

The Show Guide symbol is the same as that for the Crossover Link. Unlike the Crossover Link, however, it appears in the program information. To access the associated Web site, move the yellow box to the symbol and press Go or Return.

Many TV shows now have their own Web sites and Show Guides. There are few Crossover Links, however. In theory, this feature enables a show to point you to material about a particular story or a highlighted feature. In practice, the Crossover Links appear to take you to the same Show Guides that are available in the program listings. Keep your eyes on that corner, though. In the future, Crossover Links promise to supplement television viewing in interesting ways.

The TV Sites feature enables you to see a list of all shows that provide a related Web site. To use this feature, start by returning to your TV Home. Move the yellow box to **TV Sites** at the lower right-hand side of the screen and activate it with Go or Return.

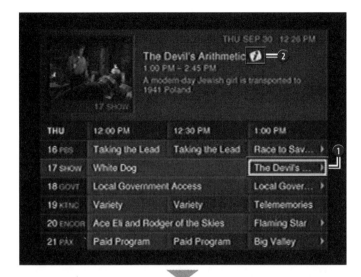

❶ *In the program listings, move the yellow box to the show that you are interested in watching. I chose The Devil's Arithmetic, to be aired later in the afternoon.*

❷ *The **i**-icon means that there is a Show Guide associated with this television show.*

▶ *Press Go or Return to see program information.*

❸ *On the Program Info screen, move the yellow box to the **i**-icon associated with the show. It tells you that it is a link to the The Devil's Arithmetic Web site. Press Go or Return.*

CROSS-REFERENCE

Need a reminder for an upcoming TV Show? See the next topic.

Watching TV with WebTV

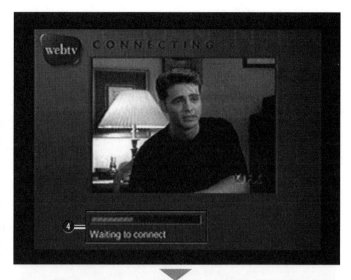

The TV Sites screen provides a list of shows, their channels, and the times those shows are displayed. Use the arrow and scroll keys to move through the list. You may find a show that features a Web site in which you have an interest. Move the yellow box to that show listing and activate it with Go or Return. WebTV moves you to that Web site. If you are not currently connected to the Internet, WebTV connects you so that you can view the Web site.

TAKE NOTE

▶ **READY WHEN YOU ARE**

Web sites associated with shows are always available. You do not need to wait until a program is being shown to view the Web site associated with it.

▶ **RETURNING TO THE SHOW**

To return to a television show from a Web site, press View. This button toggles your session between Web use and TV use.

▶ **WEBTV CLASSIC**

WebTV Classic does not support any TV Home features.

④ If you are not already connected to the Internet, WebTV connects you.

⑤ The show's Web site is displayed for you to view and explore.

FIND IT ONLINE

Visit MSNBC at **http://www.msnbc.com**.

Planning Television Viewing

There are shows that you do not want to miss the beginning of. There are shows that you simply do not want to miss. And there are shows that you think you'd like to watch, but are sure you'll never remember them when the time comes.

With WebTV you do not have to miss the beginning of a show nor the show itself. You can use TV Home to set a reminder. This reminder lets you know when your television show is about to air. Just set the **Remind** function on the Program Info page and WebTV remembers for you.

Regularly scheduled reminders

WebTV will not only remember a one-time showing, but can also learn your schedule. Whether you are interested in a recurring weekly or daily series, you can be reminded. You can tell WebTV to remind you about shows in four different ways.

First, you can request a once-only reminder. This applies to a single showing of a television program. WebTV will remind you of that one showing and leave it at that. You will not be reminded about that television show again, even if it is a recurring series.

Second, you can request a weekly reminder. If your favorite series shows on Thursday nights at 8 p.m., WebTV can act as your weekly reminder. Once you have set this option, WebTV will remember your show for you. You need never miss another *Dilbert*—assuming you're watching TV at the right time. On the other hand, if your show is canceled or you lose interest, WebTV makes it easy to remove the regular reminders.

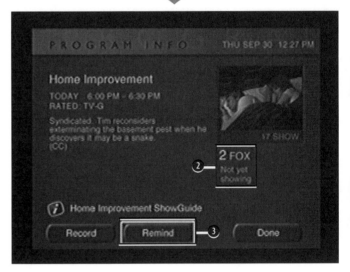

1 To remind yourself about an upcoming show, start by selecting the show that you wish to see with the yellow box. Press Go or Return to see program information.

2 These blue letters tell you whether the show is coming up soon, currently showing, or not yet showing.

3 Move the yellow box to **Remind**. Press Go or Return.

CROSS-REFERENCE

Interested in a program's Web Site? See the previous topic.

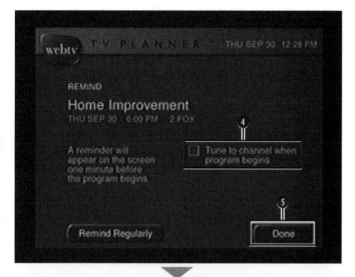

Third, you can request a weekday reminder. Some shows, such as soap operas, game shows, and news programs appear on weekdays at a regularly scheduled time. Choose this option to keep on top of a show that appears five days a week in a regular time slot.

Fourth, you can request a daily reminder. WebTV will remind you every day at a given time to tune to a certain channel. This feature helps those who watch regular religious shows and home shopping networks that follow a full-week schedule.

Continued

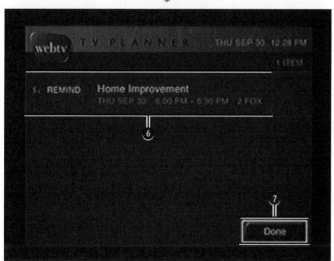

TAKE NOTE

TO TUNE OR NOT TO TUNE

I recommend selecting the **Tune to channel when program begins** option when setting a reminder. This enables WebTV to switch to the correct show if you happen to be out of the room when the show comes on.

GREEN VERSUS BLUE

You cannot set reminders for shows that appear in green, only for those that appear in blue. The reason is that WebTV colors currently displayed shows in green. There is no need to remind you in the future about a green-colored show because it is already on.

④ (Optional) Check the **Tune to channel** box if you want WebTV to switch channels for you when your show comes on.

⑤ Activate **Done** to set your reminder.

▶ (Optional) Press Back to skip the reminder.

⑥ WebTV adds a reminder for the show to your TV Planner.

▶ A reminder will appear on the screen one minute before the program begins.

⑦ Activate **Done** to return to the Program Info page.

FIND IT ONLINE

Visit CBS at **http://www.cbs.com**.

Planning Television Viewing

Continued

A minute before a show is scheduled to appear, a reminder will appear on your screen. This reminder works whether you are using the World Wide Web or simply catching a show on television. So long as WebTV is powered on and actively controlling your screen, you will see the reminder.

An important option when scheduling a reminder is **Tune to channel when program begins**. This option enables WebTV to change channels for you automatically. This is especially convenient when you have to go to the kitchen or bathroom and may miss the reminder.

With its reminder, WebTV gives you the options to **Stop** or **Continue**. If you have changed your mind about the show you have scheduled, you can always activate **Stop**. WebTV will turn off the reminder and leave you on your current channel selection. If you activate **Continue**, however, you switch automatically to the new station without having to wait for the next program to begin.

Reviewing your schedule

WebTV lets you review those shows for which you have scheduled reminders or tapings. From TV Home, activate **TV Planner**. The TV Planner page displays a list of all the programs on your schedule.

You can review these programs by moving the yellow box to one of them and pressing Go. This takes you to the TV Planner Information screen.

To remove a scheduled reminder or taping, activate **Remove**. This deletes the program in question from your TV Plans. There is no "undo" for this option, other than rescheduling the program.

8 *Shortly before the program begins, a reminder appears. If you chose the **Tune to channel** option, do nothing. WebTV will change the channel for you.*

9 *If you want to change channels immediately, activate **Go to** ....*

▶ *If you do not want to change, move the yellow box and activate **Continue**.*

10 *To review your personal TV schedule, select **TV Planner** from the TV Home page.*

CROSS-REFERENCE

Want to send an e-mail to a television show? See Section III for e-mail how-to's.

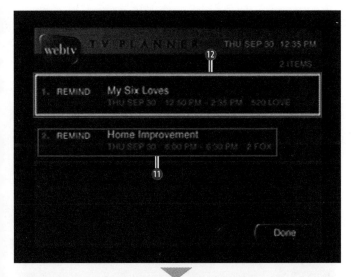

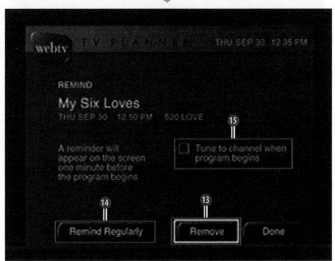

You can change the reminder schedule. From the TV Planner Information screen, activate **Remind Regularly**. WebTV will move you to the How Often screen. This screen enables you to select the frequency at which you are reminded about a show. You can select daily, weekly, weekdays, or once. This latter ensures that you will not be reminded on a regular basis.

TAKE NOTE

▶ RECORD VERSUS REMIND

If you activate **Record** rather than **Remind**, you ask WebTV to activate your VCR at the scheduled time, rather than to remind you of the upcoming show. To use this feature, you must have your WebTV Plus unit configured to work with your VCR.

▶ TAPING SCHEDULES

Setting up a VCR taping schedule follows almost identically the routine for setting up a reminder schedule. You will need to follow your WebTV and VCR manufacturers' instructions on setting up the IR controls for your WebTV and VCR units. Because of the proprietary and variable nature of this setup, specific instructions have been cheerfully omitted from this book.

▶ WEBTV CLASSIC

WebTV Classic does not support any TV Home features.

⓫ Your TV Planner lists each show that you have scheduled for reminders or for recording.

⓬ Move the yellow box to a program and press Return or Go to change the options associated with your reminder.

⓭ To remove the program from your planner, activate **Remove**.

⓮ (Optional) To remind yourself about this show on a regular basis, activate **Remind Regularly** and select a schedule from the How Often screen.

⓯ To change your mind about automatic tuning, check or uncheck the associated box.

FIND IT ONLINE

Visit NPR at **http://www.npr.org**.

Controlling Your VCR with WebTV

The difficulty many people have with programming their VCRs has been the basis of much humor. If you're one of the people who has difficulty, your WebTV Plus unit can make things a lot easier for you.

Most of you have seen the TV/VCR all-in-one units in a store or a catalog. WebTV Plus has one of these units emulated for you when you activate **VCR** on your TV Home. You'll get a TV screen in the center with the standard tape control buttons along the bottom, the Power and TV/VCR buttons on the right, and a Program button on the left.

Assuming that you have attached the Infrared (IR) unit and gone through the setup process to identify your VCR to your WebTV Plus, these controls will operate your VCR just as if you were pressing the controls on your VCR or its remote. About the only standard VCR control missing is the Eject button — you'll still have to go to your VCR remote or the VCR itself to eject and insert tapes.

Continued

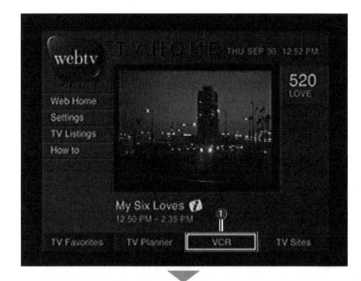

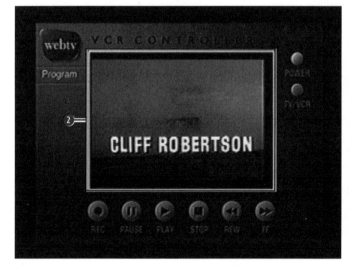

❶ To get to the VCR screen, activate **VCR** on your TV Home.

❷ You'll see your TV show or whatever your VCR is playing in the screen in center of the window. Just as with your TV Home, you toggle it to full screen by selecting it and pressing Go.

CROSS-REFERENCE

Interested in getting Reminders? See the previous topic.

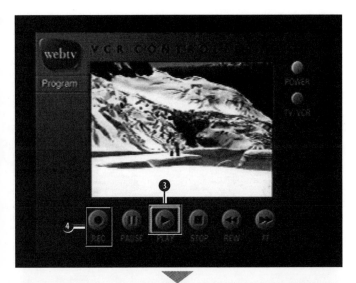

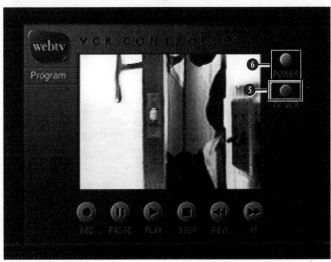

TV/VCR?

Just below the Power button is a TV/VCR button. Unfortunately, there is no indication of which state is current, so you'll probably need to toggle it to see what changes.

IS IT TIME?

The one noticeable downside to using WebTV to record shows is that it takes the time it has and bases that on when to start recording. Unfortunately, we all have seen shows that start a minute or two before the hour (or half-hour). The fact that your VCRs clock could be a little ahead or behind can add to the time-gaps. If channels in your area are known to be a little "off", I suggest making your VCR a little fast or slow to make sure you get the show you want.

GREEN VERSUS BLUE

Like a reminder, you can't program the VCR to record a show that is already on.

③ Activate the **Play** button to play a tape.

④ (Optional) Activate **Rec** to record what is currently playing on TV.

⑤ Click the **TV/VCR** control to switch your video source between the TV tuner and the VCR.

⑥ (Optional) Activate **Power** to turn the VCR on or off — unfortunately, you can't tell from looking at it whether it is on or off.

FIND IT ONLINE

Visit Nickelodeon at **http://www.nickatnite.com**

Controlling Your VCR with WebTV

Continued

Assuming that you've got all the hardware hooked up correctly (little kids and pets seem to be fascinated by the IR stick-ons and keep removing them), programming your VCR to record a show at a later time is a snap.

Just like setting a reminder, you just pick the show you want out of the TV Listing and tell your WebTV Plus that you want to record the show.

WebTV will remind you that you need to have a tape in your VCR and that the VCR needs to be turned off for programmed recording to take place. I hate to think how many times these two simple steps have caused people to miss out on recording a show (and I'm embarrassed to admit that I've forgotten the former a couple of times).

Recording and reminders

When you learned to set reminders in the previous section, you probably noticed that there was a **Record** button right next to the **Remind** button on your Program Info screen.

Since both recording and reminding use many of the same screens, they share many of the same options. You can set your VCR to record once, daily, weekly, or weekdays.

You even can set a reminder to come up just before a show is set to record.

➐ Activate **Program** on your VCR Controller screen.

▶ VCR Controller will tell you to select a program to record from the TV Listings. Activate **TV Listings** and press Go.

➑ Select the program you wish to record from the TV Listings screen. I chose the Buick Open golf tournament on ESPN.

CROSS-REFERENCE

Want to find out more about a show? Check the section on cross-over links in this chapter.

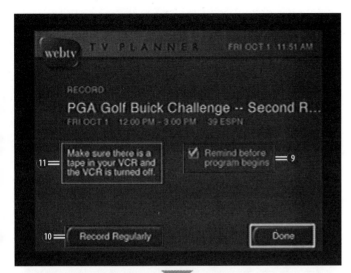

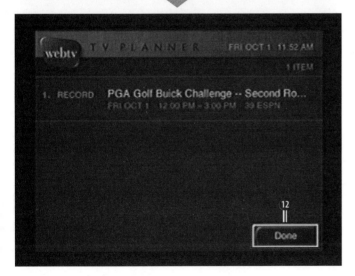

TAKE NOTE

▶ **MORE THAN JUST HARDWARE**

Remember that to use this feature you must have correctly identified your VCR to your WebTV Plus unit so that it knows what commands to send to the VCR.

▶ **CABLE DECODERS CAN BE IN THE WAY**

If you have your cable decoder ahead of the VCR in your chain of boxes, you might encounter difficulties in recording. If the VCR precedes the cable box, you might not be able to receive certain channels on the VCR. This is a Catch-22 situation. You need the decoder to get certain channels you might wish to record (maybe they're scrambled, or digital channels beyond the channel range of your VCR). Unfortunately, this makes it necessary for your VCR to be on the "play-thru" channel (usually 3 or 4); however, programming a recording will tune the VCR to the channel indicated in the listing. This will almost always result in a lost recording.

▶ **WEBTV CLASSIC**

WebTV Classic does not support any TV Home features.

---

9 (Optional). I recommend this if you have a decoder which you need to turn off.

10 (Optional) Activate **Record Regularly**. This operates identically to Remind Regularly, covered in the previous section.

11 Read the reminder, and activate **Done**.

▶ From your TV Home, activate TV Planner.

12 You'll see your scheduled recording in the TV Planner. Either select it to make changes, or activate **Done**.

FIND IT ONLINE

You can buy VCRs and other electronics at
http://www.amazon.com.

Personal Workbook

Q&A

1 What is the television equivalent to your Web Home?

_____

_____

_____

2 When might you want to retrieve TV listings manually?

_____

_____

_____

3 What are the three ways to select a television show?

_____

_____

_____

4 What are the three ways to search for a television show?

_____

_____

_____

5 How many TV Favorites can you see at once on a single screen?

_____

_____

_____

6 What does the Recent button do?

_____

_____

_____

7 What is a _Crossover Link?_

_____

_____

_____

8 How far in advance can you set a reminder for a single television showing?

_____

_____

_____

ANSWERS: PAGE 341

EXTRA PRACTICE

1 Set a reminder for a television show.

2 Set up automatic TV program listing retrieval.

3 Search for a television show by name or category.

4 Move between TV Home and the full-screen television display.

REAL-WORLD APPLICATIONS

✔ You enjoy the popular newsmagazine program *Dateline*, which has an extensive Web site. You find the show's Web site through your program listings and extend your viewing experience with associated articles.

✔ You have a particular show that you like to watch at certain times, so you take advantage of TV Home's reminder service. Whether the show appears nightly at 9:30 or weekly at 8:00 Thursdays, the reminder feature is invaluable for making sure that you catch the shows you want to see.

Visual Quiz

What is the difference between the show surrounded by the yellow box and the other channels shown in this picture?

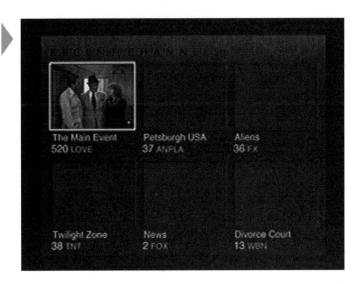

_____

_____

_____

_____

_____

_____

CHAPTER 16

MASTER THESE SKILLS

▶ **Moving Around Town**

▶ **Finding a Chat**

▶ **Finding a Newsgroup**

▶ **Creating a Web Page**

Building Community

Community involves both knowing what is going on in your vicinity and reaching out to people to form social networks. WebTV's Community feature supports both these needs. It enables you to learn about the ins and outs of your hometown, as well as join the greater Internet community. In this chapter, you learn about both.

First, you explore WebTV's Around Town, a feature that enables you to find restaurant and movie listings for your local community as well as preview special event schedules. Around Town lets you find out what's going on in your local area.

Next, you learn about Internet chats. WebTV enables you to join real-time conversations with people around the world. These "chats," which are sponsored by Talk City, permit you to make friendships and share interests in an immediate, real-time setting.

Next, you learn about Usenet newsgroups. WebTV allows you to participate in the oldest and most established Internet community — shared bulletin board postings. With newsgroups you can find thousands of people who share your passions and want to discuss them.

Finally, you learn how to create and edit your own Web pages. Having your own Web pages establishes your presence on the World Wide Web.

Moving Around Town

So, what's happening in your town or community these days? WebTV can help you find out. Its Around Town feature enables you to get local information about movies, entertainment, weather, and events. With Around Town you can keep your finger on the pulse of events in your city.

This section contains three parts: Going Out, Local Services, and Weather. Going Out is the most useful, with links to restaurant and movie listings and to event calendars. Use this information to help plan for an upcoming evening. With Going Out, you can decide what to do and where to go.

Local Services provides links to some major Internet service providers, including auctions at eBay, job searching tools from Monster Board, and White Pages searches from WhoWhere. Finally, the Weather section provides the same content available in the WebTV Centers. Checking on the weather can be a valuable tool when you're planning to attend an outdoor concert or picnic.

Used judiciously, Around Town can furnish you with valuable information about in-town happenings. For example, restaurant listings are supplied by the Zagat Survey and by Dine Site.

Going out of town

The same information that is available to you for your city is also available to you for other cities. At the bottom of the Around Town page is a section titled Change

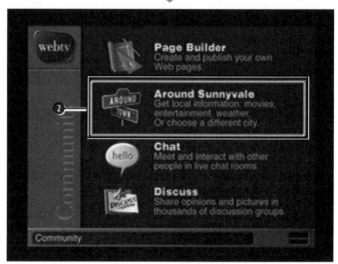

❶ From your Web Home page, activate **Community**.

❷ At the top of the Community page, activate **Around Town**, where Town is the name of your local community.

CROSS-REFERENCE

Want a better way to check the weather? Use the WebTV Centers described in Chapter 13.

City. To retrieve information for another locale, enter the city name or Zip code and activate **Change city**. This feature enables you to see the weather and local events for many other cities.

Be aware, however, that when you change cities for Around Town, you may change cities for your entire WebTV system! Make sure to change back to your home city before leaving Around Town.

TAKE NOTE

▶ **KEEP YOUR EXPECTATIONS WITHIN BOUNDS.**

Perhaps the greatest failing of Around Town is its Dining Out and Movie Listings. One would hope to find reviews rather than just listings. One finds, instead, ad copy. I quote from a local listing:"'charming' décor is a hit, as is the 'yummy' 'menu that changes daily'; diners tip their hats to the outdoor patio, 'service that's a notch above' and 'good wine list.'"

▶ **WEBTV CLASSIC**

WebTV Classic supports the same Community features as WebTV Plus.

❸ *Select from one of the four local information categories under Going Out: **Dining Out**, **Movie Listings**, **Entertainment**, and **Music Events**. For this example activate **Dining Out**.*

❹ *Scroll through the list of local restaurants. Select any one and activate it with Go or Return to retrieve further information. Results are from Dine Site. Reviews include address, telephone number, and pricing information.*

FIND IT ONLINE

Read more about it. Visit **http://help.webtv.net/ surfing/specificinfo.html.**

Finding a Chat

WebTV's Chat feature — known elsewhere on the Internet as the Internet Relay Chat — is a powerful way to meet and interact with other people. This feature is part of WebTV's Community section.

A chat involves people from different parts of the world coming together and talking to each other. This is accomplished by using special Internet programs. What you and others type is transmitted to a central location and rebroadcast to every person who is connected to the same "chat room."

Chat rooms vary. In some, people meet socially. In others, they share professional and academic information. Some people use chat rooms to play games. Other people use chat rooms to get support or share common interests. Unfortunately, there is another type of chat room behavior — that of "cyber-flirting." Some people abuse the anonymity of the Internet to carry on "cyber-affairs" with other anonymous Internet users.

Fortunately, Talk City — WebTV's official chat site associate — moderates chat rooms. You can expect many of these rooms to actually remain on-topic and relatively family friendly. Any chat room with a moderator present has a greater chance of being kept to family standards.

Continued

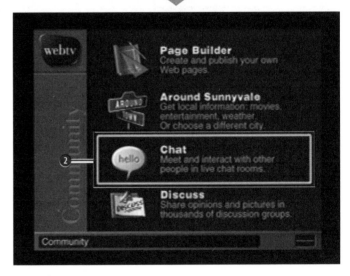

❶ *From your Web Home page, activate Community.*

❷ *On the Community page, activate Chat.*

CROSS-REFERENCE

Learn how to use newsgroups in the next topic.

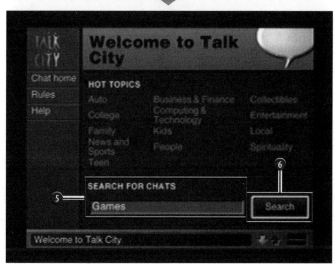

▶ NICKNAMES AND HANDLES

People in chat rooms are identified by their nicknames, also called "handles" (dating back to the CB (Citizen's Band) radio craze of the 1970s). Your nickname is the same as your Internet name. If you chose your personal name as your Internet name, you may want to create a more anonymous secondary user (see Chapter 17).

▶ ADULT LANGUAGE

Many chat rooms in Talk City, including games, are moderated. You can identify moderators and helpers by their special nicknames, which include the uppercase letters "CCC" and "TCC." For example, "AnaCCConda," "CCCat," "BewiTCChed," and so on. These moderators keep the chat rooms functioning at a family entertainment level. However, there are unmoderated chat rooms, which can become extremely raunchy and unpleasant.

▶ SPEED

Internet Chat rooms are not the place for slow readers or typists. Information goes by at a prodigious rate, often forcing you to use your scroll keys to catch the information flying by. Chat rooms are not for everyone. If the rate of communication exceeds your tolerance, do not despair, you are not alone. Many people find that chat rooms are not their cup of tea.

▶ WEBTV CLASSIC

WebTV Classic supports Chat just like WebTV Plus.

---

❸ (Optional) On the Chat page, activate **Upcoming chats at Talk City** under What's on next to see what "special events" are scheduled.

❹ Activate **Talk City** to move to the main Talk City chat site.

❺ At the Welcome to Talk City site, you can Search for Chats. Type a search phrase in the blank. In this example, our search is for "Games" to find online chat-based games.

❻ Move the yellow box to **Search** and activate it with Go or Return.

FIND IT ONLINE

Visit Talk City at **http://www.talkcity.com**.

Finding a Chat

Continued

Joining a chat involves little more than entering a chat room, reading what others have written, and entering the conversation. If you are unfamiliar with a particular chat room, or new to chat rooms in general, you may wish to lurk before participating. A lurker reads the ongoing discourse but does not add messages. Lurking gives you the time to gauge the emotional temperature of a room before joining.

You may find that when you enter a room that you are greeted by a series of people. When a new person enters a room, all others in that room are automatically notified. This notification appears in an italicized font.

Chat rooms can move very quickly, especially if there are many people in the room and if they are quick typists. To find out who is in the room, move the yellow box to people and activate it with Go or Return. WebTV shows a list of those people — or, more accurately, their nicknames — who are currently in the chat room.

A chat consists of a list of comments made by each person. Each comment is preceded by the person's nickname. To send your own message, move to the text field at the bottom of your WebTV screen, type your comment and activate **Send**.

If at any time you are involved in a Talk City chat room and are harassed by another party, you can report them. Activate **Trouble** on the left side of your screen. Your trouble reports are sent directly to a Talk City helper who will try to assist you. Use this feature only for real and serious issues.

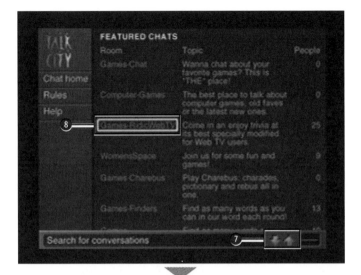

❼ You can scroll up and down through the list of Chat Rooms returned by the Talk City search engine.

❽ Activate **Games-RidicWebTV** to join the Talk City Trivia for WebTV users chat room.

❾ In this ongoing game, contestants are attempting to name items that fit the category selected by the host.

❿ Each person's comments are preceded by their nickname in bold type.

⓫ Italicized text indicates when someone enters or leaves the chat room.

CROSS-REFERENCE

Learn how to find a chat room in the previous topic.

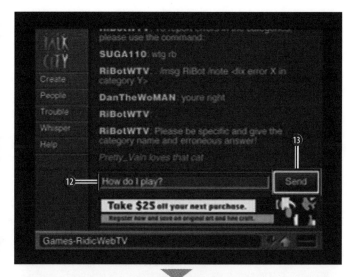

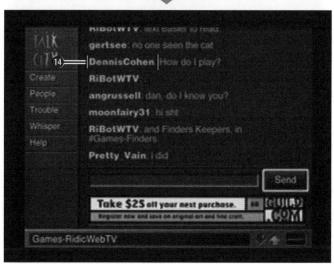

ACRONYMS

There are many acronyms found in chat. You may be unfamiliar with many of them. Here's a quick guide to some of the most common. "LOL" means laughing out loud; "ROFL" means rolling on the floor laughing; "WB" means welcome back; "TY" or "TX" means thank you; "YW" means you're welcome; "BRB" means that the person is about to leave, but will "be right back;" "CYA" or "CUL8R" means see you, goodbye or "See you later". You will find many other acronyms in use. If you are unfamiliar with one, just ask. Someone, or several people, will instruct you.

ACTIONS

A cute feature of chat rooms is "actions." Instead of typing a comment, type "/me" followed by an action. For example, if I were to type "/me looks around" in a chat room and **Send** it, the chat room would see "EricaSadun looks around." This feature enables you to add descriptive variety without actually saying anything. WebTV always sets your Talk City handle to your user name.

WEBTV CLASSIC

WebTV Classic supports the same Community features as WebTV Plus.

⑫ To talk to others in the chat room, type your comment into the text field at the bottom of the screen.

⑬ Send your comment by activating **Send**.

⑭ Your comment appears among the others, preceded by your nickname.

FIND IT ONLINE

Find out more about Talk City Games at **http://www.talkcity.com/games**.

Finding a Newsgroup

Newsgroups form one of the oldest features of the Internet. They let people communicate in a publicly shared forum. Newsgroups are made up of a series of "postings" from individuals that can stretch back for years. You can join a newsgroup at any time and read the recent messages that people have sent to each other.

Like chat rooms and mail lists, newsgroups exist for a wide range of topics. These range from the scientific to the educational, the recreational to the professional. If you have any interest whatsoever, a newsgroup probably exists that is made up of people who share your passion.

To find a newsgroup, use the **Look for** command found under the featured discussions. You can search for a wide range of topics from fishing to antiques, from medicine to Mao, and from movies to philosophy. Literally tens of thousands of Newsgroups exist on almost every topic that you can dream of. Whether you want to talk about a favorite author or a favorite hobby, chances are a newsgroup already exists with dozens, hundreds, or thousands of coenthusiasts.

If your search returns too many newsgroups for you to read through practically, remember this quick rule of thumb. Any newsgroup whose name begins with the letters "alt" is likely to be less formally organized, less well propagated, and, hence, less interesting than any non-"alt" newsgroup.

The tone of newsgroups ranges from formal to friendly to downright fierce. Some newsgroups — traditionally those dedicated to discussions about religion,

① From your Web Home page, activate **Community.**

② On the Community page, activate **Discuss**. This is WebTV's way of referring to Newsgroups. No one else on the Internet refers to them in this fashion.

CROSS-REFERENCE

Learn how to read a newsgroup in the next topic.

politics, or race — can be hostile. The Internet is open to all people, including both kind and brutal. Consider lurking before participating. To lurk, spend a few days or weeks reading a newsgroup without making any posts. Lurking permits you to gauge the emotional temperature of a newsgroup before participating.

Continued

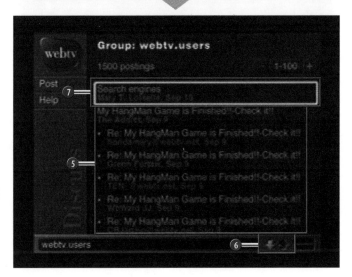

TAKE NOTE

▶ FLAMING

Some newsgroups can become hostile, especially those newsgroups about religion and politics. On the Internet, as in life, emotions can run high. An exchange of hostile comments or insulting posts is called *flaming* and comes part and parcel with newsgroups.

▶ FAQ

Most newsgroups have associated with them a list of Frequently Asked Questions or FAQ. These FAQ lists are posted at regular intervals. Make sure to read a newsgroup's FAQ before you post a question. You may find out you are the five hundredth person to have asked this question in a month.

▶ WEBTV CLASSIC

WebTV Classic supports Newsgroups the same as WebTV Plus.

③ *(Optional) You may search for a topic by typing a keyword into the text field at the bottom of the screen and activating **Look for**.*

④ *You may wish to select a featured Newsgroup; in this case, activate **WebTV**.*

⑤ *Some Newsgroups may have many postings!*

⑥ *Scroll through the current postings to see what conversations are ongoing.*

⑦ *To read a particular posting, move the yellow box to the posting and press Go or Return.*

FIND IT ONLINE

Learn how to search for newsgroups at **http://help. webtv.net/chat/discuss/search.html**.

Finding a Newsgroup

Continued

Newsgroups consist of many articles accumulated over time. Each article continues a "conversation" over time. Like e-mail, articles are listed by their subject. Unlike e-mail, articles can "time out." After a certain period of time, a newsgroup article expires to allow the newsgroup to continue to accept new postings.

Each subject in a newsgroup is called a "thread." You can follow a newsgroup thread, just as you would a thread of conversation. Be aware, however, that conversations can drift from topic to topic. Before you know it, a newsgroup discussion can veer sharply away from the purported subject. This tendency, known as "topic drift," is all too common and should not come as a surprise to the reader.

There are certain rules of thumb that you should follow when participating in a newsgroup. These rules are called "netiquette" and encapsulate the best ways people have found to get along in newsgroups.

Basic Netiquette

Be courteous. Courtesy is an important part of any conversation. When you treat others with courtesy, you are more likely to receive it in return.

Use context. When replying to a newsgroup post, be sure to summarize the post to which you are replying. You may also include selected quotes of the previous post. Place context summaries and quotes before any new text you write. Never quote the entire letter to which you are replying.

Keep your lines short. Unlike WebTV, which automatically wraps lines to fit your display, much of the world is limited to 80-character unwrapped lines. Use "hard" carriage returns (with the Return key) to keep your lines within 70 characters.

Do not SPEAK IN CAPITAL LETTERS. Mixed-case replies are easiest to read. Writing in capital letters is sure to alienate your audience and limit your ability to effectively communicate. The use of capital letters is considered "shouting" in the Net community.

Use sarcasm sparingly. Sarcasm is best conveyed by facial expression, a feature notably lacking in text-only communication. Do not assume that your readers, especially those who are not English-speakers will understand you when you use sarcasm or even humor. There are character-based equivalents for many facial expressions, called "emoticons," the most common of which is the "smiley-face" — ":)"Add context. Do not reply to a post with a vacuous followup letter. Posts of "Me too" or "I agree" are considered the worst waste of Internet resources and human time.

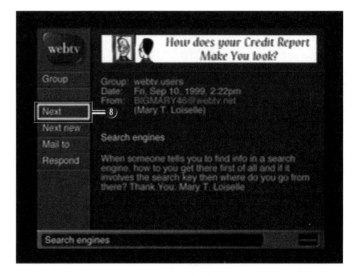

8 *Activate **Next** to see the next article in the newsgroup.*

CROSS-REFERENCE

Learn how to find a Newsgroup in the previous topic.

Get the FAQ. Make sure to read the Frequently Asked Question list associated with a newsgroup before making you first post. First impressions can last a long time. You should make your first impression your best.

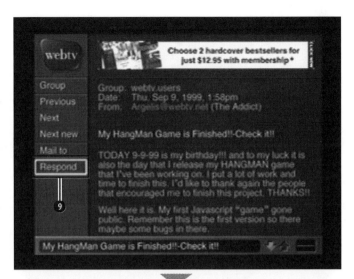

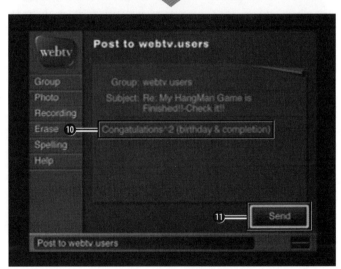

9 To reply to an article, activate **Respond**.

10 Type a follow-up article.

11 Activate **Send** to send the article to the newsgroup. Remember that any article you post may be read by hundreds of thousands, if not millions, of people.

TAKE NOTE

▶ ACRONYMS

Like chats, newsgroups tend to use lots of acronyms. Unlike chats, these acronyms tend to be vague and capricious, and apply only to specific newsgroups. The best ways to learn newsgroup acronyms are reading the FAQ, lurking, and asking for help.

▶ DEJA NEWS

Deja News, found at **http://www.dejanews.com,** archives copies of posts made to all Internet newsgroups. This archive dates back several years. You can search Deja News to find old postings and personal posting profiles.

▶ WEBTV NEWSGROUPS

WebTV's newsgroups, as opposed to Usenet's newsgroups, are private. That means that WebTV-specific discussions cannot be read by outsiders and are not archived on Deja News.

▶ WEBTV CLASSIC

WebTV Classic and WebTV Plus both enable you to access Newsgroups.

FIND IT ONLINE

Read about netiquette at **http://www.primenet. com/~vez/neti.html.**

Creating a Web Page

W hen you visit someone's Web page, you're just a tourist. When you have a Web page for others to visit, you're a resident on the Internet — that's why people call them "Home Pages." In this section, you're going to learn how to create your own Web page on WebTV.

At this time, if you have no other Internet access than WebTV, you will be using Page Builder to create your Web page. The first time you go to the Community page and choose Page Builder to create and publish your own Web page you will be presented with a license agreement. Read it through, and (assuming that yet another license agreement doesn't dissuade you) select the "I accept" box and press Go.

Page Builder then takes over and presents you with a number of page style selections. After you've selected the background style for your page, you will designate its title, the name that appears at the top of the window in which people will view your creation.

So far, you have a named page with just a background. This isn't very interesting, but you can add pictures with or without titles and captions, text, links to other pages, lists, headings, and page breaks to make it look more like the pages you're used to visiting. In the next section, we will see how to add some of these items to your page.

Continued

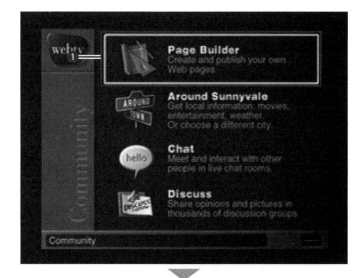

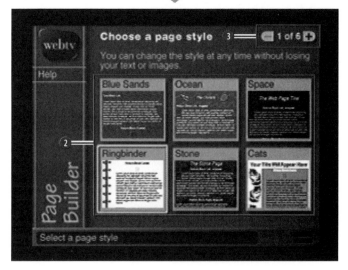

▶ From your Web Home page, activate **Community**.

❶ Select **Page Builder** on the Community page.

▶ The first time you access Page Builder, you'll be asked to accept a license agreement (not shown).

❷ You will see a series of page styles from which to choose when creating your page.

❸ (Optional) Move forward and backward through the page style choices using the navigation buttons at the top right of the screen.

CROSS-REFERENCE

Learn how to notify others of your page later in this chapter.

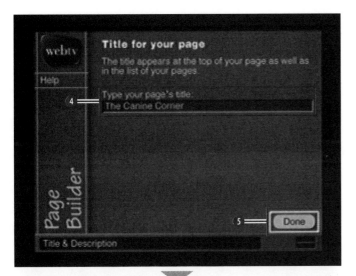

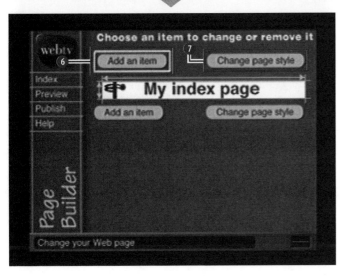

▼

④ Type the title for your page in the text box.

⑤ Select **Done** and press Go when you have entered the title.

⑥ Start adding items to your partial page by selecting one of the **Add an item** buttons and pressing Go.

⑦ (Optional) If you wish to change the page style, select either of the **Change page style** buttons and press Go.

TAKE NOTE

▶ **HTML**

Web pages are really text files, part of which are specially formatted instructions telling a Web browser (like WebTV) how to display the text and where the pictures are stored and where they go on the page. HTML stands for Hypertext Markup Language.

▶ **PAGE BUILDER**

Page Builder is what is known as a graphic Web page editor. This means that you don't need to know HTML to create a Web page. Page Builder will translate your instructions into HTML for you.

▶ **WEBTV CLASSIC**

WebTV Classic supports Page Builder the same as WebTV Plus.

FIND IT ONLINE

Learn about HTML at **http://www.utoronto.ca/ webdocs/HTMLdocs/NewHTML/index.html**.

Creating a Web Page

Continued

Page Builder gives you a choice of six item types to add to your page: pictures, text, links, headings, lists, and page breaks.

Pictures for your Web pages are just like pictures that you attach to your e-mail (see Chapter 8) and can come from the same sources: video capture, your scrapbook, or the WebTV Art Gallery. Once you have selected the picture, Page Builder will ask you if you wish to provide a title and/or a caption for the picture. A title is centered above the picture and a caption is a block of text that appears below the picture, left-justified.

Text items are also just as they are in e-mail — blocks of text where you can specify a size and a style.

You select links on Web pages to go to other pages without having to type in the new page's address. Page Builder lets you specify a descriptive name for your visitors to select to get to a desired Web address.

Headings are just blocks of text that you can specify as starting a new section of your page. You can add a dividing line either before or after the heading, which is displayed left-justified on your page.

Page breaks are clues to Page Builder to divide your page into two (or more) pages, which your visitors can move between by selecting the Next page or Previous page items which Page Builder will provide as navigational aids.

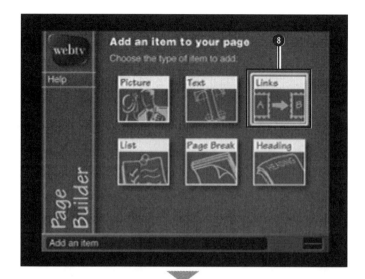

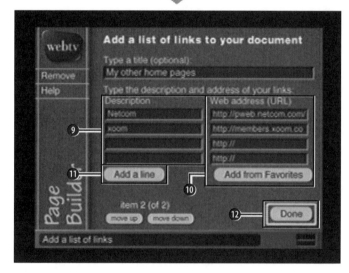

8 Choose one of the six item types to add to your page. In this example, we choose to add links.

9 Enter descriptive names in the Description boxes.

10 Type the URL in one of the Web address boxes, or select **Add from Favorites** to pull the Web address from your stored Favorites.

11 (Optional) If you wish to add more than four links, click **Add a line.**

12 Select **Done** and press Go when you are finished.

CROSS-REFERENCE

Learn how to add pictures in Chapter 8.

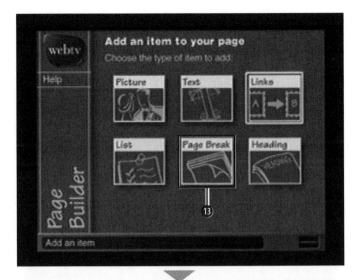

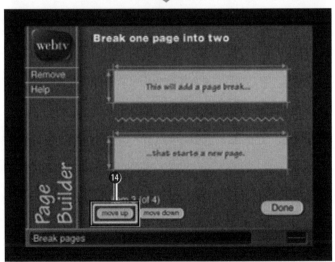

Lists are standard, bulleted sequences of items with an optional title. If, for example, you wish to list members of your family one to a line, you would use a list to do so.

TAKE NOTE

▶ JUSTIFICATION

Page Builder determines whether items are centered, left-justified, or right-justified by the item type. HTML allows for any of these alignments; however, Page Builder uses its own preferences and doesn't give you any control.

▶ TABLES

One of the most common items used in Web page design for the formatting of blocks of text and display of tabular information is a table. Page Builder, at this writing, provides no support for you to create tables; however, it uses tables internally to lay out your pages.

▶ WEBTV CLASSIC

WebTV Classic and WebTV Plus both enable you to access Page Builder.

---

⑬ If your page is getting too long for convenient scrolling, you can split it into multiple pages by selecting **Page Break.**

⑭ Use **move up** and/or **move down** to position the page break before the item you wish to have start the new page.

FIND IT ONLINE

Read about Dynamic HTML at **http://www. webdeveloper.com/html/html_dhtml_1.html.**

Creating a Web Page
Continued

Once you have placed the desired items on your Web page, arranged them in the order you want, and put in the page breaks to ease navigation you will want to check it out and let people know that you have new material for them to peruse.

Page Builder has a Preview function where you see your page as it will appear in your WebTV browser. If anything is not to your liking, just press the Back button, select the item you wish to change, and press Go. Edit or move the item and check again.

After you've verified that the page looks the way you want it to look, it is time to Publish your page. When you publish a page, Page Builder passes it off to WebTV's Web server and you're told of the page's URL. Page Builder then asks you whether you want to notify people of the new page, add the page information to your e-mail signature, and/or change the title or description. If you choose to send mail announcing your new page, you are taken to e-mail with the subject being the title of your new page and a link to the page in the message body. Just add the addressees you wish to notify and, if you wish, some added text to the body of the e-mail telling people about the new page. When you're ready to do something else, select Done and press Go.

You can go back at any time and modify the pages that you have in your public list of pages. Once you have at least one Web page, invoking Page Builder will initially bring you to an index of your published pages. Select the one you wish to modify (or remove) and proceed as previously described.

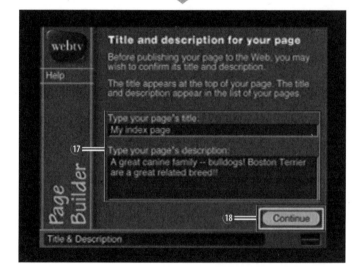

⑮ Select **Preview** and press Go to see what your page will look like to a visitor.

⑯ Select **Publish** and press Go to add this page to your list of pages, making it available to visitors.

⑰ Page Builder will ask you to confirm (or update) the title and description for your page. If you wish to change either, select the appropriate text box and edit the text.

⑱ Select **Continue** and press Go.

CROSS-REFERENCE

Learn about URLs in Chapter 4.

At every step of the way while creating, modifying, and publishing your pages, Help is available in Page Builder.

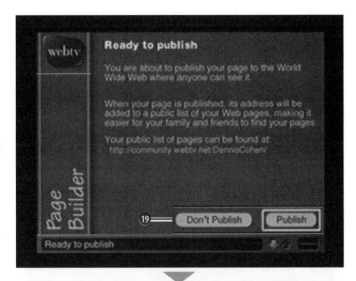

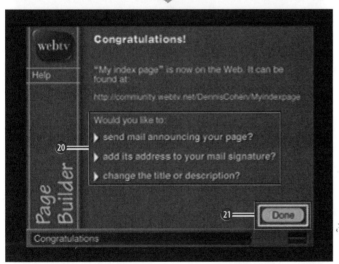

⑲ *Page Builder will give you one more chance to change your mind, as well as inform you of where your public list of pages can be found. Select **Publish** or **Don't Publish** and press Go.*

⑳ *(Optional) Your page is now available on the Web. If you would like to send mail announcing the page to some friends or relatives, include the page address in your mail signature, or change the title or description of the page, select that item and press Go.*

㉑ *Select **Done** and press Go.*

TAKE NOTE

▶ PUBLISHING

WebTV maintains an index for you of all your published pages. This index is what your visitors will see when they go to your WebTV personal Web site unless they specify a specific page on your site.

▶ ANNOUNCING

Publishing your pages does not get them listed with a search engine such as Yahoo, Alta Vista, or Excite. For a search engine to catalog your pages, they must contain what are called META tags in the HTML header formatted with the information that the search engine's "spider" will extract. Page Builder creates the META tags for you; however, you will need to go to the various search engines and notify them of your new pages — eventually, they should show up in the search (typically 2-4 weeks).

▶ WEBTV CLASSIC

WebTV Classic and WebTV Plus both enable you to access Page Builder.

FIND IT ONLINE

List your page with Yahoo at **http://docs.yahoo. com/info/suggest/**

Personal Workbook

Q&A

1 If you change your city in Around Town, do you change your city for your entire WebTV system?

_____

_____

_____

_____

_____

2 What information can you find under Going Out in the Around Town feature?

_____

_____

_____

_____

3 How is your chat nickname assigned in Talk City?

_____

_____

_____

_____

4 What is _Netiquette?_

_____

_____

_____

_____

_____

5 In a chat room thread, what does "brb" mean?

_____

_____

_____

_____

6 What does it mean when a person in a Talk City chat room has a nickname such as GrinCCC?

_____

_____

_____

_____

_____

ANSWERS: PAGE 341

EXTRA PRACTICE

1. Pull up an Around Town listing for a local restaurant you are familiar with.

2. Find a chat room that interests you.

3. Join a chat room and talk with others.

4. Find an interesting Newsgroup.

5. Browse through the Newsgroup postings.

REAL-WORLD APPLICATIONS

✔ You have a technical question that you need help with. You search for and find a newsgroup that discusses this topic and pose your question. (Of course, you were sure to check the newsgroup FAQ before asking.)

✔ You want to have some fun so you join one of Talk City's daily games. You test your wit, knowledge of trivia, and verbal skill against others.

✔ You are going on a trip. You use Around Town to find an event schedule for the city you'll be visiting.

Visual Quiz

Which Talk City category under Hot Topics might appeal to a football enthusiast?

_____

_____

_____

_____

_____

CHAPTER **17**

MASTER
THESE
SKILLS

▶ **Adding a Secondary User**
▶ **Removing a Secondary User**
▶ **Switching Users**
▶ **Checking Your Billing Information**
▶ **Switching Onscreen Keyboard Styles**
▶ **Enjoying Background Music**
▶ **Adjusting Font Sizes**
▶ **Asking WebTV for Help**

Administrating Your WebTV Account

As the Primary WebTV user in your household, you may have to take on some administrative duties, such as expanding or customizing your current account. This chapter teaches you those skills that will make administering your account more reasonable.

First, you learn to add and remove secondary users. Your WebTV account can support one primary and five secondary users. You may also want to limit the way secondary users access the Internet. This chapter shows you how to perform user-related tasks for your WebTV account.

Second, you may need to set or update billing information for your WebTV account. This chapter teaches you to adjust your billing when your name, address, or method of payment changes. You will also learn how to cancel your WebTV account.

Next, you learn to specify a number of WebTV settings. These settings can enhance or individualize your WebTV surfing experience. You learn to change onscreen keyboard styles, set background music, adjust font sizes, and enter and leave demonstration mode.

Finally, you learn to use WebTV's built-in help center to learn how to perform new or unfamiliar tasks. By the time you have finished this chapter, you will be familiar with those basic skills that are necessary to administer your WebTV account.

Adding a Secondary User

Each WebTV account supports a primary user and five secondary users. All six users are covered in the standard monthly fee. The primary user is the party responsible for billing and for receipt of official notifications.

Secondary users have the same abilities as the primary user. Each secondary user has an individual mailbox, an e-mail address, and a set of favorite Web links. However, the primary user is responsible for the actions of the secondary users of the account. The primary user may restrict what secondary users can do or see on the Internet. This enables parents to limit their children's ability to access chat rooms, e-mail, or adult Web sites.

The primary user can set up a password for each user. While the primary user does not have access to a secondary user's password, he or she can change that password if necessary.

The primary user may also restrict a secondary user's ability to create Web pages.

Expanded possibilities

You may find that you wish to add secondary users beyond the number of people in your account. Secondary users provide your WebTV account with possibilities. There are several advantages for creating "utility" secondary users.

You may find the 2-megabyte mailbox size-limit restrictive. Each secondary user is created with an additional mailbox. This means that a single WebTV account supports not just 2, but up to 12 megabytes of mail storage. This additional storage space may prevent the nightmare of repeated "your mailbox is full" messages and the ensuing heartaches of deciding which mail is

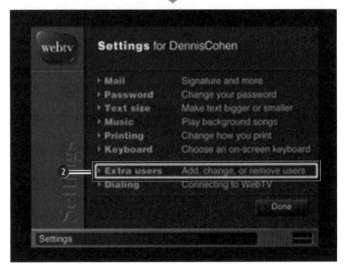

❶ *From your Web Home page, activate* **Settings***.*

❷ *On the Settings for page, find the heading* **Extra users***.*

CROSS-REFERENCE

Read how to remove a secondary user later in this chapter.

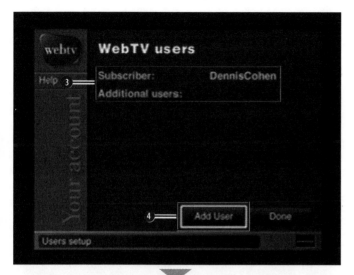

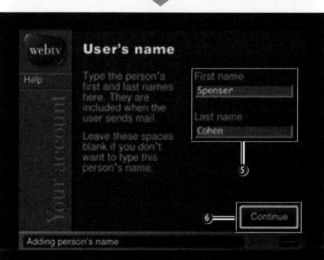

still precious and which must be discarded. Forward your treasured letters to a secondary user and you create a mail archive. Similarly, you can multiply the space available for your Web pages by the number of secondary users you create.

You may want to surf the Internet with greater privacy. If your Internet name is based on your personal name, a secondary user presents another, more anonymous, way to access the Internet. Whether you wish to use chat rooms, e-mail, or Usenet newsgroups, a secondary user name may protect your personal privacy.

Continued

TAKE NOTE

► USER NAMES MAY BE TAKEN

When choosing an Internet name for a secondary user you may find that name has already been taken. Consider appending a number to a favored name. For example, the Internet name "JaneDoe" may not work, but "JaneDoe99" might.

► INTERNET NAMES

You can pick arbitrary Internet names that have no connection to personal names. For example, if you like baking, you might choose "CookieMan," "BreadBaker," or "TheCook." Be creative, but pick something easy to remember and easy to type.

► WEBTV CLASSIC

You can add secondary users on WebTV Classic just as you do on WebTV Plus.

③ *WebTV shows you the current users of your WebTV account on the WebTV users setup screen.*

④ *Activate the **Add User** button at the bottom of the screen.*

⑤ *On the User's name screen enter the First name and Last name of the new user. (You can leave these spaces blank if you choose.)*

⑥ *Activate **Continue**.*

FIND IT ONLINE

Read more about primary and secondary users. Visit
http://wecare.webtv.net/newusers/accounts.html.

Adding a Secondary User

Continued

Restrictions

One of the restrictions that can be imposed on secondary accounts is e-mail blocking. Some parents consider it inappropriate for their child to engage in unsupervised correspondence with strangers. This restriction does not prevent the child from using his or her parent's primary account to send and receive e-mail. It does, however, introduce a level of parental control and oversight.

Another restriction involves access to chat rooms. Many Internet chat rooms include adult language and sexual themes. Again, the parent's primary account may be used to access chat rooms under a more supervised context. Although most Talk City chat rooms are moderated, with content kept to a "family acceptable" level, many non-Talk City chat rooms are not. Involving the primary user, the parent, in the child's experience with chat rooms provides another safety valve for Web access.

SurfWatch is another restriction. When SurfWatch is active, Web sites are screened for adult content before they can be accessed. WebTV will display only family friendly sites. This service limits access to sites that are sexually explicit or that include hateful speech.

Together, these restrictions combine to make the WebTV experience more family oriented and, most importantly, safer for your children. Recent news features about Internet stalking and other dangers should make you more aware of the perils, as well as the rewards, associated with the World Wide Web experience.

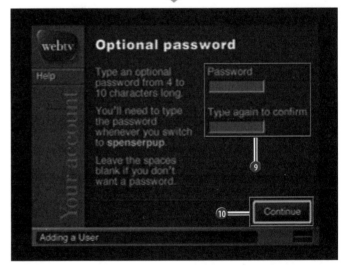

⑦ On the User's Internet name screen enter an Internet name for the new user. Internet names can contain letters and/or numbers, but not spaces.

⑧ Activate **Continue**.

⑨ (Optional) If you wish, you may enter a password for the user's account. You must type the password again to confirm. You need not use a password with WebTV if you do not wish to.

⑩ Activate **Continue**.

CROSS-REFERENCE

Read how to switch users later in this chapter.

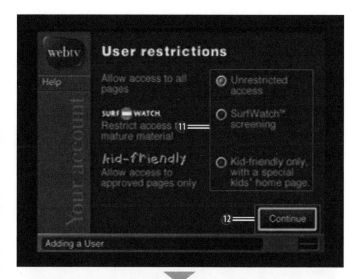

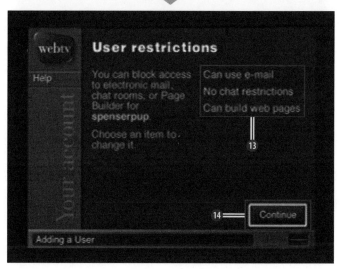

TAKE NOTE

RESTRICTIONS CAN BE LIFTED

Restrictions can be lifted. If you add a restriction to a secondary user, but later wish to change your mind, you can. You may wish, however, to check current restrictions on precocious children on a regular basis.

RESTRICTIONS CAN BE ARBITRARY

Some early surf-watching software made the news when they restricted access to cancer-survivor groups and Web sites because they contained the phrase "breast cancer." Recent updates to these packages have improved their capability of distinguishing between the acceptable and the unacceptable. Some restrictions, however, are still arbitrary and unfathomable. Your child may be unable to access certain sites that contain completely unobjectionable material. In this case, consider sitting down with your child and using your account rather than lifting your child's account restrictions.

WEBTV CLASSIC

WebTV Classic supports secondary users. Adding, selecting, and removing secondary users operates similarly to WebTV Plus.

⑪ *Select a level of user restriction that best matches your user's needs and sensibilities. SurfWatch restricts access to mature material; Kid-friendly enables access to approved pages only.*

⑫ *Activate* **Continue**.

⑬ *WebTV lists your user's restrictions. You may activate the blue-colored restrictions to change them.*

⑭ *Activate* **Continue**. *WebTV finishes the new user procedure by displaying a confirmation page.*

FIND IT ONLINE

Want to restrict a user's e-mail? Visit **http://wecare. webtv.net/abuse/plusrestrict.html**.

Removing a Secondary User

At some point, you may wish to remove a secondary user. Someone may have moved away from home. You may wish to create a fresh account. You may want to remove someone's computer privileges. For whatever reason you choose, WebTV lets you remove a user from your account.

When you delete a user, whether intentionally or by accident, you remove all the information associated with that user. This information, including the mailbox, favorites folder, and so on, cannot be recovered. Take enormous care when removing a user from your account. If you wish to save any information — such as e-mail or Web Favorites — transfer it to another user before undertaking the removal.

The only user account that you cannot remove is that for the primary user. If at any time you wish to cancel your WebTV service, you must call 1-800-GoWebTV and request service termination. For any other secondary user, however, you have control on both user creation and removal.

This feature proves especially useful when you have visitors. When you have not used the maximum number of secondary users, you can create a temporary user name for your visitor. This enables your visitor to surf the Web and, if their e-mail provider permits a POP3 retrieval of electronic mail, to check and reply to their mail as well.

Remember two things when creating a short-term secondary account. First, the secondary user must inform any e-mail correspondents that the e-mail address he or she uses is temporary and that they are *not* to

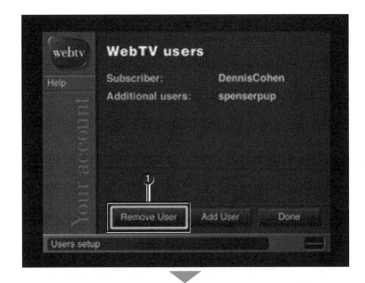

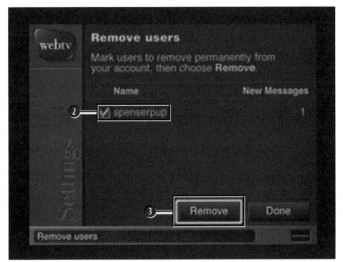

▶ To remove a User, open the WebTV users' screen. To reach this screen, activate **Settings** from your Web Home page and then **Extra users**.

❶ Activate **Remove User**. This option will not appear if your WebTV account does not have at least one secondary user.

❷ Select the user you wish to remove with the arrow keys and place a check before his or her name by pressing Go or Return.

❸ Activate **Remove**.

CROSS-REFERENCE

Want to add a secondary user? See the previous topic.

respond to that account after a certain date. This date, of course, will approximate when you remove that secondary user. Second, try not to find or use a particularly special user name. When testing out a WebTV unit, I created a user name I fell in love with. After I removed that secondary user and returned to my primary WebTV account, I found I could not resurrect that user name.

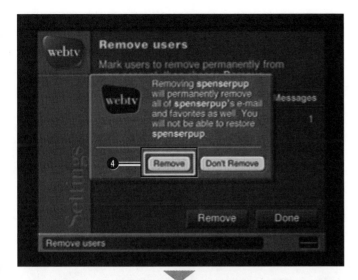

④ *WebTV will ask you to confirm this action. Removing a secondary user permanently destroys that user's mailbox, favorites, and preferences. If you are sure that you wish to remove this user, confirm **Remove**.*

▶ *WebTV removes the secondary user.*

⑤ *Activate **Done** to finish this task.*

TAKE NOTE

▶ YOU CAN STILL HAVE SIX USERS

After removing a user, you can create a new secondary user. While you cannot exceed six users per account, you can remove one user and replace him or her with another user.

▶ SLEEP ON IT

Because removing users cannot be undone, take a break to reconsider before performing a user removal. Also, remember that you may not be able to reuse a user name once you have removed it from your account.

▶ DISAPPEARING OPTIONS

The Remove User option will not appear unless your account has at least one secondary user.

▶ WEBTV CLASSIC

WebTV Classic enables you to remove secondary users just as with WebTV Plus.

FIND IT ONLINE

Read about changing user information at **http://wecare.webtv.net/newusers/change.html**.

Switching Users

When multiple users exist for a single WebTV account, WebTV always prompts you to select a user when powering on. To select a user, simply move the yellow box to the desired Internet name and activate it with Go or Return. If you have set a password for the account, you are prompted to enter it.

You can also switch users during the middle of a WebTV session, although it is a slightly more involved process. WebTV enables you to select which user is active without having to power your unit off and on again. This permits you to "turn over" the console to another person, perhaps regaining it yourself at a later time.

Whenever more than one user has been added to a WebTV account, a new Switch User option is added to each user's WebTV home page. This option adds quick access to the user-changing feature. When you activate it, WebTV moves you to the Choose your name screen. Here, you are prompted to select from a list of all Internet names actively associated with the WebTV account.

WebTV will restart with this name as the current user. Once again, if a password is associated with that primary or secondary user, you will be prompted to enter it before you may gain access to the account. When the restart procedure has finished, the WebTV home page for the new user will have been selected. The new user may continue with the WebTV session.

The Choose your name screen gives you a quick update of which users have new e-mail in their mailbox. In the example on the facing page, Spenser has received

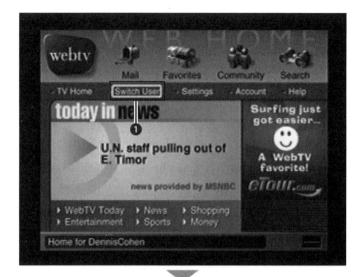

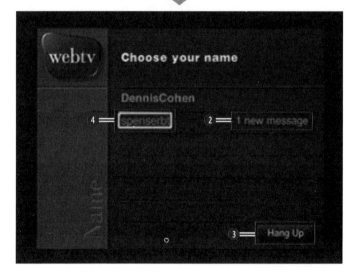

❶ From your Web home page, activate **Switch User**.

❷ On the Choose your name screen, WebTV tells each inactive user whether they have e-mail messages waiting and how many.

❸ (Optional) Instead of selecting a new user, you can also choose to **Hang Up**.

❹ Select the next user with the yellow box. Then press Go or Return.

CROSS-REFERENCE

Want to add or remove a secondary user? See the previous topics.

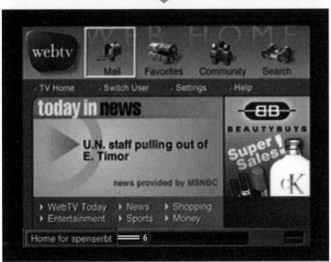

5 *WebTV restarts.*

6 *When the new user becomes active, his or her Web Home page is displayed.*

one new letter. When a family member asks you, "Did I get any new mail?," you can quickly and easily check by looking at this screen without having to actually change users.

TAKE NOTE

▶ **YOU ONLY CALL ONCE**

When switching users, WebTV should not have to redial. An existing connection should be maintained for you. Sometimes redialing may occur when you have already "timed out" before the switch-user process is complete, or when you have chosen to hang up.

▶ **HANGING UP**

When prompted to select a user, you may also choose to activate **Hang Up**. This lets you terminate your WebTV call, but leave the power on. You may also find this feature in the Options menu.

▶ **SELECTING THE WRONG USER**

If you have pressed Go or Return after selecting the wrong user name, you may need to repeat this procedure to return to your own account.

▶ **WEBTV CLASSIC**

WebTV Classic enables you to switch users in the same fashion as WebTV Plus.

FIND IT ONLINE

Read how to activate Surf Watch. Visit **http://wecare. webtv.net/abuse/classicsurfwatch.html**.

Checking Your Billing Information

WebTV enables you to update your Billing information at any time. You can change your credit card number, phone number, address, or billing method. Simply select the item to change and enter the new information.

Even though you may update your billing information at any time, WebTV can take up to a month to process your changes. This means that you should try to avoid changing your billing information more than once a month.

In Spring 1999, WebTV introduced a new billing feature: the e-mail statement. Now you can request WebTV to send you your account information directly by electronic mail. WebTV account summaries include current information about your WebTV account including balance, payment method, monthly charge, last payment date, and address as of the date the information was requested. See the Find It Online section below for the WebTV address to request e-mail statements.

Payment

You may pay your WebTV service fee by a variety of methods. WebTV accepts credit and debit cards, money orders, and checks. Valid credit cards include American Express, Discover, MasterCard and Visa. WebTV also accepts MasterCard and Visa debit/checking cards. WebTV

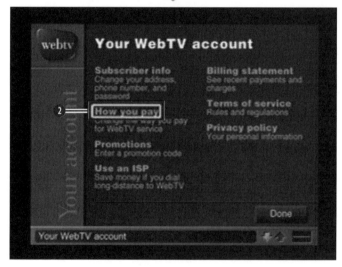

▶ You must be the Primary User to change billing information.

❶ From the Web Home page, activate **Account**.

❷ On the Your WebTV account page activate **How you pay**.

CROSS-REFERENCE

Read more about electronic mail in Section III.

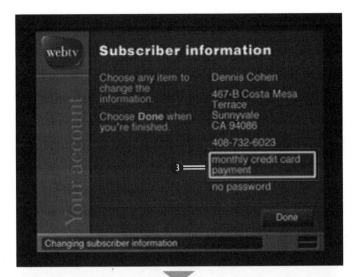

also supports an Automatic Check Payment service that lets you pay for monthly service through automatic withdrawals from a checking account. This last feature, however, is not currently available in Canada.

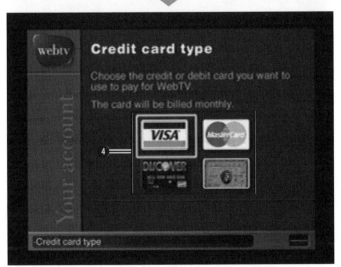

❸ *The Subscriber information screen shows the name and address of the Primary user. Select an item to change with the yellow box. Activate it with Go or Return.*

❹ *Selecting an item to change brings up a sequence of screens that lead you through the selection process. In this example, the credit card types are shown.*

▶ *Follow these screens. When finished, you are returned to the Subscriber information screen. From there, activate* ***Done.***

FIND IT ONLINE

Sign up for automatic e-mail statements. Visit:
http://help.webtv.net/billing/billingstmt.html.

Switching Onscreen Keyboard Styles

With WebTV, you can select either a traditional (typewriter) or alphabetical layout for your onscreen keyboard. People familiar with touch-typing generally prefer the traditional layout. Other people may prefer the alphabetical layout.

The traditional layout follows the QWERTY style. That is, the first six keys on the upper left of the keyboard are Q, W, E, R, T, and Y. Most typing keyboards are laid out this way. If you own the optional remote keyboard, you'll find it also has this layout. Anyone well versed with standard keyboards will find the traditional layout familiar.

The alphabetical layout follows, unsurprisingly, the alphabet. The letters go A, B, C, D, and so on. A bit of trivia: This layout is the one most often used on entry systems on factory floors and by traveling salesmen. Those unfamiliar with touch-typing can easily locate and activate keys in a reasonably efficient manner. This technique builds on people's familiarity with the alphabet and is surprisingly effective.

Selecting either format is not permanent. You can move back and forth whenever you wish. This lets you try each style to determine which best matches your data entry style.

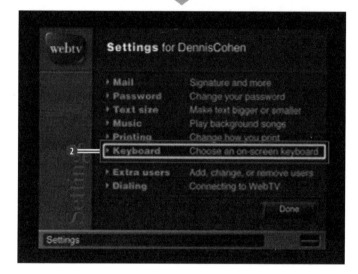

❶ Activate **Settings** on your WebTV Home page.

❷ On the settings screen, activate **Keyboard** from the list of options.

CROSS-REFERENCE

Learn how to use the onscreen keyboard in Section I.

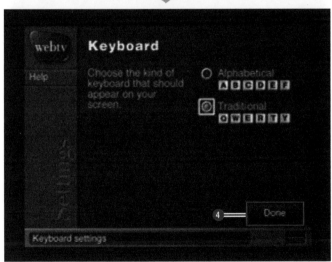

❸ *Use the yellow box to select either the Alphabetical or Traditional radio button. Press Go or Return to activate the red light.*

❹ *Activate **Done.***

TAKE NOTE

▶ BUY A KEYBOARD

You may wish to buy a keyboard if your unit did not come with one rather than use the onscreen one. Most WebTV users prefer to use the physical device rather than the onscreen version. They claim this improves efficiency and lowers stress.

▶ SAVE YOUR NECK

Some users, especially seniors, report that using the onscreen keyboard helps reduce strain on their necks. They insist that the onscreen keyboard is easier for them to use than the physical one. Instead of repeatedly looking down at the remote keyboard and then up again at the screen, eyes (and neck) remain in a more fixed position. These users, for the most part, are not touch typists and need to search the keyboard for each key to type.

▶ QWERTY MYTHS

According to Darryl Rehr, the QWERTY layout was not invented to slow typists down (as is the usual explanation for the keyboard layout). Instead, Mr. Rehr suggests, the keys that were used often in combination (such as "T" and "H") were placed on separate parts of the keyboard to avoid jamming when pressed in quick succession.

▶ WEBTV CLASSIC

WebTV Classic enables you to select a keyboard style in the same fashion as WebTV Plus.

FIND IT ONLINE

Read more about the history of QWERTY. Visit **http://home.earthlink.net/~dcrehr/index.html.**

Enjoying Background Music

I f you enjoy music, WebTV can provide soothing background melodies during your WebTV session. This feature is little known, but easy to use. You can set your WebTV to provide real-time background melodies in a variety of styles from Funk to Classical to Ragtime to Pop.

This feature is available from the WebTV Settings screen. To gain access, activate **Music** and check the Background Music option.

Until you turn this option off, WebTV will play background instrumental tunes during your online sessions.

Musical tastes vary. I recommend that you pick selections that will not disturb others who may be sharing room space with you. I have not found any of WebTV's music to be objectionable, although I do find some of it extremely tedious. Experiment with this feature when others are out of the house before inflicting it on an unsuspecting audience.

Do not expect symphonic-quality selections. WebTV background music is based on the MIDI (Musical Instrument Digital Interface) standard. This means that WebTV plays the melody in much the same way a music box would — a single instrument plucking out a melody with some rhythm. You will find harmony and expression quite limited. On the up side, the music is almost universally pleasant and fades nicely into the background as you work.

Any time you turn on the TV window (using ⌘+W, if you have a keyboard), the background music turns off enabling you to better hear the program in progress. When you remove the TV window, the music returns after a few seconds.

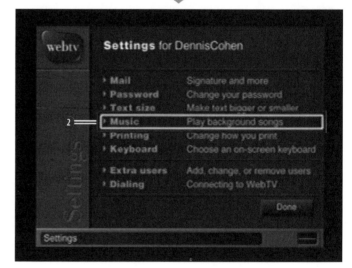

❶ Activate **Settings** on your WebTV Home page.

❷ Activate **Music** from the list of options on the Settings screen.

CROSS-REFERENCE

Learn to use WebTV's Karaoke feature in Section II.

▶ SEE THE MUSIC, HEAR THE MUSIC

From the Background music styles page, you can activate the blue-colored name of any music style to see a list of music selections in that category. Activate any blue-colored selection to hear that piece.

▶ REPETITION

Although, in theory, this feature should randomly move through a variety of music during an online session, I find that it often gets stuck. After hearing "Für Elise" for the fiftieth time, I discovered that my particular WebTV unit had to be powered off and on to choose another random music selection. Your WebTV unit may mimic this behavior, or it may act more properly in providing a jukebox for you. Be aware.

▶ TV HOME

WebTV background music plays during online sessions, but not while you are using your TV Home.

▶ WEBTV CLASSIC

WebTV Classic lets you listen to background melodies in the same fashion as WebTV Plus.

③ Check the Background Music box to turn on the background music feature.

④ Activate **Choose Music Styles** to select the styles of background music that you want to hear.

⑤ WebTV offers a variety of music styles. Place checkmarks next to those styles you wish to hear, and remove them from those you do not.

⑥ Activate **Done** to finish selecting music styles. Then activate **Done** on the Music page to finish setting up background music.

FIND IT ONLINE

Read more about it. Visit **http://wecare.webtv. net/setup/music/classicsetup.html**.

Adjusting Font Sizes

Television screens tend to be small. In theory, however, you need not strain your eyes to view WebTV. WebTV allows you to select a font size that best suits your vision and TV. You may choose to display characters in a small, medium, or large font.

The larger the font that you select, the easier it is to read characters on your television screen. However, the larger the font, the less the amount of information that can fit on a single screen at one time. Smaller fonts let you display more information at once, but are, at the same time, harder to read.

Even at the "large" setting, many senior citizens or visually challenged people may find it difficult to discern detail — and not everyone can afford to buy larger television sets to remedy the situation.

WebTV uses a special technology to try to make all characters as visually distinct as possible. Certainly this technology bridges the gap between illegibility and legibility on most television screens. Font size selection adds an extra dimension to improve visual comprehension. If you find your WebTV screen hard to understand, experiment with a larger font size.

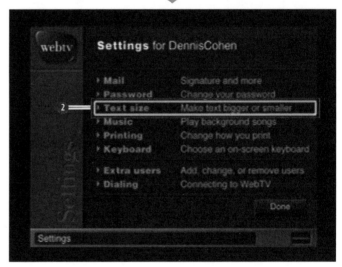

❶ Activate **Settings** from your WebTV home page.

❷ Activate **Text size** from the Settings screen.

CROSS-REFERENCE

Learn to use WebTV's Around Town feature earlier in Chapter 16.

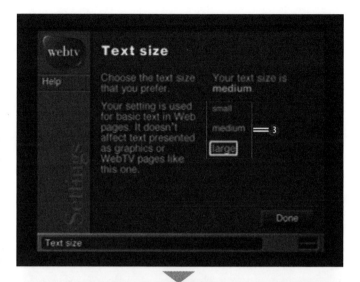

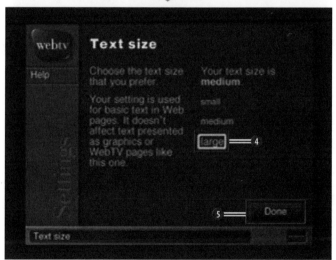

Please note that text size on many World Wide Web pages, those not directly owned or managed by WebTV, are not affected by this option. Web page designers often specify font size when creating pages. These design specifications override your WebTV preferences when you visit these pages. However, when a page designer does not specify font size, and for all main WebTV pages, your defaults *will* affect the way WebTV displays that page. WebTV service pages (such as the ones displayed to the right) are not affected because they are designed to be displayed in large type.

TAKE NOTE

▶ **TV HOME**

Setting a default font size affects only some of the listings shown on your TV Home.

▶ **WEBTV CLASSIC**

WebTV Classic enables you to set font size, as does WebTV Plus.

❸ *Examples of small, medium, and large text are displayed.*

❹ *Use the yellow box to select small, medium, or large, and confirm your choice with Go or Return.*

❺ *Activate **Done** to confirm your new font selection.*

FIND IT ONLINE

Read more about it. Visit **http://wecare.webtv.net/ surfing/plustextsize.html.**

Asking WebTV for Help

There comes a time in everyone's life when you need to ask for help. Fortunately for WebTV users, WebTV has an online help center. This help center enables you to ask questions — in English! — and get immediate access to online help files.

This center is called Ask WebTV. It is located at askwebtv.webtv.net. To find it, you must use the Go To button or select **go to** from the options menu. When the Address dialog box appears, as seen on the facing page, type **askwebtv.webtv.net** into the address line and activate **Go to Page**. These steps are necessary because, surprisingly enough, there is no "help" key built into the keyboard or remote!

The Ask WebTV help center is powered by a system called "Ask Jeeves." This system uses "natural language processing" to help translate your English-language questions into a form that the computer can understand. It works well. For example, my question "How do I spell-check mail?" was easily understood and a number of help topics were returned by the help center.

If you wish to skip typing a whole sentence, you are welcome to do so. Ask WebTV works as well with "Spell Check" as it does with "How do I spell-check mail?" Feel free to type a single word or phrase into the query line. You need not type sentences unless you feel more comfortable doing so.

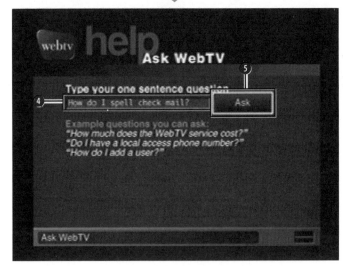

① *From your Web Home page, press the Go To button on your remote to bring up the Go to an address screen.*

② *Type **askwebtv.webtv.net** in the address line.*

③ *Activate **Go to Page**.*

▶ *You enter the WebTV Help Center.*

④ *Move the yellow box to the text area and type a question for WebTV.*

⑤ *Activate **Ask**.*

CROSS-REFERENCE

Learn more about basic WebTV Skills in Section I.

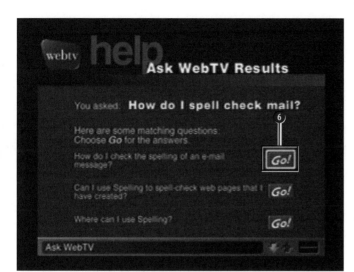

6 *Select a help topic that best matches your question and activate **Go!***

▶ **ONLINE NEWSLETTER**

WebTV publishes a helpful monthly newsletter called Club WebTV. You can find this newsletter at **http://www.webtv.net/corp/clubwebtv/ newsletter/.** This newsletter, which includes tips and how-to's, is updated monthly. Many issues include late-breaking news and editorials from WebTV's corporate offices.

▶ **GLOSSARY**

Are technical phrases confusing you? Do you want to know what WebTV thinks a particular word means? WebTV maintains a Web Terms list, which, to normal humans, means an online glossary of Internet-related terms and phrases. You can visit this glossary at **http://help.webtv.net/glossary.html.**

▶ **CALL FOR HELP**

If you cannot find help in any other fashion, you may call WebTV directly. You can find a person to talk to at 1-800-GoWebTV. Make sure to ask for Technical Support at the start of your phone call. WebTV's support service is not available at all hours of the day. If you call outside of normal hours, you will be unable to talk to a representative, and will have to listen to a prerecorded message instead.

▶ **WEBTV CLASSIC**

WebTV Classic supports full access to the Ask WebTV site.

FIND IT ONLINE

Try it out. Visit: **http://askwebtv.webtv.net**.

Personal Workbook

Q&A

1 How many users can coexist in one WebTV account?

_____

_____

_____

2 If you remove a user, can you recreate his or her account later?

_____

_____

_____

3 Can you pay for your WebTV service by money order?

_____

_____

_____

4 How do you cancel your WebTV account?

_____

_____

_____

5 What types of onscreen keyboard styles are available with WebTV?

_____

_____

_____

_____

_____

6 If you activate background music, when does it play?

_____

_____

_____

_____

_____

7 How many font sizes does WebTV support?

_____

_____

_____

_____

ANSWERS: PAGE 342

EXTRA PRACTICE

1. Add a secondary user to your account — use an Internet name that you do not care whether it is lost.

2. Switch back and forth between your primary user and this secondary user.

3. List your billing information.

4. Set your onscreen keyboard style to "alphabetical."

5. Turn background music on, and then off.

6. Adjust your font size.

REAL-WORLD APPLICATIONS

✔ Your spouse or child wants to use WebTV. You add him or her to your WebTV account as a secondary user. When adding a child, you use the special "kids" or "surf watch" features to safeguard his or her experience on the Internet.

✔ You've got a fancy to listen to some music. You turn on WebTV's background music feature and select musical styles that appeal to you and experiment with the background music option.

Visual Quiz

How many more users can you add to this WebTV account?

_____

_____

_____

_____

_____

_____

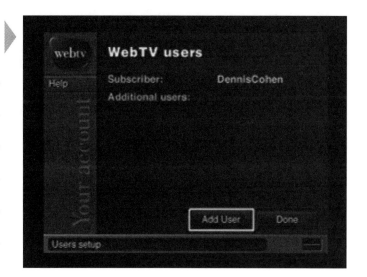

Personal Workbook
Answers

Chapter 1

See page 20

❶ How do you power on your WebTV unit?

A: Press Power on your remote or keyboard.

❷ Can you use WebTV without buying the optional keyboard?

A: Absolutely. WebTV is designed to be fully usable without a keyboard. Still, consider getting the keyboard. It makes a huge difference in ease of use.

❸ What does the onscreen keyboard do?

A: The onscreen keyboard allows remote-only users to enter text into WebTV.

❹ How do you make the onscreen keyboard display?

A: Press Go on the remote when the yellow cursor is blinking.

❺ How do you finish typing with the onscreen keyboard?

A: Activate Continue.

❻ How do you "activate" a WebTV feature?

A: Move the yellow box to a feature and press Go or Return.

❼ What does Home on the keyboard do?

A: Pressing this key moves you to your Web Home page.

❽ If the yellow cursor is not blinking, how do you activate a text-entry space?

A: Press Edit.

Visual Quiz

Q: How do you make this onscreen keyboard disappear?

A: Press Back or activate **Continue**.

Chapter 2

See page 36

❶ When you press Delete, which character is removed?

A: The character directly to the left of the yellow blinking cursor is removed.

❷ What happens if you press Delete while the yellow cursor is positioned before the entirety of your text?

A: Nothing happens. The Delete key will not remove text positioned to the right of the cursor.

❸ How do you highlight text with the arrow keys?

A: You can highlight text with the arrow keys by pressing and holding the Shift key at the same time.

Personal Workbook Answers

4 **How do you cut highlighted text?**

A: Press and hold the ⌘ key and tap X. The highlighted text will be cut.

5 **What is the difference between cutting and copying text?**

A: In terms of copying information to WebTV memory, they both work the same. However, copying text does not change the original, while cutting text will remove the original selection.

6 **What does ⌘+A do?**

A: This key combination selects the entire text.

7 **What happens if you type ⌘+A several times in sequence?**

A: The text will alternately be all selected, none selected, all selected, none selected, and so forth.

8 **Do you execute the commands to add an accent before or after the letter it will be attached to?**

A: Add it before.

Visual Quiz

Q: How do you type the one-half character?

A: Press and hold the Alt key. Tap 6.

Chapter 3

See page 56

1 **When you encounter a list in which a radio button precedes each item, how many items may you select at once?**

A: Radio buttons indicate you may select only one option at a time.

2 **When you encounter a list in which a square box precedes each item, how many items may you select at once?**

A: Check boxes indicate you may select any number — from zero to all — of options at a time.

3 **What does a rounded gray rectangle with a downward-pointing triangle indicate?**

A: This indicates a pull-down list.

4 **How many items may you select from a pull-down list at once?**

A: You may select only one item from a pull-down list at any time.

5 **How do you identify a scrolling list?**

A: You can identify a scrolling list by the down- and/or up-pointing triangles.

6 **How do you move through a scrolling list?**

A: You can use the up and down arrows as well as the scroll keys to navigate through a scrolling list.

7 **What do you see when entering information into a password field?**

A: You see a series of dots.

8 **What happens when you activate the Reset button in a form?**

A: You reset the form to the original (default) values.

Visual Quiz

Q: What does the yellow arrow on the right-bottom corner of this box mean?

A: It indicates that you are looking at an "Image Map" and can use the arrow to point to a part of the picture.

Personal Workbook Answers

Chapter 4

See page 72

1 **What is URL an acronym for?**

A: It stands for Uniform Resource Locator.

2 **What is a more common name for URL?**

A: A Web address is the same as a URL.

3 **What does http:// mean?**

A: This acronym stands for Hypertext Transfer Protocol. It is the way most Web addresses begin.

4 **What is a *hyperlink*?**

A: A hyperlink allows you to move directly between Web pages without having to manually enter Web addresses.

5 **How do you detect hyperlinks?**

A: Any image or text you can surround with a yellow box is potentially a hyperlink.

6 **What is the difference between the Back and Recent buttons?**

A: The Back button lets you move back one page. The Recent button permits you to select from one of the 12 most recently visited pages.

7 **How do you know when a Web page is unsecure?**

A: If pressing the Info button does not reveal a **Security Details** option, then the page is not secure.

Visual Quiz

Q: **Is this Web page secure?**

A: No, it is not. No Security Details option is displayed in the information.

Chapter 5

See page 92

1 **What is the difference between a Web address and a Web page?**

A: The Web address tells WebTV where to find the Web page.

2 **How do you add a Web address to your Favorites?**

A: Use the Save key. Then choose the folder in which you want to save the page. Press Save Page.

3 **What are F keys?**

A: The F keys are the seven keys labeled F1 through F7, found at the upper-left of your WebTV remote keyboard.

4 **How many Favorites folders does WebTV let you maintain?**

A: WebTV permits you to maintain up to 20 Favorites folders.

5 **How many favorites may you store in a single folder?**

A: You may store up to 32 favorites in a single folder.

6 **If you rename a Web site favorite and later wish to resume the former name, what can you do?**

A: You can always return to the site, resave it and discard the renamed version.

7 **Why might some people prefer to omit site snapshots?**

A: Omitting snapshots enables you to view more favorites at once.

8 **If several sites seem to have a common theme, what is a way to organize them?**

A: Create a new folder and move those favorites to it.

Personal Workbook Answers

Visual Quiz

Q: Which site is assigned to an F key? Which F key?

A: The games-tcgames site is assigned to F2.

Chapter 6

See page 108

1 How do you tell WebTV that you wish to begin searching the World Wide Web?

A: A search begins by pressing Search or by activating **Search** from your WebTV home page.

2 Why do you find Web pages that include only subsets of the search phrases you used?

A: By default, WebTV and Infoseek will find pages that include many, but not necessarily all, of the phrases that you search for.

3 Which will produce more Web pages: a search for *burgundy* or a search for *Burgundy*?

A: The lowercase search will produce more matches. It will match both upper- and lowercase. The uppercase search will match only those Web pages with the uppercase usage.

4 What is the difference between searching for *top cat* and *"top cat"*?

A: The latter search ensures that the two words will appear together within a Web page.

5 How might you search for the Gettysburg Address, if you are unsure how to spell Gettysburg?

A: Try searching for "four score and seven years ago."

6 What's a good way to search for song lyrics by Gilbert and Sullivan?

A: You might wish to search for Gilbert Sullivan +lyrics.

7 If you wish to find information about the Golden Gate Bridge, which query should you use: *San Francisco attraction +golden +gate +bridge* or *+San +Francisco +attraction golden gate bridge?*

A: Use the former query, it uses + to restrict the more desired and more specific terms.

8 How might you search for information about Camels but exclude pages that talk about the cigarettes?

A: You could search for camels –cigarettes.

Visual Quiz

Q: How could you view sites about pasta recipes?

A: Move the yellow box to Pasta Recipes under Best Bets and activate it with Go or Return.

Chapter 7

See page 120

1 How do you find WebTV's Explore feature?

A: Activate Explore from your WebTV home page.

2 What is *Karaoke?*

A: Karaoke involves singing prompted words to a prerecorded soundtrack.

3 What is the difference between MIDI and MIDI Karaoke?

A: The former does not include words. The latter does.

4 What's a good way to search for MIDI Karaoke songs?

A: Use the search techniques that you mastered in Chapter 6 and search for "MIDI karaoke". Notice the lowercase usage of "karaoke." This enables you to match more sites.

5 What sorts of free expertise can you find on the Internet?

A: You can find expertise ranging from hobbies to gardening, law to medicine, religion to music.

Personal Workbook Answers

6 **How reliable is the free expertise that you find on the Internet?**

A: The expertise will vary from priceless to worthless. You do, in general, get what you pay for.

Visual Quiz

Q: **How can you change the pitch on this song?**

A: Highlight and activate the plus or minus buttons in the pitch area to raise or lower the pitch. The indicator to the right serves as a guide.

Chapter 8

See page 148

1 **What does an e-mail address look like?**

A: Username@domainname.domaintype.

2 **Why does the red message light on your WebTV unit illuminate?**

A: The red message light illuminates when you have mail.

3 **How should you address an e-mail when you are sending it to more than one person?**

A: Separate names with a comma followed by a space.

4 **What is *spam*?**

A: Spam is unsolicited or unwanted mail.

5 **What should you do about spam?**

A: Ignore it.

6 **What does it mean when the Previous option is displayed in very dim blue rather than yellow?**

A: You are at the first letter in the mail list.

7 **What does it mean when both the Previous and Next options are displayed in very dim blue rather than yellow?**

A: You are at the only letter in the mail list.

8 **When should you not send a sound recording attached to an e-mail?**

A: If you have not received permission in advance or if the person cannot hear .WAV files on their personal computer.

Visual Quiz

Q: **How could you read the letter from SpenserPup?**

A: Highlight it with the yellow box and press Go or Return to open the message.

Chapter 9

See page 164

1 **How many addresses can you store in an address book?**

A: You can store up to 150 addresses.

2 **How can you store an old and a new address for a friend?**

A: Make sure the names are slightly different.

3 **How can you send an e-mail to more than one person using the address book?**

A: Check more than one name when addressing mail.

4 **How can you change your mind about sending mail to someone when using the address book?**

A: Choose their name a second time and the check mark will be turned off and their name will be removed from the list of recipients.

5 **Why should you print your address list before removing a name?**

A: To provide a record of the address you are about to remove, helping insure against mistakes.

Personal Workbook Answers

6 **When should you update names and addresses?**

A: When addresses and names change. For example, when people change jobs, marry, and so forth.

7 **When should you remove names?**

A: When people move, change addresses, or otherwise drop out of sight.

8 **What might be the problem when you are unable to find someone's e-mail addresses?**

A: They may not be on the Internet or they may not have been "found" by search engines.

Visual Quiz

Q: How can you add Bruce Leak's name and address to your address book?

A: Highlight the name or e-mail address and press Go or Return. Confirm that you want the name added to your address book.

Chapter 10

See page 188

1 **Why do people use e-mail signatures?**

A: To save time and keystrokes when writing e-mail. Signatures add an identifying message. They allow people to skip "signing" every letter with identical information.

2 **Why do people use different e-mail ordering?**

A: Mostly for familiarity. Some people are accustomed to most-recent-first or least-recent-first ordering.

3 **What difference is there between sending a letter to person X with a cc: to person Y and just sending the letter to both X and Y?**

A: Using cc: is a matter of style. The mail arrives to both people either way.

4 **When should you "Reply to all"?**

A: When you are involved in a group conversation.

5 **Why do people include e-mail in a reply?**

A: To provide context for the reply.

6 **Why might someone erase a letter that they are writing?**

A: All sorts of reasons, but mostly because they do not want to send that letter.

7 **What does it mean when you get a letter from the "Post Office?"**

A: It means a letter you wrote could not be delivered.

8 **Why are most letters returned to you by the "Post Office?"**

A: Most letters are returned because the address was incorrectly specified.

Visual Quiz

Q: You are in the middle of writing the following letter. How can you take a break?

A: Power off your WebTV unit. When you turn it back on, press the Mail button and then activate **Write**. You can pick up where you left off.

Chapter 11

See page 206

1 **What does WebTV's Storage option enable you to do?**

A: Enabling storage allows you to create and access saved, discarded, and sent messages.

2 **How many storage areas does WebTV provide?**

A: WebTV provides four storage areas: the Mail list and the Saved, Sent, and Discarded folders.

3 Is discarding a letter from the Mail list a permanent action?

A: Yes and no. Messages discarded from the Mail list can be recovered from the Discarded mail storage folder if and only if storage has been enabled.

4 How long is saved mail kept?

A: Saved mail is kept indefinitely until you remove it.

5 How long is discarded mail kept?

A: Discarded mail is kept for seven days.

6 How long is sent mail kept?

A: Sent mail is kept for seven days.

7 How much storage is allocated to each WebTV user?

A: Two megabytes.

8 How can you determine how much space a letter takes up?

A: The Clean up screen shows the size of a letter as a percentage of available storage space.

Visual Quiz

Q: How much space do these sent messages take up?

A: They take up about 3.1 percent of 2 megabytes, or about 62,000 bytes.

Chapter 12

See page 220

1 If you set WebTV to automatically check e-mail at 11 a.m., at what time will WebTV automatically check your e-mail?

A: If the phone line is free, WebTV will check your e-mail sometime between about 10:30 a.m. and 11:30 a.m.

2 How can you set two times to check e-mail?

A: With WebTV Plus, set a second time to retrieve new TV listings. This will check for new e-mail at the same time.

3 The red message light went on, but no e-mail was received. Why?

A: The message may belong to another user on your WebTV account.

4 What kinds of picture attachments can WebTV display?

A: WebTV can display GIF and JPEG pictures.

5 How do you send a message with very large characters?

A: Use embedded HTML and set the font size high.

6 You have another e-mail account and it supports POP3. Can you use WebTV to read that e-mail?

A: Yes, but only if that account's POP3 server permits it.

7 What happens if you "send" a Web page to yourself?

A: You will receive an e-mail message with a hyperlink containing the Web page's address.

8 What do blue-colored words in an e-mail message mean?

A: Blue-colored words indicate embedded hyperlinks. You may activate them with the yellow box and pressing Go or Return.

Visual Quiz

Q: What happens when you activate To:?

A: Your address book will appear and prompt you to select an address.

Personal Workbook Answers

Chapter 13

See page 232

1 **What is the difference between an administrative address and a list address?**

A: Send subscription requests to the administrative address. Send on-topic letters to the list address.

2 **Which search term will find more lists, "Bicyc" or "Bicycling"?**

A: Bicyc will find lists on Bicycles, Bicycling, and so on. Bicycling will not find lists about Bicycles.

3 **What is *lurking?***

A: Lurking refers to monitoring an e-mail list discussion without participating.

4 **What is a *mail list digest?***

A: A digest is a compilation of all list messages received in one day.

5 **Why might some people prefer digests?**

A: Digests reduce strain on your mailbox. You receive only one message a day rather than ten or a score or even a hundred.

6 **Which is better Liszt or ListServ?**

A: Neither. Liszt is easier to use. ListServ is older and has a widely accepted base of use.

7 **How can you temporarily stop mail from your mail list if you have to go away from your WebTV unit for a period of days or weeks?**

A: Set your e-mail list subscription to "no mail" or its equivalent. You can put a hold on your mail list just as you would with your newspaper.

8 **If you unsubscribe from a list, can you resubscribe to it at another time?**

A: Yes.

Visual Quiz

Q: **This is part of Liszt search for "Opera". How would you narrow the search to find lists likely to interest a soap opera enthusiast?**

A: Ignore the lists about Cooperative Cataloging, Bowling Center Operations, The Linux Operating System, and so on, and focus, instead, on *Days of our Lives*, *Guiding Light*, *All My Children*, and such.

Chapter 14

See page 254

1 **How do you get to MyWebTV?**

A: Activate the MyWebTV bar at the lower right-hand corner of your WebTV home page.

2 **What topics are covered in MyWebTV?**

A: Topics include News, Weather, Stocks, Sports, and Entertainment.

3 **How do you choose which topics to track?**

A: Activate Change Settings on the top-right corner of your MyWebTV Screen.

4 **What happens if you choose no topics to track?**

A: You end up with a very boring MyWebTV screen.

5 **What are the two ways that you can use to specify a city for weather forecasts?**

A: You can specify either by city and state or by Zip code.

6 **Can you get weather forecasts for Canadian cities?**

A: Not at this time.

Personal Workbook Answers

7 **How many stocks can you track at a time?**

A: You can track up to 75 stocks at one time.

8 **How do you find the details behind a final sports score?**

A: Activate the score to bring up a play-by-play article.

Visual Quiz

Q: You are about to visit Denver on vacation. What should you pack?

A: Whatever you pack, make sure its warm! Snow is in the forecast.

Chapter 15

See page 288

1 **What is the television equivalent to your Web Home?**

A: The equivalent is your TV Home.

2 **When might you want to retrieve TV listings manually?**

A: When you are using TV Home for the first time or when you have moved between cities.

3 **What are the three ways to select a television show?**

A: Select from the TV listings, from your Favorites, or by setting a reminder.

4 **What are the three ways to search for a television show?**

A: Search by name, search by date and time, or search by category/topic.

5 **How many TV Favorites can you see at once on a single screen?**

A: You can see six favorites at once. Use the scroll keys to view more favorites.

6 **What does the Recent button do?**

A: Shows you recently viewed channels

7 **What is a *crossover link*?**

A: Crossover links move you to a Web site that is associated with a television show.

8 **How far in advance can you set a reminder for a single television showing?**

A: You can set a once-only reminder one week in advance because WebTV retrieves a week of television listings at a time.

Visual Quiz

Q: What is the difference between the show surrounded by the yellow box and the other shows shown in this picture?

A: The show surrounded by the yellow box is active, showing movement and sound. The other shows are seen as still shots.

Chapter 16

See page 308

1 **If you change your city in Around Town, do you change your city for your entire WebTV system?**

A: Yes. Make sure to return to your old city before leaving Around Town.

2 **What information can you find under Going Out in the Around Town feature?**

A: Features include Dining Out, Event Tickets, Music Events, and Movie Listings.

3 **How is your chat nickname assigned in Talk City?**

A: Your chat nickname is the same as your Internet name.

Personal Workbook Answers

4 **What is *spam?* How might you get some?**

A: Spam is unsolicited or unwanted mail. If you post to Usenet Newsgroups, you may get Spam.

5 **What is *Netiquette?***

A: Netiquette is set of rules that govern how people can courteously communicate with each other in Usenet Newsgroups.

6 **In a chat room thread, what does "brb" mean?**

A: "BRB" is chat shorthand for "be right back."

7 **What does it mean when a person in a Talk City chat room has a nickname such as GrinCCC?**

A: It means he or she is a Talk City moderator.

Visual Quiz

Q: Which Talk City category under Hot Topics might appeal to a football enthusiast?

A: Perhaps "News and Sports" might fit the bill.

Chapter 17

See page 330

1 **How many users can coexist in one WebTV account?**

A: You may have one primary and five secondary users assigned to any WebTV account.

2 **If you remove a user, can you recreate his or her account later?**

A: No, you cannot. All personal information is deleted along with the mailbox and Favorites folders. Additionally, it is unlikely that you will be able to reuse the Internet name.

3 **Can you pay for your WebTV service by money order?**

A: Yes, but you must pay for six months in advance.

4 **How do you cancel your WebTV account?**

A: Call 1-800-GoWebTV to cancel your account.

5 **What types of onscreen keyboard styles are available with WebTV?**

A: You can select either alphabetical or traditional keyboard styles.

6 **If you activate background music, when does it play?**

A: Background music plays when you are online with WebTV.

7 **How many font sizes does WebTV support?**

A: WebTV currently supports three font sizes: small, medium, and large.

8 **What is a *power-off code?***

A: A power-off code is a signal sent to WebTV when your unit is powered off.

Visual Quiz

Q: How many more users can you add to this WebTV account?

A: You can add four more users to a total of six.

Index

+ delimiter, 104–105
.AIFF, 215
.AU, 215
.com domains, 69
.gov domains, 69
.org domains, 69
.SND, 215
.WAV format, 145
@ sign, 15, 216

A

abbreviated title, 66
absolute address, 69
accented characters, 32
account address, 219
account information, 6
account name, 216
accounts, administering
    billing information, 320–321
    font size, adjusting, 326–327
    Music, 324–325
    online help center, 328–329
    onscreen keyboard, switching styles, 322–323
    overview, 311
    secondary user, 312–315, 316–317
    switching users, 318–319
acronyms, 35
acronyms, chat rooms, 297
acronyms, newsgroups, 301

actions, chat rooms, 297
activate image map, 52
acute accent, 32
Add, 82
Add button, 152
Add to Message option, 144
Address, 62
address book, 127
    adding to from electronic mail, 154–155
    adding to manually, 152–153
    addressing electronic mail with, 156–157
    finding addresses, 162–163
    limits, 153
    overview, 151
    printed version, 161
    removing entries from, 160–161
    updating, 158–159
addresses, electronic mail, 130–131
addresses, searching for, 162–163
Addresses option, 152, 156
Adobe Acrobat PDF files, 215
adult content, 314
advertising, 116
advice services, 116–117
Aiwa DM-H100, 145
aliases, 218
AllExperts.com, 116
alphabetical layout, 322
Alt key, 32–33
    acute accent (Alt+apostrophe), 32
    Alt Command List, 32
    cedilla (Alt+C), 33
    Greek character mu (Alt+M), 32

Index

Alta Vista, 107, 307
alternate spellings, 269
Amazon, 82
American Express, 320
amusing quotes, 169
anonymity, 163, 313
antenna, 261
antiques, 223
Apple, 100
archives, 301
Around Town, 292–293
arrow keys
    deselect highlighted text, 26
    image map, 53
    keyboard, 10
    navigate listings, 264
    password, 50
    pull-down lists, 44
    recent page, 66
    remote control
    scrolling list, 46, 48
    select text, 26
    yellow box, 12
    yellow cursor, 14
arthritis, 223
ASCII clip art, 169
Ask Jeeves, 328
Ask WebTV, 328
assign F key, 80–81
at-sign (@), 130
Attach original message feature, 179, 180–181
attachments, 141, 214
attribution, 169
attribution, remembering to include, 29
auctions, 292
audio-in jacks, 138, 143
audio-out jacks, 138
audio-visual output cable, 138
authentication, 51
Automatic Check Payment service, 321

automatic e-mail check, 210
automatic wrap, 133

B

Back, 65, 66
Back button, 17
back key, 79
Background Music option, 324–325
background style, 302
backward compatibility, 66
bandwidth, 141
banking service, 70
Barnes and Noble, 82
baseball, 250
basic skills, overview, 5
basketball, 250
Battleship game, 114
Be, 100
best bet, 105
billing information, 6, 320–321
birthdays, 143
black and white pictures, 139
blind carbon copies, 174
blinking vertical line. *See* yellow cursor
blurring, 141
board games, 114
books, 96, 252
Boolean negation, 33
border, image map, 53
boxes, checking, 42
brackets, 179
brand names, 104
browsing, 106–107
Business, 244
By day and time, 266
By program title or category, 268

C

cable decoder, 287

cable service, 258, 273

caller identification, 6

cancel your WebTV service, 316

canceling service, 7

capitalize, single letters, 17

caps indicator, 17

caps lock, 18

carbon copies (cc:), 172–173, 174–175

card games, 114

carriage returns, 18, 300

cassette player, 144

catalogs, 96

CBS Sportsline, 251

CD-player, 144

cedillas, 32, 33

CGI. *See* Common Gateway Interface

chain letters, 127, 137

Change button, 34

Change city, 293

Change sports, 250

changing cities, 261, 263

channels, changing, 119

Chat feature, 294–297

check mark, 43, 46, 49

checkbox, 43

chess, 114

children's shows, 270

Choose Address, 212

choose city, 248

choose stocks, 246

Choose your name screen, 318

circumflex, 32

city name, 293

classical music, 113

Clean up, 196, 198, 201

cleaning up saved messages, 195

Clear, 62

Clear All, 271

clothing, 252

Club WebTV, 329

cmd key, 18
    copy text (cmd+C), 28–29
    cut (cmd+X), 28
    deselect (cmd+A), 27
    paste text (cmd+V), 28
    select text (cmd+A), 26
    view hyperlink (cmd+Ctrl), 65

cmd+A, 89, 204

cmd+arrow key, 265

cmd+C, 89, 204

cmd+R, 247

cmd+V, 89

coaxial cable, 139

comma, placing between addresses, 133

command (cmd) key combinations, 205

commercial electronic mail packages, 171

commercial sites, 76

Common Gateway Interface (CGI) protocol, 55

common words, 99

Community feature
    Around Town, 292–293
    Chat feature, 294–297
    Newsgroups, 298–301
    overview, 291

complete address, 69

COMPLETE STORY, 242

compressed archives, 214

compression, 147

computer memory, 141

confidential information, 71

contests, 163

context, 300

Index

context-checking, 35
convenient reference material, 78
Copy, 89
copy and paste, 204
copy text, 18, 28–29
copyright, 144
copyright issues, 113
copyright symbol, 33
Corporate Homepage, 7
correspondence, 42
courtesy, 300
courtesy copies. *See* carbon copies (cc:)
Create a storage area option, 177
creating new passwords, 51
credit card information, 70
credit card number, 320
Crossover Links, 259, 278–279
cut and paste, 30–31
cut text, 18
cyber-flirting, 294

D

daily listings, 260
daily reminder, 281
data entry style, 322
data files, 214
date, Web page, 68
debit cards, 320
default selection, 47
Deja News, 301
Delete key, 24–25
Delete option, 158
Description tag, 106
deselect all, 27
designers, 64
Detach, 180
Detailed Instructions, 146
diamond-with-an-I symbol, 264

dictionary, 35
dieresis, 32
Digital Cable, 265
digital cameras, 139
digitized format, 214
Dilbert Zone, 65
dim option, 129
Dine Site, 292
disable options, 193
Discard button, 86
Discard option, 129, 158, 196
Discarded folder, 200, 202
Discover, 320
Discovery Channel, 82
disregarding matches, 105
diversity, 230
doctors, 116
documents, 214
domain name, 216
domains, 69
Done, 80, 88, 91
Don't Erase, 184
Dow Jones average, 239
down arrow, 158
download current listings, 260
downtimes, mail servers, 187

E

E! Online, 240
earphones, 142
eBay, 292
eCommerce, 252
edit, 14
Edit button, 15
edit, address book, 158–159
Edit key, 17
Edit Message, 212
Edit Message option, 186

Index

editing site names, 88
Eject button. *See* Infrared (IR) unit
electronic library, 61
electronic mail, 77
 addresses, 127, 130–131
 advanced techniques, 209
 attachments, 214
 carbon copies (cc:), 172–173, 174–175
 checking automatically, 210–211
 cleaning up Mail list, 198–199
 context, 178
 discarding a letter, 196–197
 enabling storage, 192–193
 erase, 184–185
 forwarding, 136–137
 Help function, 146–147
 hyperlinks, 212–213
 include, 178–179, 180–181
 intermediate skills, 167
 Mail list, moving through, 128–129
 misaddressed, 186–187
 multiple recipients, 132–133
 order, Mail list, 170–171
 overview, 125
 pause, 182–183
 permanently discarding, 200–201
 pictures, 138–141
 reading, 126–127
 Reply all feature, 176–177
 replying, 134–135
 resending sent messages, 204–205
 retrieving discarded letters, 202–203
 retrieving from other accounts, 216–219
 sending, 132–133
 sending to yourself, 213
 signatures, 168–169
 sound clips, 142–145
 spam, 135
 storage, overview, 191
 storing a letter, 194–195
 time outs, 135
 undeliverable, 186–187
 video, 138–141
 writing, 130–131
e-mail, 14. *See* electronic mail
 checking, 44
e-mail blocking, 314
e-mail lists
 grammatical mistakes, 229
 joining, 226–227
 leaving, 230–231
 ListServ, 224–225
 Liszt, 228–229
 offensive posts, 227
 overview, 223
 replying, 229
 rules, 227
e-mail statement, 320
emoticons, 300
encoding, electronic mail, 154
encryption, 70
Enter button, 118
entertainment, 237, 240–241, 292
episode summaries, 264
Erase, 30, 183, 184–185
erase information, 54
erasing in-progress e-mail, 185
Esc key, 80
Eudora, 217
event calendars, 292
Excel spreadsheet, 215
excess bandwidth, 168
Excite, 107, 307
exploring the Web
 advice services, 116–117
 MIDI Karaoke, 112–113
 online games, 114–115
 overview, 111
 while watching TV, 118–119
Extras, 192
Extras section, 177, 178

Index

F

F keys, 19, 80–81
fair use copyright law, 144
Family, 76
family pictures, 213
family standards, 294
FAQ. *See* Frequently Asked Questions (FAQ)
Favorite Channels screen, 272
favorites
    adding folders, 82–83
    adding pages, 76–77
    discarding sites, 86–87
    F keys, 80–81
    folder limits, 77
    frequency of use, 79
    moving between folders, 76, 90–91
    overview, 75
    removing, 76, 84–85
    renaming sites, 88–89
    selecting, 78–79
    unassign, 81
Feature, 240, 252
feedback, 54
Fetch, 218
fetch remote mail, 217
File Transfer Protocol (FTP), 216
film strip, 181
filter-before-download option, 217
Financial, 244
Find a celebrity box, 240
Find key, 27
flame, 231
flame wars, 177
flaming, 299
florist, 252
fn key, 18
folders
    accidental deletion, 87
    adding, 82–83

    moving sites between, 90
    organizing, 91
    removing, 84–85
font size, adjusting, 326–327
font size, setting default, 44
food, 252
football, 250
For today, 264, 267
foreign correspondents, 32
foreign currency symbols, 32
forms, 163
    default selection, 41, 45, 47
    gray triangle, 44
    gray, rounded rectangle, 44
    multiple choice scrolling lists, 48–49
    overview, 39
    predetermined selections, 41
    pull-down list, 44–45
    radio buttons, 40
    red dot, 40
    Reset Form, 54–55
    rows versus columns, 43
    scrolling lists, 46–47
    selecting many options, 42–43
    selecting one option from many, 40–41
    square box, 42
    Submit Form, 54–55
forms, filling out, 8
forward, 193
forward button, 112
Forward option, 129, 136
four-line rule, 168
fractions, 32
free advice, 117
Freeze feature, 139
freeze-frame display, 140
frequent correspondents, 160
Frequently Asked Questions (FAQ), 146, 299
From line, 127, 154, 204
FTP. *See* File Transfer Protocol (FTP)
Fun, 82

Index

G

gambling games, 114
game shows, 281
games, 295
    addictive qualities, 115
    Battleship, 114
    multiple players, 114
    shared worlds, 114
    Yahoo, 114
garden supplies, 252
gardening, 224
Gardening folder, 83
General MIDI, 215
Getting Started, 146
GIF, 215
GIF format, 214
GIF89a Animation, 215
gisting, 178
Go button, 8
Go To key, 62
Go to Page, 63
Going Out, 292
golf tournaments, 270
graphic Web page editor, 303
grave accent, 32
gray triangles, 44
green arrows, 78
green background, 26
green-colored displays, 281
greetings, recording, 142–145
groups, electronic mail, 157

H

handles, 295
Hang Up, 319
hardware, 66

header, electronic mail, 154
headers, 205
headlines, 237
Health, 244
help, 328
help center, 328–329
Help function, 146–147
help key, 81
highlighting text, 26–27
hobby, 61, 76
hockey, 250
Home, 135
home key, 18, 275
Home Pages, 302–307
Home Schooling, 106
home shopping networks, 281
hotline, 7
How Often screen, 283
HTML. *See* Hypertext Markup Language (HTML)
http. *See* hypertext transfer protocol (http)
humidity, 248
humor, 137
hyperlinks, 53, 96, 169, 212–213
    overview, 64–65
    revisit pages, 66–67
Hypertext Markup Language (HTML), 209, 303
hypertext transfer protocol (http), 62. *See* Post Office
    Protocol version 3 (POP3)

I

illegal operations, 13
image maps, 52–53, 64
image movies, 214
image retention, 277
important phone numbers, 194
incorrect addresses, 186

Index

Info button, 55, 68–69
info key, 19
information box, 69
Infoseek, 97, 98, 102, 107
Infrared (IR) unit, 284
Instructional, 270
interactive content, 259
international copyright law, 113
internationalizing Web sites, 52
Internet
    establish connections across, 62
Internet etiquette, 168
Internet names, 313
Internet provider, 130
Internet Relay Chat, 294–297
Internet service providers (ISPs), 195, 209, 216
Internet-related terms, 329
IR. *See* Infrared (IR) unit
IR-Blaster, 266
ISP. *See* Internet service providers (ISPs)

J

jewelry, 252
job applications, 39
job searching tools, 292
job title, 42
jokes, 137
JPEG images, 214, 215

K

karaoke, 112–113
keyboard, remote
    alt key, 18
    arrow keys, 10, 18
    back button, 18
    benefits, 10
    caps lock, 18
    cmd key, 18
    functions, 18
    navigation, 18
    options button, 18
    overview, 18–19
    Power button, 6
    Return key, 10, 12
    shift keys, 18
keyword associations, 271

L

last payment date, 320
late-breaking information, 237
laughing out loud (LOL), 297
lawyers, 116
Learning, 106
Leave messages on server, 218
light-blue box, 52
lights, 140
line wraps, 17
line-of-sight, 10
lines, deleting, 25
link
    activating, 12
links. *See* hyperlinks
Listing option, 170
Listings setup, 260
LISTSERV REFCARD, 227
Liszt, 225, 228–229
Living & Travel, 244
Local News & Weather, 244
local phone numbers, 6
Local Services, 292
LOL. *See* laughing out loud (LOL)
Look for:, 224

lowercase, 17
low-light conditions, 140
lurking, 226, 296, 299
Lycos, 99

M

Mace 3:1 compression, 215
Mace 6:1 compression, 215
Macintosh, 147
Macromedia Flash 1.0, 215
magazines, 96
Magnavox, 9
Mail, 14
mail archive, 313
Mail buttons, 26, 126
Mail Help, 146
mail information, 54
Mail key, 30
Mail list, 24, 196
    moving through, 128
    overview, 126
Mail list screen, 218
mail lists, 224
mail server downtime, 187
mailbox size-limit, 312
mail-check time, 211
mailing lists, 176
mall, 252
manifolds, 116
Mark all, 198–199
marketing, 42
MasterCard, 320
mathematical research, 116
mathematicians, 32
medical advice, 116
membership, e-mail lists, 225
memory, 89

Message light, 126, 210
message ordering, 170
Message Watch feature, 210
META tags, 307
Mic jack, 142, 144
microphones, 142, 144, 145
Microsoft Word documents, 215
middle initials, 103
MIDI. *See* Musical Instruments Digital Interface
MIDI Karaoke, 112–113, 215
minijack-to-RCA adapter, 143
mini-plug, 142
ministers, 116–117
mini-to-mini cable, 144
misaddressed electronic mail, 186
misspellings, 105, 269
mixing case, 100–101
model numbers, 104
moderators, 295
Money, 82, 246–247
money orders, 320
Monster Board, 292
monthly charge, 320
monthly newsletter, 329
MOOs, 114
More Details About option, 162
more results, 97
Moved, 6
movie reviews, 237
Movies, 82, 270, 292
moving fast, 19
MPEG movies, 215
MPEG-2 Audio, 215
MPEG-3 Audio, 215
MSNBC, 242, 243
MSNInvestor, 246
MUDs, 114
multiple-choice scrolling list, 46, 48–49

Index

MUSHes, 114
Musical Instruments Digital Interface
(MIDI), 112–113, 324

N

Nagel, Katherine, 230
name changes, 159
names, 35
    searching for, 103
names, selecting for address book, 155
names, Web sites, 88–89
NASA, 69
natural language processing, 328
navigating, 15
neck muscles, straining, 11
netiquette, 168, 300
new customers, 6
New Movies In Theaters, 240
New Movies on Video, 240
new units, 6
newbie, 230
newest-first order, 170–171
News, 76, 78, 82, 242–243, 270
news articles, 77
news headlines, 88
Newsgroups, 298–301
NeXT, 100
next 10, 98
Next option, 128–129
Next page, 304
nicknames, 103, 295
No Shortcut, 80, 81
No video signal message, 140
NoMail, 231
non-WebTV account, 218
non-WebTV e-mail account, 146

O

occupation, 61
odd characters, 15
oldest-first order, 170–171
once-only reminders, 280
ongoing phone calls, 210
ongoing shows, 278
online banking service, 70
online forms, 6. *See* forms
online glossary, 329
online help center, 328–329
online shopping, 252
onscreen keyboard
    hide, 17
    introduction, 16–17
    key layouts, 16
onscreen keyboard, switching styles, 322–323
onscreen program listings, 258
oops!, 54
Opinion, 244
Option button, 239
Options, 62
Options button, 258
Options control panel, 118
order confirmation pages, 77
ordered subsets, 102
orders, online, 70
Organize, 80, 86, 88
original letters, attaching to replies, 178
outgoing phone call, 210
outreach programs, 116

P

page authors, 64
Page Builder, 302

page changes, 135
pages
    date last changed, 68
    loading, 65
    peeking at Web page information, 68–69
    recent list, 66–67
    security information, 68
    security rating, 70
partner merchants, 252
passwords, 50–51, 216, 218, 219, 312
Paste, 89
paste text, 18, 28–29, 30–31
path, electronic mail, 154
Pathfinder mission, 69
pause, 182
pause button, 112
payment method, 320
PBS, 82
peek feature, 68–69
personal advice, 116–117
Personal folder, 76, 82, 90
personal information, 55, 70
personal messages, 194
personal privacy, 313
pet, 252
petitions, 127
Philips M62080, 145
Philips-Magnavox, 66
phone numbers, 6, 320
photo capture from video, 138–141
Photo option, 138
physical storage, 194
picture-in-picture box, 118
picture-in-picture capability, 140
pictures, 138–141, 181, 214
pictures, selecting from, 52–53
pitch bar, 112
Play feature, 142
play-thru channel, 287

plurals, 102
POP3. *See* Post Office Protocol version 3 (POP3)
popular choices, 258
portals, 258
Possible Misspelling box, 34
Post Office, 186
Post Office Protocol version 3 (POP3), 216
Power button, 8
powering on, first time, 6–7
prebuilt folders, 82
predefined categories, 106–107
predefined categories, television, 270
Preview function, 306
Previous, 34
Previous option, 128–129
Previous page, 304
priests, 116–117
primary account, 194
primary user, 312
primary user accounts, 85
Print, 203
printer, 160, 194
privacy, 55, 70, 183
private newsgroups, 301
professional organizations, 225
programming your VCR, 286
PS/2-style keyboard, 9, 11
public domain, 113
publisher, 243
punctuation marks, 32

Q

QuickTime Audio, 215
quotation marks, 103
quoted phrases, 102–103
quotes, 247
QWERTY, 16, 18
QWERTY style, 322

Index

R

rabbis, 116–117
racing events, 270
radio, 144
radio buttons, 40
Radio Shack 33-1067, 145
ragged edge effect, 242
ranked results, 97
RCA Audio jacks, 142
RealAudio, 215
Recent, 66
recent button, 28, 258
recent channels, 276
recent pages, 66–67
recipients, selecting from address book, 156
Recommended folder, 76, 82
reconditioned units, 6
reconnect rectangle, 10
Record, 266, 268, 286
Recording, 142
recover deleted letters, 192, 203
rectangle, gray and rounded, 44
red caps indicator, 17
red check mark, 156
red dot, 40
red light, 186
red Message light, 126, 171, 210, 211
redialing, 260, 319
reduce selection, 27
reenable options, 193
Reference, 82
refresh, 247, 248
registration process, 6
regularly scheduled reminders, 280–283
relative address, 69
religious shows, 281
reload, 239
reload Web page, 19
Remind, 266, 268, 286

Remind Regularly, 283
reminder feature, 259, 280–283
remote control
  arrow keys, 8
  Go button, 8, 12
  Power button, 6, 8
Remote mail option, 216
Remove, 84–85
remove secondary user, 316–317
Remove User option, 317
removing addresses, 160–161
Rename, 88
replies, 178
Reply All button, 172, 176–177
Reply function, 160
Reply option, 129, 134–135, 136
required phrases, 104–105
Reset form, 54–55
reset to default, 54
restaurant listings, 292
restrictions, secondary users, 314
Return key, 10, 12, 133, 300
reusing text, 28, 185
review outgoing messages, 192
rewind button, 112
ROFL. *See* rolling on the floor laughing (ROFL)
rolling on the floor laughing (ROFL), 297
routing, electronic mail, 154
rule, cursor and box, 15

S

safety, 314
sales calls, 42
sales slips, 39
Samples, 82
sarcasm, 300
satellite service, 258, 273

Index

save important mail, 192
Save key, 76
Save Page, 76
save screen space, 45
Saved folder, 194, 202
Saved mail, 196
scholarly advice, 116–117
screen snapshot, 78
screen space, 44
Scroll Down, 136
scroll keys, 265
Scroll Up, 136
scroll up key, 18
scrolling lists, 46–47
Search, 105
search engines, 96, 161, 162–163
Search key, 96–97, 102
Search the Web, 102
Search TV Listings, 268
searching
    + sign, 104–105
    best matches first, 99
    browsing categories, 106–107
    built-in access, 97
    Infoseek, 97, 98
    limiting, 99, 100–†101
    mixed case, 100–†101
    ordered subsets, 102
    overview, 95
    quoted phrases, 102–103
    required phrases, 104–105
    results, 97
    Search key, 96–97
    search phrases, 98–99
    strategies, 98
secondary e-mail account, 218
secondary user, 312–315, 316–317
secondary user accounts, 85, 194, 196
secure ordering pages, 70
secure socket layer (SSL) protocol, 70–71
security, 50, 55, 70–71, 192, 200, 217, 219

Security Details, 19, 70–71
select, 89
select all, 26
selecting passwords, 51
selecting text, 26–27
Send, 212
Send button, 14
send my feedback, 54
Send option, 131
sensitive mail, 200
Sent folder, 202
Sent mail, 196
Series, 270
service termination, 316
Settings, 192, 216
Settings option, 168, 170
set-top units, 214
Setup Favorites, 272
shift, 17
shift key, 18
    select text, 26
shipping information, 70
Shockwave Audio, 215
shopping, 71, 252
Shopping Center, 107
Shopping Guarantee, 252
Shortcuts, 80
short-term secondary account, 316
shouting, 300
Show Current, 62
Show Details option, 186
Show Guides, 278–279
Show Last, 62
show listings, 264
sign up process
    concerns about, 7
    keyboard, 10–11
    remote control, 8–9
signals, blocking, 10
signal-to-noise ratio, 230
signature, electronic mail, 168–169

Index

Signature option, 168
single-choice scrolling list, 46
six degrees of separation, 96
Skip Word, 34
slanted diamond, 278
slow times, 263
snapshot, 66
soap operas, 281
soccer matches, 270
social gathering place, 223
social networks, 291
social security number, 70
songs, 113
Sony, 66
Sony F-V5, 145
Sony FV410, 145
Sony Walkman earphone set, 142
Sony WebTV units, 143
sorting, addresses, 152
sound clips, 142–145
sounds, 181
space limitations, 201
spacebar, 18
spam, 135
speakers, 143
special characters, 32–33
Specials, 270
spell-checker, 34–35
Spelling, 34–35
splitting folders, 90
Sports, 244, 250–251, 270
sports scores, 237
Sprint, 100
squares, scrolling lists, 46
SSL. *See* secure socket layer protocol
stagnation, 231
start and stop times, 264
Start the Search!, 224
Stay on channel while browsing listings option, 264
stock trades, 70

stocks, 237, 239, 246
Storage, 192–193, 194
storage, electronic mail
    Clean up option, 198–199
    Discard, 196–197
    enabling, 192–193
    overview, 191
    permanently discarding, 200–201
    quota, 194
    resending sent letters, 204–205
    retrieving discarded letters, 202–203
    Saved folder, 194–195
strategy games, 114
subcategories, 106–107
Subject: line, 15, 30, 130–131, 132
Submit form, 54–55
subscription, e-mail list, 226
summaries, Web site, 97
Surf Watch, 314
Switch User option, 318–319
system administrator, 155

T

tab, 18
tables, 305
Talk City, 294
Talk Radio, 41
tax forms, 39
technical terms, 35
Technology, 244
telephone, hanging up, 210
tempo bar, 112
terminate, 319
text
    boxes, 16
    entry areas, 16

Index

free-form areas, 16
    insert, 14
    multiline, 14
    paragraphs, 16
    slots, 16
text, editing
    copy, 28–29
    cut, 28, 30–31
    Delete key, 24–25
    highlighting, 26–27
    insert, 25
    introduction, 23
    overwrite, 25
    paste, 28–29
    remove an entire line, 25
    select, 26–27
    undo, 25
text-based clip-art, 169
theological advice, 116–117
thread, 230, 300
threatening electronic mail, 155
tilde, 32
time gaps, 285
time out, 10, 135, 319
time zones, 239
times, program listings, 262
To line, 130, 132
Today home page, 238
toll calls, 6
toll-free numbers, 6
Top Stories, 240, 244, 252
topic drift, 300
touch-typing experience, 11
toys, 252
trading online, 71
triangles, scrolling lists, 46
tripod, 140
Trouble, 296
Tune to channel when program begins option, 281
TV, watching while Web surfing, 118–119

TV Favorites, 274
    setting up, 272–273
    using, 274–275
TV Guide Web site, 261
TV Home, 12, 258–259, 262
TV input, 139
TV listing updates, 211
TV listings
    date and time, 266–267
    downloading, 44
    retrieving, 260–261, 262–263
    searching, 268–269, 270–271
TV Planner, 282
TV Sites, 267, 278
tv window, 118
TV/VCR button, 285
type of show, 270
typewriter layout, 322
typographic error, 24
typographical errors, addresses, 156

U

unauthorized charges, 253
unavailable computers, 186
undo, 25, 87, 88
uniform resource locator (URL), 62
unlisted e-mail addresses, 163
unmoderated chat rooms, 295
unrelated favorites, 90
unwanted electronic mail, 155
unwanted favorites, 76
unwrapped lines, 300
up arrow, 158
update address book, 158–159
URL. *See* **uniform resource locator**
Use remote mail screen, 218
Usenet newsgroups, 163, 225, 301

Index

user interface, 170
user-centered design, 170
utility passwords, 51
utility secondary users, 312

VCR, connecting, 138
VCRs, 266, 268, 283, 284–287
verb case, 102
vertical space, 17
video, 138–141
VIDEO input, 139
video-in jack, 138
video-out jack, 138
View button, 279
View TV Listings options, 267
viewing agenda, 262
viewing planner, 258
Visa, 320
vital information, 78

Wall Street, 239
Warner Brothers, 82
WAV sound recordings, 214
WB. *See* welcome back (WB)
weather, 237, 248–249, 292
Weather Channel, 248
weather forecast information, 88
Web addresses, 62–63
    case insensitive, 63
    typing correctly, 63

Web Home option, 258
Web Page, creating your own, 302–307
Web page address. *See* Web addresses
WebBattleship, 114
WebTV Art Gallery, 304
WebTV Centers
    Entertainment, 240–241
    hotline feature, 238
    Money, 246–247
    News, 242–243, 244–245
    overview, 237
    Shopping, 252–253
    Sports, 250–251
    Today home page, 238
    using, 238–239
    Weather, 248–249
WebTV Classic
    address book, 153
    advice services, 117
    Ask WebTV site, 329
    background music, 325
    browsing, 107
    carbon copies, 175
    change subscriber information, 321
    Chat, 295
    check box options, 43
    clean up mail, 199
    Commuity feature, 293
    copying and pasting, 29
    create new folders, 83
    cutting and pasting, 31
    delete functions, 25
    discard letters, 197
    Entertainment, 241
    Favorites folders, 79
    font size, 327
    forms, 41, 45, 55
    forward saved letters, 205
    forwarding electronic mail, 137
    games, 115

Index

highlight text, 27
hyperlinks, 213
image maps, 53
inclusion, electronic mail, 179
Infoseek, 101
keyboard, 9, 11, 19
keyboard style, 323
limit searches, 103
Mail Help, 147
Mail list, 129
Mail list ordering, 171
Message Watch, 211
MIDI Karaoke, 113
misaddressed letters, 187
Money, 247
multiple choice lists, 49
multiple recipient addresses, 133
News, 243
Newsgroups, 299
onscreen keyboards, 17
Page Builder, 303
passwords, 51
Picture option, 139
POP3, 219
power on, 7
reading electronic mail, 127
recover discarded letters, 203
remote-control, 9
remove favorites folders, 85
Reply all, 177
replying to electronic mail, 135
saving letters, 195
scrolling, 47
Search feature, 97
secondary users, 313
Security Details option, 71

Shopping, 253
signatures, 169
sound recordings, 145
special characters, 33
spell-checking, 35
sports, 251
storage activation, 193
switch users, 319
Today, 239
TV Home, 259
TV picture-in-picture, 119
weather, 249
World Wide Web access, 63
writing electronic mail, 131
yellow box, 13
yellow cursor, 15
WebTV mailing address, 321
WebTV Plus
   address book, 153
   advice services, 117
   Ask WebTV site, 329
   background music, 325
   browsing, 107
   carbon copies, 175
   change subscriber information, 321
   Chat, 295
   check box options, 43
   clean up mail, 199
   Community features, 293
   controlling VCRs, 284–287
   copying and pasting, 29
   create new folders, 83
   Crossover Links, 278–279
   cutting and pasting, 31
   delete functions, 25
   discard letters, 197
   Entertainment, 241
   Favorites folder, 79
   font size, 327
   forms, 41, 45, 55

Continued

Index

WebTV Plus (*continued*)

forward saved letters, 205

forwarding electronic mail, 137

games, 115

highlight text, 27

hyperlinks, 213

image maps, 53

inclusion, electronic mail, 179

Infoseek, 100

keyboard, 9, 11, 19

keyboard style, 323

limit searches, 103

Mail Help, 147

Mail list, 129

Mail list ordering, 171

Message Watch, 211

MIDI Karaoke, 113

misaddressed letters, 187

Money, 247

multiple choice lists, 49

multiple recipient addresses, 133

News, 243

Newsgroups, 299

onscreen keyboard, 17

overview, 257

Page Builder, 303

passwords, 51

photo capture, 138

POP3, 219

power on, 7

reading electronic mail, 127

recently viewed TV shows, 276–277

recover discarded letters, 203

Remind function, 280–283

remote-control, 9

remove favorites folders, 85

Reply all, 177

replying to electronic mail, 135

retrieving TV listings, 260–261, 262–263

saving letters, 195

scrolling, 47

Search feature, 97

searching TV listings, 268–269, 270–271

secondary users, 313

Security Details option, 71

selecting television shows, 264–265

Shopping, 253

signatures, 169

sound recordings, 145

special characters, 33

spell-checking, 35

sports, 251

storage activation, 193

switch users, 319

Today, 239

TV Favorites, 272–273, 274–275

TV Home, 258–259

TV picture-in-picture box, 119

viewing TV listings, 266–267

weather, 249

World Wide Web access, 63

writing electronic mail, 130–131

yellow box, 13

yellow cursor, 15

webtv.net

support page, 11

weekday reminder, 281

weekly reminders, 280

welcome back (WB), 297

westerns, 270

White Pages searches, 292

white starburst, 52

WhoWhere, 292

WhoWhere search engine, 162

Windows, 147

wine enthusiasts, 223

wireless keyboard. *See* **keyboard**

World Wide Web

general page information, 68–69

hyperlinks, 64

overview, 61

revisit pages, 66–67
security, 70–71
Web addresses, 62–63
Write, 14, 26, 30
Write a message display, 156
Write a message screen, 24
Write option, 130, 132

x-headers, 174

Yahoo!, 107, 307
yellow arrow, 52

yellow box
example, 8
hyperlink, 64
introduction, 12–13
move, 12
yellow connected light, 210
yellow cursor
arrow keys, 14
location, 14

Zagat Survey, 292
Zip code, 293

my2cents.idgbooks.com

Register This Book — And Win!

Visit **http://my2cents.idgbooks.com** to register this book and we'll automatically enter you in our fantastic monthly prize giveaway. It's also your opportunity to give us feedback: let us know what you thought of this book and how you would like to see other topics covered.

Discover IDG Books Online!

The IDG Books Online Web site is your online resource for tackling technology — at home and at the office. Frequently updated, the IDG Books Online Web site features exclusive software, insider information, online books, and live events!

10 Productive & Career-Enhancing Things You Can Do at www.idgbooks.com

- Nab source code for your own programming projects.

- Download software.

- Read Web exclusives: special articles and book excerpts by IDG Books Worldwide authors.

- Take advantage of resources to help you advance your career as a Novell or Microsoft professional.

- Buy IDG Books Worldwide titles or find a convenient bookstore that carries them.

- Register your book and win a prize.

- Chat live online with authors.

- Sign up for regular e-mail updates about our latest books.

- Suggest a book you'd like to read or write.

- Give us your 2¢ about our books and about our Web site.

You say you're not on the Web yet? It's easy to get started with IDG Books' *Discover the Internet*, available at local retailers everywhere.